Ferdinand Zirkel

Microscopical Petrography

Ferdinand Zirkel

Microscopical Petrography

ISBN/EAN: 9783337077778

Printed in Europe, USA, Canada, Australia, Japan

Cover: Foto ©ninafisch / pixelio.de

More available books at **www.hansebooks.com**

PROFESSIONAL PAPERS OF THE ENGINEER DEPARTMENT, U. S. ARMY.

No. 18.

REPORT

OF THE

GEOLOGICAL EXPLORATION OF THE FORTIETH PARALLEL

MADE

BY ORDER OF THE SECRETARY OF WAR ACCORDING TO ACTS OF
CONGRESS OF MARCH 2, 1867, AND MARCH 3, 1869,

UNDER THE DIRECTION OF

BRIG. AND BVT. MAJOR GENERAL A. A. HUMPHREYS,

CHIEF OF ENGINEERS,

BY

CLARENCE KING,

U. S. GEOLOGIST.

I-II

VOLUME VI.

UNITED STATES GEOLOGICAL EXPLORATION OF THE FORTIETH PARALLEL.
CLARENCE KING, GEOLOGIST-IN-CHARGE.

MICROSCOPICAL PETROGRAPHY

BY

FERDINAND ZIRKEL.

SUBMITTED TO THE CHIEF OF ENGINEERS AND PUBLISHED BY ORDER OF THE SECRETARY OF
WAR UNDER AUTHORITY OF CONGRESS.

ILLUSTRATED BY TWELVE PLATES.

WASHINGTON:
GOVERNMENT PRINTING OFFICE.
1876.

TABLE OF CONTENTS.

LIST AND EXPLANATION OF PLATES.

PLATE I.

FIG. 1. Double inclusion, consisting of an external (solid) zone (*a*), of liquid carbonic acid (*b*), and of a bubble (*c*); in the quartzes of many gneisses and granites.

FIG. 2. Inclusion of a saturated solution of chloride of sodium, containing a sharp, little salt cube (and bubble); in the quartzes of many granites and gneisses.

FIG. 3. Inclusion as in Fig. 2, containing also thin, pale-green microlites of hornblende, resting upon the walls of the including quartz, and projecting into the interior of the fluid.

FIG. 4. Same inclusion in the quartz of granite; black microlites accompanying the salt cube.

FIG. 5. Same fluid-inclusion, containing grains and microlites of hornblende and plates of blood-red oxyd of iron, beside the salt cube; in the quartz of granite-porphyries of Franklin Buttes, Nevada.

FIG. 6. Apatite prisms, broken into many pieces and thrown into a curved bow; in many gneisses and granites.

FIG. 7. Apatite, with microscopic fluid-inclusions; in gneiss and granite.

FIG. 8. Apatite, filled with cylindrical pores, which lie parallel to the chief axis of the crystal, and confined to its middle; longitudinal and transverse section; from granites of Wachoe Mountains, Nevada.

FIG. 9. Apatite, containing strange dust-like material, arranged in short lines, which are combined in broom, and tuft-like forms; in andesite of Kamma Mountains, Nevada.

FIG. 10. Section of apatite, with a black prismatic core through its whole length; six thin line-like prisms are affixed to the six vertical edges of this stouter individual; in rock from Basalt Hill, near White Plains, Nevada.

FIG. 11. Section of a hornblende crystal, not a homogeneous individual, but built up of many accumulated thin microlites, with distinct signs of aggregation from all sides; in diorite from New Pass, Nevada.

FIG. 12. Skeleton-like or cross-formed groups of magnetite crystals, arranged according to the axes of the regular system; in the basalts from near Wadsworth.

FIG. 13. Glass-inclusion in the olivine of basalt, from the head of Clan Alpine Cañon, Augusta Mountains; the inclusion is pressed flat, stretching out many dendritical arms, which carry near their terminations small, dark bubbles.

FIG. 14. Aggregations of microscopical tridymite in the reddish-gray (later) trachytes from Mount Rose and the Sugar Loaf, Washoe, Nevada.

FIG. 15. Hexagonal glass-inclusion, representing the form of quartz in which it is imbedded; a six-radiated, faint star over it, the rays of which apparently protrude beyond the border of the inclusion; in quartz of rhyolite from Carico Valley, Nevada.

FIG. 16. Glass-inclusion, the bubble of which is sac-like, curved, and twisted; in quartz of rhyolite from New Pass, Desotoya Mountains, Nevada.

FIG. 17. Hornblende-microlite, partly surrounded by a bubble-bearing glass-drop, and itself containing two little glass-inclusions; in quartz of dacite from Shoshone Peak, Nevada.

FIG. 18. Glass-inclusion, containing, beside the bubble, many black, short microlites, resting on the periphery, and stretching into the interior in parallels; in olivine of basalt from Buffalo Peak, North Park, Colorado.

FIG. 19. Microlites of augite, on both sides of which are affixed many subtile prickles of augite at different angles, like the needles of a fir-tree; in basalt from Snowstorm Cañon, Black Rock Mountains, Nevada.

FIG. 20. Colorless crystallites, the ends of which are terminated in two acicular points, or in regular stair-like serrations, or irregularly lobed; in globular pearlite of Montezuma Range, Nevada.

Fig. 21. Section of leucite, with a concentric ring of glass-inclusions and augite grains; in the leucite rock from the Leucite Hills, northwest of Point of Rocks, Wyoming.

Fig. 22. Section of leucite, with radially interposed, club-formed augite prisms; from last-named locality.

Fig. 23. Section of leucite; green augite-microlites projecting into its substance; last-named locality.

PLATE II.

Fig. 1. Mica-schist, west slope of Humboldt Range, Nevada, containing quartz, brown mica, white mica, and singular knots, which consist of a dense web of microlites of fibrolite (disthene), imbedded in a quartz-mass.

Fig. 2. Mica-schist, Spruce Mountain, Pequop Range, Nevada, consisting of quartz, much deep-green and little white mica; the laminæ of biotite contain innumerable extremely thin microlites, which sometimes show a hexagonal arrangement.

Fig. 3. Stanrolite in a silver-white mica-slate from Red Creek, Colorado, partly consisting of color-less, rounded quartz grains; an arm of the mica-slate, with microscopical tourmaline and specular iron projecting into the staurolite-crystal.

Fig. 4. Granite dike from north of Summit Springs, Havallab Range, Nevada; quartz filled with black, hair-like microlites; cleavable hornblende and lamellated biotite, showing a curious interlacing and interwreathing; also brown titanite and dusty apatite.

PLATE III.

Fig. 1. Structure of feldspar, filled with microscopical interpositions (plates, lamium, microlites, grains) resembling those of true labradorite; from coarse-grained granite of Havallah Range.

Fig. 2. Hornblende, of syenitic granite-porphyry, from the divide between Bingham Cañon, Oquirrh Mountains, and Tooelle Cañon; altered (with outlines conserved) into an aggregation of a leek-green substance (viridite), calcite, with rhombohedral cleavage, epidote, and black magnetite; all clearly observable secondary products.

Fig. 3. Hornblende of diorite, from the southwest end of Winnemucca Peak, Nevada, altered into green viridite, epidote and geode-like calcite, with residua of original hornblende.

Fig. 4. Greenish-yellow nests of concentrically radiating epidote, showing, in their aggregation, the original form of the hornblende by the alteration of which they have been produced; in diorite from east end of Winnemucca Peak, Nevada.

PLATE IV.

Fig. 1. Hornblende rock; dike in granite of low hills northeast of Havallah Range; consisting of colorless quartz, delicate green particles, and larger crystals of hornblende.

Fig. 2. Mechanically altered crystals of hornblende, surrounded by black border; in hornblende-porphyry of Augusta Mountains, Nevada.

Fig. 3. Melaphyre, from Berkshire Cañon, Virginia Range, Nevada, with transverse section of an amygdule, composed of regularly arranged quartz and green-earth.

Fig. 4. Propylite, from Independence Valley, Tuscarora, Nevada, with characteristic greenish, pro-pylitic groundmass, zonally built crystals of plagioclase, and two kinds of hornblende; the predominating green one (somewhat fibrous and without a black border, altering into epidote), and a rarer brown form (strongly dichroitic, surrounded by black border, eminently cleavable, and entirely fresh); the latter playing the rôle of an accessory, almost a foreign element.

PLATE V.

Fig. 1. Brown biotite, in the quartziferous propylite of Wagon Cañon, Cortez Range, Nevada, con-taining interposed layers of pellucid calcite in the direction of the lamellation.

Fig. 2. Very much broken and shivered hornblende-crystals, surrounded by dark border (probably a product of the chemical attack of the molten magma); from hornblende-andesite of Augusta Cañon.

Fig. 3. Hornblende-andesite, from the Anule Creek, Cortez Range, with large, schistiform feldspars, containing innumerable glass-inclusions, arranged in regular bands.

Fig. 4. Leucite rock, from the Leucite Hills, Wyoming; many rounded or eight-sided leucites, with grain-rings in their interior; prisms and microlites of pale-green augite; larger laminæ of peculiar, brownish-yellow mica, dusty apatite, black microlites; no feldspar.

PLATE VI.

FIG. 1. Structure of rhyolite: pearlitic cracks run as a network through a light homogeneous glass, associated on both sides with a narrow zone of microfelsitic substance, with imbedded crystals of feldspar; north of Wadsworth, Nevada.

FIG. 2. Structure of rhyolite: fluidal bands of dark-brown grains form contorted undulations, which include axiolitic fibrous portions; from foothills of Virginia Range, northwest of Wadsworth, Nevada.

FIG. 3. Structure of rhyolite: fluidal lines of dark-brown grains run in contorted undulations, and envelop homogeneous glass portions; from last-named locality.

FIG. 4. Rhyolite from the ridge at the head of Louis' Valley, Nevada, with lamellated brownish biotite plates, broken and shivered into single leaves.

PLATE VII.

FIG. 1. Rhyolite of the Black Rock Mountains, Nevada; microfelsite (with some polarizing particles), containing single axially fibrous or axially cuneate bodies (axiolites) with distinct middle suture.

FIG. 2. Rhyolite from Pahkeah Peak, Pah-tsou Mountains, Nevada, presenting a ramifying network of axially cuneate strings, in the meshes of which concentric, radially fibrous sphærolites are placed; fractured and contorted biotite; quartz and feldspar with glass-inclusions.

FIG. 3. Rhyolite, northwest from Black Cañon, Montezuma Range, consisting of a confused aggregation of bunch-formed systems of parallel fibres, repeating the true structure of artificial porcelain; stripes of colorless, polarizing, angular grains run through this mass.

FIG. 4. Rhyolite from the Mopung Hills, west of Humboldt Range; yellowish and grayish-brown, axially fibrated, tall-formed strings of longer or shorter extension, and with distinct middle suture, run through a light-gray, ferrite-bearing groundmass, which is in the undeveloped crystalline state.

PLATE VIII.

FIG. 1. Rhyolite from Hot Spring Hills, Pah-Ute Range; fluidal stripes, composed of brown grains, and set with ciliated, thorn-like hairs, forming a network the meshes of which consist of axially or concentrically fibrous portions.

FIG. 2. Rhyolite from the pass north of Chataya Peak, Pah-Ute range; presents a delicate alternation of contorted, darker-brown, glassy layers (set with short, dark hairs), and of lighter microfelsitic or half-crystalline ones; crystal of feldspar, with glass-inclusions.

FIG. 3. Rhyolite, summit of ridge south of Squaw Valley, Nevada; groundmass a dense aggregation of finely fibrous sphærolites, which partly consist of thicker, reddish-brown ferritic needles in concentric grouping; feldspars and quartzes with glass-inclusions.

FIG. 4. Obsidian from Truckee Ferry, Truckee Cañon, Nevada, consisting of laminæ and layers of a nearly colorless and of a pale-brownish glass, which are entangled and kneaded together in the most confused manner.

PLATE IX.

FIG. 1. Glassy rock from Truckee Range; the small, granular globulites in the glass are coagulated into little lumps, stars, needles, tendrils, spider-like forms, etc.

FIG. 2. Pearlite from the Pah-tsou Mountains, with globulites, aggregated into the form of crystallitic needles, and of cuneate and tendril-like bodies; large crystals of brown hornblende.

FIG. 3. Pearlite from Grass Cañon, west side Pah-tsou Mountains, with colorless and black microlites (belonites and trichites), drawn straightly or twisted, arranged in parallels by fluctuation. This microlitic devitrification is quite independent from the pearlitic shell-texture, which produces concentric crack-lines in the section.

FIG. 4. Pearlitic rock from Montezuma Range, west of Parker's Station, devitrified into subtile black trichites, usually sharply contorted, often curled into little indistinct flocks; the stronger ones sometimes powdered with pale, pellucid grains of extreme minuteness; distinct arrangement in parallel linear paths by fluctuation.

PLATE X.

FIG. 1. Obsidian from the Ombe Butte, Utah, consisting of yellowish-red and of nearly colorless glassy stripes, which are much contorted and kneaded through each other; long thin pores appear like black lines; quartzes with large inclusions of orange-colored glass.

FIG. 2. Half-glassy rock from East Goose Creek Mountains, Nevada, containing quartz, sanidin, plagioclase, lamellated brown biotite, greenish augite, rare dark-brown hornblende, and magnetite in a mass, which consists of a throng of microlites, imbued with glass, and presents excellent phenomena of waving, damming, and encircling fluctuation.

FIG. 3. Basalt, north of American Flat Creek, Washoe, Nevada, characteristic type, containing larger microscopical or even macroscopical crystals of feldspar and olivine, both contrasting with an extremely fine-grained crystalline mixture of rounded, drop-like or crippled augite grains of pale color and black sharp grains of magnetite. The aggregation of these two ingredients, which contains no perceptible glassy base, plays the rôle of a groundmass. Olivine only appears as larger porphyritical crystals; angite, on the other hand, only as a subtile constituent of the groundmass. Borders of the feldspar ledges not very sharply defined. Extremely minute angite grains interposed in the larger feldspars, forming lines which correspond to the triclinic striation. Olivine partly decomposed into greenish serpentinoous matter.

FIG. 4. Basalt from Lower Truckee Valley, containing characteristic typical feldspars, a comparatively large number of which are sanidins, irregularly shaped angites, and larger, partly metamorphosed olivines, imbedded in an unindividualized amorphous base, which consists of a glass substance and of extremely small, dark globulitic grains (globulitically devitrified glass). This base is characteristically crowded in between the diverging crystalline elements in cuneiform points.

PLATE XI.

FIG. 1. Altered basalt: the globulitic base is metamorphosed into amygdaloidal nests, consisting in the section of undulated and curled concentric rings, with an alternately lighter and darker grayish or brownish-yellow color. Mountain Wells Station, Overland Road, Augusta Mountains, Nevada.

FIG. 2. Augite-andesite from Susan Creek Cañon. The large feldspar consists of spots which are almost wholly glass, the light-brownish inclusions being really woven together on the sides, so that the feldspar substance scarcely appears between them; yet the bubbles of the single particles which have been welded together are distinctly recognizable.

FIG. 3. Basalt from the divide between North and Middle Parks, with large olivine, partly altered into serpentineous matter, which forms strings and veins.

FIG. 4. Basaltic rock of the Egyptian Cañon, River Range, Nevada, with peculiar crystallitic ingredients. (See text.)

PLATE XII.

FIG. 1. Fragment of rhyolite, having resinous lustre, from rhyolitic breccia of Mullins Gap, Pyramid Lake, Nevada; pale-brownish-violet glass, with lighter spots; the glass containing delicate microlites, dark gas-pores (stretched out in the direction of fluctuation), and most remarkable fluid-inclusions, with moving bubble up to 0.012^{mm} in diameter. The colorless prismatic crystal in the middle (apatite) contains a glass-inclusion, which itself holds a liquid particle with moving bubble.

FIG. 2. Chalcedony from Grass Cañon, Pah-tsou Mountains, chiefly consisting of splendidly polarizing siliceous sphœrolites, which are made up of radiating fibres; figure in polarized light.

FIG. 3. Palagonite-tufa, southeast from Hawes' Station, Nevada; hyaline-breccia of differently colored glass fragments, containing crystals of plagioclase and dark-bordered gas-cavities, in many of which the inner walls and the immediately environing palagonite mass have been altered into a fibrous aggregation of short needles.

FIG. 4. The same between crossed nicols; the isotrope, glassy mass becomes entirely dark, the altered walls of the cavities presenting excellent aggregate polarization, showing even a colored cross, which changes its position and color by turning the object or the analyzer. The plagioclases show variously colored stripes.

October, 1876.

GENERAL: Herewith I have the honor to transmit Volume VI of the report of this Exploration.

While American palæontologists have materially aided field-geologists by their systematic assignment of fossil remains to proper horizons, the important study of petrography has suffered complete neglect, save by a few exceptional workers.

Believing that the establishment of definite American rock-types could only be satisfactorily accomplished by minute comparisons with those of Europe, and that the refinements of microscopic investigation were essential to success, I naturally turned to Europe for aid.

I am sure American men of science will welcome the present volume, from the distinguished pen of Prof. Ferdinand Zirkel, as one of the most important contributions ever made to our geology, and will give it the cordial intellectual greeting due so eminent a guest as its author.

Very respectfully, your obedient servant,

CLARENCE KING,
Geologist-in-Charge.

Brigadier-General A. A. HUMPHREYS,
Chief of Engineers, U. S. Army.

SIR: Sending you herewith my report on the crystalline rocks along the Fortieth Parallel in the Western United States, I cannot fail to gratefully acknowledge how much invaluable assistance I owe to you and to your excellent fellow-workmen, Messrs. S. F. Emmons and Arnold Hague. You well remember that happy time in New York when for many weeks we made together the preliminary examination of that vast collection of rocks you had gathered under such difficulties, but with such eminent geological taste.

You then enabled me to become acquainted with the geological distribution, relative age, and reciprocal connections of the rocks; and if I have been able to study their mineralogical and chemical constitution from a geological point of view, and to present more than a sterile and dry petrographical description, the merit is originally yours. Since the greater part of this investigation is directed to the microscopical composition and structure of rocks, it has appeared appropriate to offer in the beginning some brief general remarks upon that subject.

You know that when we examined the collection macroscopically I entirely agreed with the determination and nomenclature you and your able colleagues had already arrived at in the field. There were only some doubtful occurrences, whose true nature could not at that time be decidedly cleared up. Now, after having carefully studied more than twenty-five hundred thin-sections under the microscope, I have only to testify again that your original designations should almost never be altered or corrected.

May the results of this report as an American contribution to the general science of rocks, fulfil the expectation you cherished when you entrusted your classic collections to me.

With sincerest respect,

F. ZIRKEL.

To CLARENCE KING,
United States Geologist.

CHAPTER I.

INTRODUCTORY.

Former examinations of the microscopical structure of rocks which are not clastic have established the existence of certain large and well-defined groups. These general divisions of micro structure are entirely independent of the mineralogical composition of the rock and the special nature of its ingredients. They are the following:

I. Purely crystalline type: rocks composed simply of macroscopical[1] or microscopical crystalline individuals, which are in direct contact with one another, there being no amorphous substance between them. Granite is an excellent macroscopical example of this type of structure. Not only the apparently homogeneous mass of some so-called cryptocrystalline rocks, free from macroscopical crystals, but the groundmass of many porphyries, belong to this kind of microscopical structure. Moreover, although the entire absence of unindividualized substances is the strongest characteristic of this group, we must still class with it those members in which there is a minute quantity of a substance between the largely predominating crystalline ingredients.

II. Half-crystalline type: the crystalline individuals are either macroscopical and microscopical, or microscopical alone, and constitute only a part of the rock. The rest is composed of an unindividualized amorphous substance of greatly varying character and quantity. This unindividualized mass exists microscopically in rocks of the second group, and in a certain sense plays the *rôle* of a foreign substance, is opposed to the

---

[1] It is time this admirable word gained a fixed place in American petrography, and I have determined to use it throughout this geological series, with the accepted European signification.—O. K.

1 M P   1

crystalline ingredients and varies much in its behavior, especially possessing the following constitution:

a. Purely glassy, consisting of a lighter or darker yellowish-brown, a
grayish or a nearly colorless glass, which is simply refracting, yielding
no colors in polarized light; some of the half-crystalline rocks being
comparatively very rich in this pure glass, while in others it only imbues
and impregnates the aggregation of predominating crystalline elements.

b. Partly devitrified by the secretion of strange grains or needles,
which do not belong to the crystalline constituents of the rock, but
are of an entirely different nature. In this type, the unindividualized
substance is not pure glass, but a glass in which sharply shaped, rounded,
yellowish-brown or dark-brown grains, or black, hair-like needles, are imbedded. The diameter of these somewhat translucent grains seldom exceeds
0.005^{mm}, and they are often densely crowded together, almost totally replacing
the glass. Since they do not polarize, they can only be considered as
glass somewhat richer in iron. They are similar to the dark-green grains
so often found in the colorless mass of the artificial, green slags of iron-
furnaces. They belong to the so-called crystallites, and have been named
by Vogelsang "globulites".[1] This granulated or globulitic devitrification
of the amorphous mass is common in the half-crystalline basalts, melaphyres,
and other basic rocks, but it seems to be rare in rocks rich in silica. The
dark, almost wholly opaque needles or trichites, are usually aggregated within
the glassy portions of the rock into branches, confused flocks, or singular
skeleton-like nets.

c. Such a dense aggregation of extremely small grains, needles, and
hair-like bodies that very little glass, or none at all, appears between
them. These little bodies, of which the very plentiful inclusion indicates
an advanced stage of devitrification, are of quite an indistinct nature, not
properly individualized, and certainly cannot be identified with the crystalline ingredients of the rock, for they belong to the intermediate kingdom
of undeveloped crystallites. This peculiar behavior of the amorphous mass
may be termed the micro-crystallitic. It is, of course, connected by passage-
members with the former.

[1] H. Vogelsang, Die Krystalliten, 1875, 115.

d. A peculiar amorphous substance, which, on the one hand, lacks the glassy appearance, possessing no transparency, and yet, on the other, cannot be resolved into single actually individualized particles. This microfeldsitic mass is usually composed of indistinct and imperfect little grains which blend into one another, or of well-nigh obliterated fibers. A typical development of this variety is generally perfectly dark between crossed nicols, but it sometimes sends out a very feeble, vague, general light. In places, the incomplete, undeterminable grains and fiber show a tendency to incomplete radial grouping. A light-grayish or yellowish mass of this sort specially enters into the composition of highly-silicated rocks, such as quartz-porphyries and rhyolites, but they are hardly ever developed in the basic rocks. The four principal types of the unindividualized substance in the half-glassy rocks are therefore the purely glassy state, the globulitic and trichitic, the microcrystalline, and the microfeldsitic devitrification.

III. Uncrystalline type: the rock consisting of an unindividualized amorphous substance, which is sometimes in the glassy and often in the microfeldsitic state, as obsidians free from crystals, tachylyte, and some feldsite rocks. But just as those rocks in whose crystalline aggregation there is a trifle of glass may properly enough be named crystalline, so these which include a few small and rare secreted crystals in the largely predominating amorphous mass, are rightly called uncrystalline. Perhaps it is not superfluous to add that a rock which owes its specific place and name to the mineralogical nature of its ingredients, or to its macroscopical structure, does not of necessity always belong to one of these three types of microstructure. The basalts, which are characterized by the amount of plagioclase, augite, olivine and magnetite they contain, are, for instance, in one place developed as a purely crystalline, and in another as a half-crystalline rock, the included amorphous mass varying in its condition. Even in the same coherent rock-mass, forming a geological whole, the behavior of the microscopical structure often entirely changes in very small distances. The well-defined differences of these types cannot therefore be depended upon in the general or special classification of rocks, which, in the first place, must always be founded upon the mineral nature of the individualized constituents as the characteristic of most constant importance; the development of the microscopical structure of the mass being wholly independent of the quality and combination of these.

To prevent confusion, it seems best to employ the word "groundmass", in consonance with its present use, in the macroscopical sense only, signifying a mass which for the most part contains larger porphyritical crystals, appears.to the unaided eye homogeneous (dense) and insoluble, however it may behave under the microscope. That substance, however, which appears under the microscope as the proper unindividualized ground-paste, the bearer and holder, if one may say so, of both the microscopical and the macroscopical crystals, evidently merits a distinctive appellation, and has been named the "base",[1] by which, therefore, a purely microscopical conception is meant. In the groundmass, the base is very often accompanied by crystals. The base may be glassy, globulitic, microfeldsitic, etc., but never crystalline-granular. If the macroscopical groundmass is actually homogeneous throughout, as in many obsidians, of course both conceptions fail.

In the glassy and half-glassy rocks, it is a widely-spread phenomenon for the colorless green and black, needle-formed, microscopical elements to be grouped together into strings, bands, and flocks. There are bodies among them which have the appearance of undulated and bent streams, damming up before a larger crystal, and flowing around it to unite on the other side, (giving the crystal something the appearance of an eye,) often also really scattered and dissipated by one of them. These appearances evidently indicate that the fluctuations happened in the stiffening glass magma, after the microlites or little needle-formed crystals had been solidified. Analogous phenomena of motion, fluctuation or fluidal structure, invisible to the naked eye in the hand-specimens, are very often observed in the thin sections of partly or almost wholly crystalline massive rocks, such as basalts, trachytes, phonolites, melaphyres, and greenstones. The smallest ledge-formed sections of orthoclastic or plagioclastic feldspars, prisms of hornblende or augite, microlites of a variety of kinds; in short, all the microscopical bodies possessing a longitudinal axis, are locally grouped parallel to one another, and form undulating streams which diverge in the form of fans or ice-flowers. Where larger crystals lie in the paths of

---

[1] F. Z., Die mikroskopische Beschaffenheit der Mineralien und Gesteine, 1873, 268.

these crowded bands, the little needle-formed crystals encircle them on all sides with a tangential arrangement, are turned aside into different paths, or come to an abrupt end before them, as if by a shock, the microlites being thrown asunder in all directions. Observations of these phenomena of fluidal microstructure are best made between crossed nicols, for the single crystals are then colored and exhibit their characteristic direction much better than in ordinary light. A low magnifying power best enables one to overlook at once a larger portion of the thin section, and thereby to follow the lines of fluctuation. The shape of the little crystals is not without importance in the distinct observation of the form of the fluctuations. If they are needle-like or ledge-formed, even feeble movements of the mass will be unmistakably expressed; if, on the contrary, they are of a roundish, granular form, it often happens that strong fluctuations which have taken place fail to leave a trace of their action. In some rocks, especially the rhyolites, this wavy structure is produced by small dark grains grouped into lines and bands. These lines of grains undulate in a most remarkable manner, so that the figures of their curvature resemble marbled paper. There are also curled and twisted stripes of felsitic material, differing in color and behavior, which render the waving motion evident.

Three important points present themselves upon which light is thrown by this remarkable microstructure, connected with the fluctuations of the solidifying mass. It proves that the rock was at one time a magma, in a plastic state, and that, after larger crystals had been secreted, a shifting and displacement of the small microlites happened. Soon afterward, the mass seems to have been so suddenly solidified that the streams became fixed, and their fluctuation preserved for our observation. And, from these facts, the conclusion follows that the large and small crystals were not formed exactly where we perceive them, but that they have been thrown into their present place by the purely mechanical action of the surrounding plastic mass. It is worth mentioning that those rocks whose microfluidal structure is particularly distinct, are generally proportionately rich in broken crystals, shivered into detached, sharply angular fragments. And, lastly, this structure proves that the smallest crystals of the rock have not altered their mutual grouping and form, which date back to their solidification; and that, although secondary decompositions may have occurred in the lapse of time, these metamorphic influences have by no means been sufficient to obliterate the original characteristic structure.

It is well known that the non-fragmentary, so-called crystalline rocks, are divided petrographically into the simple and the mixed. The latter are grouped, according to their general characteristics of structure, under the two names *massive* (not slaty, but for the most part granular) and *slaty* rocks. By far the greater number of the massive rocks contain feldspar, which is either orthoclase or plagioclase, or a representative of feldspar in the form of nepheline or leucite. But a very small part of them, like such comparatively very rare rocks as eclogite, tourmaline-rock, and cherzolite, is free from feldspar. It may be desirable to present in this place the complete arrangement of the feldspar-bearing rocks according to the present mode of classification, and to add some considerations and remarks. The names which are not italicized are of rocks whose eruption antedates the Tertiary age, the ante-Tertiary and old massive rocks: those printed in italics have outflowed since the beginning of that age, and comprise the Tertiary and recent eruptive rocks.

I. Orthoclase rocks. *a.* With quartz or excess of silica: granite, granite-porphyry, felsite-porphyry, *rhyolite, glassy* and *half-glassy rocks* rich in silica, *obsidian, pearlite, pumice,* and *pitchstone.* *b.* Without quartz, with plagioclase: syenite, augite-syenite, quartzless orthoclase-porphyry, *trachyte,* and *augite-trachyte.* *c.* Without quartz, with nepheline or leucite: foyaite and miascite, liebenerite, orthoclase-porphyry, *phonolite, leucite,* and *sanidin* rocks.

II. Plagioclase rocks. *a.* With hornblende: quartz-diorite, diorite, porphyrite, hornblende-porphyrite, *quartz-propylite, propylite, dacite,* and (*hornblende*) *andesite.* *b.* With biotite: mica-diorite. *c.* With augite: diabase, augite-porphyry, melaphyre, *augite-andesite, feldspar-basalt* (with *dolerite* and *anamesite*), and *tachylyte.* *d.* With diallage: gabbro. *e.* With hypersthene: hypersthenite. *f.* With olivine: (serpentine) forellenstein.

III. Nepheline rocks: *nephelinite* and *nepheline-basalt.*

IV. Leucite rocks: *sanidin-leucite* rocks and *leucite-basalt.*

The rocks printed in italics are those of the true mineralogical and chemical, Tertiary and post-Tertiary, equivalents of the previously-mentioned ante-Tertiary rocks. It is curious that proper nepheline and leucite rocks are not met with until the Tertiary age, no analogous types being known in older time.

Some of the names of rocks require a more extended explanation. Felsite-porphyry has been preferred to the synonymous term of quartz-porphyry, because many of these rocks which are chemically identical with others do not contain macroscopical quartz, while the felsitic nature of the groundmass is common to all.

The name rhyolite was proposed early in 1860 by v. Richthofen[1] for certain rocks frequently occurring in Northern Hungary, distinguished mineralogically from trachyte, which they otherwise resemble, by the presence of quartz as an essential ingredient, and an almost infinite variety of texture, bearing clearer evidence than other rocks of having once flowed in a viscous state. He also united under this term the natural glasses, such as obsidian, pumice-stone and pearlite, which are geologically closely related to, and chemically identical with, the others.

A long time before this (in 1820) Boudant had described certain non-glassy varieties of these rocks as trachytic porphyries. In 1861, the name liparite was given by J. Roth[2] to the same rock division, including the glassy modifications, of which well-characterized members occur in the Lipari Islands. Rocks of this kind, which certainly deserve to be separated from the trachytes, have been found in many parts of the globe, everywhere possessing one characteristic behavior. They are met with in Iceland, the Euganean Hills, Northern Italy; the Siebengebirge in Rhenish Prussia; the Aegaic Islands in New Zealand. Other geologists have subsequently named the non-glassy members quartz-trachytes. In a very valuable memoir presented to the California Academy of Sciences,[3] on the Natural System of Volcanic Rocks, v. Richthofen proposes the following as

---

[1] Studien aus den ungarisch-siebenbürgischen Trachytgebirgen, Jahrb. d. geolog. Reichsanstalt, XI, 1860.

[2] Die Gesteinanalysen in tabellarischer Übersicht und mit kritischen Erläuterungen, Berlin, 1861.

[3] Vol. i, part ii, San Francisco, 1868, translated in the Zeitschrift der d. geolog. Gesellschaft, XX and XXI.

subdivisions of the rhyolite group: *a.* nevadite, or granitic rhyolite, in which large macroscopical crystalline ingredients like quartz, sanidin, plagioclase, biotite, and hornblende predominate over the groundmass; *b.* liparite, or felsitic and porphyritic rhyolite, in other words, the liparite proposed by J. Roth for the whole class, has been by v. Richthofen retained for those varieties which resemble quartz-porphyry. or felsite-porphyry, possessing a porphyritic or felsitic structure; *c.* rhyolite proper, or hyaline rhyolite, which includes the eminently glassy modifications, such as obsidian, pumice-stone, and pearlite.

But this nomenclature does not seem to be suited to the natural manner of occurrence of the rocks, for, so to speak, the centre of gravity of the group appears rather to lie in the second series. The felsitic and porphyritic varieties seem more to merit the name of proper rhyolite than the glassy ones, which are always merely local, and are quantitatively inferior equivalents of the others. From this point of view, then, the division would be as follows:

a. Nevadite, or granitic rhyolite.

b. Proper rhyolite, the felsitic and porphyritic.

c. Glassy rhyolite, obsidian, etc.

Trachyte is a rock which repeats during the Tertiary age the mineral combination of the older syenite, being characterized by the predominance of sanidin over plagioclase, and by the absence of quartz as an essential ingredient. This being the general apprehension, it is strange that v. Richthofen should, in the memoir alluded to, admit an oligoclase (*i. e.*, plagioclase) trachyte. This variety does not belong petrographically to the trachytes, but to the hornblende-andesites, for it presents a groundmass in which the principal imbedded crystals are striated feldspar and hornblende. It is essential to limit the name trachyte to the sanidin-bearing rocks. The sanidin is indeed generally accompanied by hornblende; but the examination of the trachytes of the Fortieth Parallel has proved that, in some cases, the black constituent, rich in lime, magnesia, and iron, and poor in alumina and the alkalies, is augite instead of hornblende. A new division, under the name augite-trachyte is therefore introduced into the petrographical system; and this classification is sustained by the fact that G. von Rath has shown that among the old syenites of Tyrol and Norway, always considered as combinations of orthoclase and hornblende, there are real augite-syenites. This contemporaneous but independent enlargement of the older series and its newer equivalent is most interesting.

In Hungary and Transylvania there occur singular rocks which in mineral composition closely resemble the old diorites, while they are intimately allied to the volcanic rocks geologically. They have, moreover, a commercial importance as the bearers of rich metallic veins; for instance, that of Kapnik, Nágybánya, etc. Having sufficient evidence of the Tertiary age of these rocks, in 1860 v. Richthofen designated them greenstone trachytes; for at that time rocks with prevailing plagioclase were still named trachytes. But subsequently he found rocks of the same distinctive petrographical behavior and the same geological position at Washoe and Silver Mountain; and since they have re-opened the eruptive activity of the Tertiary age, in all the localities where they have been met with, he called these precursors of all the Tertiary volcanic rocks propylites. Nevertheless, they always present the petrographical features of the old dioritic porphyries.

In later periods of the Tertiary age, in Hungary and Transylvania, as well as in the western regions of the United States, has appeared another rock, which, like propylite, is chiefly composed of plagioclase and hornblende—hornblende-andesite. It was formerly called gray trachyte by v. Richthofen. The rock is also found in many other parts of the globe. It is the best proof of v. Richthofen's eminent geological perception that he should have separated these two rocks from each other, although he could not exactly explain the petrographical difference between them.

"It escapes description. It may, at this present time, safely be founded on what the botanist would call 'habitus', a certain general character which is as easy to recognize by the eye as it is difficult to describe it in words and impossible to define its causes. It is probable that observations, such as Sorby has made in reference to those minute differences of texture which can only be detected with the aid of the microscope, and H. Rose in regard to the modifications of silica and their causes, aided by exact chemical analyses and experiments made with the view of inquiring into the differences of origin of such eruptive rocks as differ from each other in texture, will, if further prosecuted, reveal the true nature and cause of the properties which distinguish these rocks."[1]

The vagueness of this diagnosis, founded upon geological properties alone and wanting well-defined, characteristic lithological distinctions, has prevented the propylite of v. Richthofen from receiving any considerable acknowledgment among European geologists, who doubted its specific independence or the necessity of separating it petrographically from hornblende-andesite. But careful examination of the characteristic and typical propylites of the Western Territories of the United States has been the means of establishing a considerable number of constant microscopical peculiarities, sufficient to make it easy to discriminate between the two rocks, at least as they occur here. That petrographical differences exist between propylite and hornblende-andesite cannot be any longer doubted.

Both these rocks have their quartz-bearing equivalents, agreeing with the old ante-Tertiary diorite and quartz-diorite. G. Stache was the first to discover[2] that rocks which were classified by v. Richthofen partly as greenstone trachytes (propylites) and partly as gray trachytes (hornblende-andesites) contained quartz. He separated these rocks into greenstone-like quartz-trachytes and andesitic quartz-trachytes, and proposed dacite[3] as a name for both, and also for the granito-porphyric quartz-trachytes, although the last are really rhyolites or nevadites, with predominating sanidin. But because the assumed difference between greenstone-trachytes (propylites) and andesitic trachytes (hornblende-andesites) was not sufficiently obvious to geologists generally, the name of dacite is mostly confined to those quartz-bearing rocks which are marked by other peculiar-

---

[1] Natural System of Volcanic Rocks. F. von Richthofen, Mem. Cal. Acad., 1867.

[2] Fr. v. Hauer and G. Stache, Geologie Siebenbürgens, Wien, 1863, 44, 102.

[3] The name of dacite was chosen because typical varieties of these rocks occur in the ancient Roman province of Dacia. v. Richthofen is wrong when he says—Zeitschr. d. d. geol. Ges., XX, 1868, 692—that Stache's dacite is generally quartziferous propylite. Misunderstanding the observations of Austrian and other geologists, he assumes dacite and quartz-propylite to be identical, and fails to recognize in his groupings the quartz-bearing member of the hornblende-andesites—his own gray trachytes.

ities as belonging to the proper hornblende-andesites.[1] Dacite is now always used in this sense where the specific existence of propylite has been established, and so it is not proper to apply it to the quartz-bearing members of both rocks. It may be proposed to limit the term dacite to the quartz-iferous hornblende-andesites, and to call the equivalent member of propylite quartz-propylite.

The differences between augite-andesite and feldspar-basalt will be hereafter explained under the proper heads.

v. Richthofen has shown that the succession of massive eruptions during the Tertiary and post-Tertiary ages in widely-separated parts of the earth has uniformly occurred in the following general order:

a. Propylite, with quartz-propylite.
b. Andesite, with dacite.
c. Trachyte.
d. Rhyolite.
e. Basalt.

This order of succession is also observable in the vast areas of Tertiary eruptive rocks along the Fortieth Parallel.

It is, of course, not designed to describe generally in this place the microscopical peculiarities of ordinary rock-composing minerals; the diagnostic characters of single species being made a subject of occasional detailed statement in the following text. But this introductory chapter would seem to be the proper place for some remarks upon certain microscopical bodies which cannot always be identified with macroscopically-known minerals, and whose mineralogical nature is left more or less in doubt by the absence of distinctly characterizing features. It has been proposed (chiefly by H. Vogelsang) to designate the most frequent occurrences with special preliminary and subsidiary names.

Microlites are thin, needle-formed, mostly cylindrical individuals. Many minerals are apt to occur in this imperfectly crystallized form, such as feldspar, augite, hornblende, apatite, and mica. In many cases, it can be ascertained with perfect certainty to what mineral a microlite belongs, when the qualifying

[1] For instance, Doelter, Tschermak's Mineralog. Mittheilungen, 1873, 102.

word is added, like feldspar-microlite, hornblende-microlite, etc. But, on the
other hand, there occur a great many needle-formed products in the rocks
which cannot be certainly referred to any macroscopically known mineral,
either because they do not occur macroscopically or are not sufficiently well
characterized. In such cases, where the closer signification is not to be determined, the general group-name of microlite will be found very useful. The
more minute the microlites are, the more the peculiarities of those belonging to
different minerals are blended, until they are almost or entirely indistinguishable. Sometimes the microlites have very curiously dichotomous,
acicular, curled, and twisted dismembered forms, which will be described
in detail hereafter. The regular crystals, like garnet and noscan, do not
have a tendency to form microlites, on account of the isometric relation of
their axes, and this is also true of the minerals which, like specular iron,
occur macroscopically in lamellar plates. Microlites are generally the first
product in the secretion of crystals from a molten mass. Sometimes one is
inclined to think the microlites are the real embryos of crystals. It would,
indeed, be possible, in the case of crystallographically and chemically
closely related minerals, like hornblende and augite, or orthoclase and plagioclase, that the microlites should occasionally show a stage of primary
development where the characteristic properties of neither have had time
to assert themselves. For instance, a microlite may have been solidified
so early that it failed to develop the characteristics of either hornblende
or augite, say, but in a measure combines those of both; so that it
really belongs to neither, having in a certain sense not decided which to
become.

Belonites are colorless, *trichites*, black and impellucid microlites.
Both are of an uncertain mineralogical nature, and they very often occur
in glassy rocks, like obsidian.

Opacite: black, entirely opaque, amorphous grains and scales, which
often appear as metamorphic products, resulting from the decomposition of
other minerals. These little bodies may be of very different substances,
formless magnetite, earthy silicates, amorphous metallic oxyds (especially
oxyds and hydrous oxyds of titanium and manganese), graphite, etc.

Ferrite: yellowish, reddish, or brownish amorphous earthy substances, which are not infrequently pseudomorphous after iron-bearing minerals. In most cases, this rust-colored, powder-like material doubtless consists of sesquioxyd of iron free from water or in the hydrous state, but it cannot usually be identified with any mineral.

Viridite: green and transparent substances in the form of scaly or fibrous aggregations, which very often result from the decomposition of hornblende, augite, or olivine. Their composition is not always the same. They may belong chiefly to silicates of monoxyd of iron and of magnesia. The scales for the most part belong to a chloritic, the fibers to serpentinous or delessite-like mineral.

These names have been offered merely for the sake of convenience to obviate the necessity of repeated long descriptions, and will serve only so long as our ignorance of the proper mineralogical nature of the substances in question shall continue.

CHAPTER II.

CRYSTALLINE SCHISTS AND RELATED ROCKS.

Of the metamorphic rocks of the Washoe district, through which diorites and afterward Tertiary volcanic rocks of the Virginia range have protruded, there may be only mentioned in this connection a slaty hornblende rock [1],[1] which occurs on the hills above American City. It consists of a colorless quartz-ground, in which are distributed an innumerable quantity of small crippled prisms and irregular laminæ of pale-green hornblende, some lobes of brown mica, and only a very few striated plagioclases.

The gneiss from the north end of the Lake Range, Nevada [2], represents a remarkable variety, which not infrequently reappears among the crystalline schists of Nevada and Utah, but which is otherwise very rare and has not yet been particularly studied. The feldspar is almost entirely triclinic plagioclase, the colorless fresh sections of which bear the most rich, delicate, and variegated striation in polarized light. There is only a very little unstriated orthoclase present. Beside the brown mica (biotite) and quartz, this gneiss also contains beautiful green hornblende, so that it really becomes an equivalent of quartziferous mica-diorite, in the same manner as the common mica-gneiss corresponds to granite, and the usual hornblende-gneiss to quartz-syenite. With reference to the nature of its feldspars, it may indeed be named a diorite-gneiss. To this rock seem to be allied the gneisses rich in oligoclase, which Fischer has observed at Todtmoos

---

[1] The actual hand-specimens from which these descriptions are written will receive, beside the collection-number, a special number corresponding to the bracketed numeral throughout this memoir. When, therefore, the collection finds its permanent resting-place in the National Museum, students will be able to identify, not only the species, but individual rocks, described by Professor Zirkel.—C. K.

14

and Gropbach in the Münsterthal of the Black Forest, and v. Hochstetter at Adams' Peak in Ceylon; yet they differ by containing more orthoclase and less or no hornblende. The brown mica of this rock is, as always, easily to be distinguished by its excellent lamellation, by its strong dichroism, and by its powerful absorption when examined with one nicol. For the hornblende, which shows also important but somewhat less dichroism, the distinct cleavage according to the obtuse angle of the prisms (∞ P) is highly characteristic. The transverse sections of the biotite plates become nearly black when the direction of their lamellation forms an angle of 90° with the short diagonal of the polarizer. The quartzes of this gneiss are strikingly poor in microscopical fluid-inclusions, those which are present being exceptionally large; on the other hand, both quartzes and plagioclases contain the most finished, sharply edged, brown laminæ of mica, whose diameter often decreases to a few thousandths of a millimeter. The enormous quantity of microscopical apatite prisms found in this rock is remarkable, as in all gneisses which abound in hornblende.

A series of curious crystalline slates occurs in Trinity Cañon, Montezuma Range, Nevada, and in some adjacent hills [3, 4, 5]. To the naked eye, they look almost wholly homogeneous or without any distinct constituent; they have a dark, grayish-black color, a finely glittering lustre, and are not easily fissile; so that at first sight they might be mistaken for certain fine-grained anamesites or basalts. The microscopical analysis discovered a wholly crystalline mixture of quartz, brown mica in large proportion, white mica (muscovite), black particles of magnetite, and a few grains and prisms of a pale-green mineral which seems to be a kind of hornblende. The brown and white mica laminæ show a remarkable phenomenon, which has never been elsewhere observed, but which often reappears in the mica-bearing rocks of this region.[1] The same microlites are also imbedded in the mica of the Kersanton from Brest in Brittany. They often contain very numerous, thin, delicate microlites, which have a tendency to cross each other after the manner of a net, and uniting in hurdles in the middle of the micas, or forming stars and groups whose members radiate from a centre. These microlites are often dichotome on the ends, and always spread out in

[1] See representation of another rock, Plate II, fig. 2.

the plane of lamination. Their proper color is not distinguishable, and their mineralogical nature must remain uncertain, but they may belong to the above-mentioned green mineral, for some varieties of these rocks exist [4] in which the latter is wanting, and here the laminæ of the brown mica are found to be entirely pure.

The variety from the ridge west of Pahkcah Peak, Pah-tson Mountains, Nevada, contains, beside the brown and white micas, an oil-green mica in thin laminæ, larded with fine, limpid quartz grains. None of these rocks contain a trace of either monoclinic or triclinic feldspar.

A similar metamorphic rock is found in the ridge east of Pahkcah Peak, Pah-tson Mountains [6]. Quite crypto-crystalline and almost homogeneous, light greenish-gray in color, it shows under the microscope a colorless quartz-ground, in which an immense quantity of very pale-green hornblende prisms have been associated and crowded together in single heaps, which are often elongated in one direction. As in the previously described rock, feldspar is here wanting.

The Humboldt Range offers an excellent field for the study of the Archæan crystalline schists. On the west slope of these mountains, there occurs a brown mica-schist [7] with curious yellowish-gray knots which reach a diameter of 8^{mm}. The chief mass of the slate itself (Plate II, fig. 1) is a mixture of quartz, brown and colorless mica, the latter being remarkably laminated, so that its transverse sections, in ordinary light, might be mistaken for polysynthetic plagioclase; yet between the nicols, of course, in spite of the striation, no variegated lineation appears, only monochromatic polarization. A few very distinct crystals of plagioclase are also present. Under the microscope, the knots present a very intimately entangled web of extremely thin, colorless, needle-formed microlites, heaped together primarily in bunches, which are again woven together. On the exterior of the knot-sections, the felt becomes looser, and, as may be clearly seen, is imbued with water-clear quartz. The outward margin consists of quartz, in which are isolated needle-tufts. As to the nature of these microlites, it is highly probable that they belong to fibrolite or bucholzite, which, if not identical with sillimanite or disthene, is only a variety. The bucholzite from Bodeumais in Bavaria is a mineral so similar in every respect that it might be mistaken under the microscope for these Humboldt microlites.[1] These fibrous bunches possess a further striking resemblance to those in the cordierites of the Saxon gneisses (Göhren near Wechselburg, environs of Rochsburg, Galgenberg near Mittweida), and especially the cordierite in that from Bodenmais, and which, according to all appearances, belongs likewise to the fibrolite.[2] In the American specimen, the needle-bunches also lie abundantly in the independent quartzes and brown micas of the rock, just as both also occur in the gneiss from Bodenmais. Where the microlites are heaped together into sheaves, they are often curved, crooked, and dismembered into single short pieces as in similar European rocks. Hydrous oxyd of iron has penetrated narrow fissures of these clots, and given them a yellowish tinge. At Spruce Mountain [8], Peoquop Range, Nevada, another mica-slate occurs which exactly agrees with this interesting variety.

Clover Cañon in the Humboldt Mountains yields an excellent and rich assemblage of varieties of Archæan crystalline schists. The gneisses are generally composed of orthoclase, quartz, brown mica, and some hornblende. Their feldspars are distinguished by the contained fluid-inclusions, which, as is well known, are elsewhere not often found in this rock-constituent. Here the feldspars in some instances contain more liquid-inclusions and empty cavities than the granitic quartzes, being actually surcharged with them. Here also the feldspars are decidedly richer in fluid-particles than the quartzes of these rocks: the inclusions have a rectangular or irregular shape, with numerous ramifications and branches, while those of the quartz are either rounded or more regular in form. This interesting peculiarity in the structure of feldspar, hitherto supposed to be very rare, is surprisingly common through the gneisses, granites, and younger eruptive rocks of the Fortieth Parallel; but it can, of course, only be observed where the feldspar-substance remains clear and unaltered. Many fluid-inclusions which were once present in other feldspars may have been obliterated by decomposition, to which this mineral falls an easy prey.

Most of the gneisses from Clover Cañon may also be distinguished by the

[1] See F. Z., Mikroskopische Beschaffenheit der Mineralien und Gesteine, 1872, 200.
[2] Ibid., 209.

2 M r

surprising quantity of proportionally thick and strong individual prisms of microscopical apatite, which often have a length of 0.5^{mm}, are glaring and dazzling, and are frequently traversed by basic cracks, broken into several pieces, dismembered into single joints which lie behind each other in a straight line or show the phenomenon of reciprocal dislocation. Some of the small members are moved out of a straight line, which sometimes breaks the apatites into a dozen pieces and throws them out of an even row into a curved bow behind each other (Plate I, fig. 6). Many of the larger of these apatites also show traces of the well-known fine, dust-like material rendering the interior impure, generally accumulated in the form of a thin strip along the chief axis; but here, as elsewhere, this interposed substance is so fine that its nature cannot be determined. Long, cylindrical cavities are often visible in these apatites. All the prisms seem to be very sharply-featured, for the hexagonal sections of the transversely cut, vertically standing, or somewhat inclined columns (which let through a dazzling light) are very regularly edged, while in the other rocks these hexagons are nearly rounded. These apatites are found included in all rock-constituents, in the quartzes, feldspars, micas, and hornblendes; and they also show in this crystalline schist the familiar peculiarity of being gathered in numerous individuals upon a limited space, as if the phosphoric acid had not at the outset been equally spread through the rock-material. Moreover, it is remarkable that apatite should occur with such strikingly similar behavior in rocks which differ so widely in their genetic history. The apatites of the basalts and phonolites are, as such, not in general distinguishable from those in the crystalline slates, which, whatever may be the opinion as to their origin, have certainly been formed differently from basalts or trachytes.

In Clover Cañon, there also occurs a gneiss [9] poor in mica, whose quartzes contain the very curious double inclusions, the interiors of which consist of liquid carbonic acid, (Plate I, fig. 1). Seen from above, they present three circular lines arranged concentrically. The outermost line is often somewhat angular, and marks the limit of the whole inclosure; the middle one is the external limit of the carbonic acid; the innermost circle is the bubble which lies in this fluid. There is not the slightest doubt that this liquid b is really carbonic acid, for the bubble c within it shows one of the most characteristic reactions. When subjected to a rising temperature, a heat of only 31°C., it disappears by condensation, and reappears when, by cooling, that point of temperature is again reached. There is no other liquid, except nitrous oxyd, which possesses at so low a degree such an enormous expansive power.

Vogelsang has shown, by a series of ingenious experiments, that quartzes containing a liquid having these peculiarities immediately gave, in a spectrum-apparatus, the excellent and characteristic lines of carbonic acid. The mineral decrepitates upon being heated in an exhausted tube. Such quartz, powdered in lime-water, causes a precipitate of carbonate of lime, owing to the presence of the carbonic acid in little hollows.[1] Nearly at the same time that Vogelsang demonstrated the above, Sorby was engaged in showing, by measuring its expansive force, that the curious fluid in some sapphires is also carbonic acid.[2] As to the external zone *a* which surrounds the fluid and separates it from the quartz, Brewster has observed in Brazilian topazes inclusions analogous to these, and he believed that there were two distinct liquids, one outside the other.[3] But as against this explanation is the fact that by heating our inclosures even to and above the high temperature of 120° C., the external boundary-line of the interior carbonic acid never shows either dilation or contraction, or, indeed, any alteration whatever, which probably ought not to be the case if the environing substance were likewise a liquid. Vogelsang, therefore, believed that the external zone was a solid, and he was inclined to regard it as a topaz substance of different density, which may have been produced by the expansive nature of the interior fluid. If this interpretation is right, we should see in the external zones of our inclusions a quartz substance in a somewhat different state of pressure; but it will be evident that upon this supposition the very sharp outermost boundary-line of the whole inclusion is somewhat striking. Moreover, all these inclusions are very similar to the elsewhere-occurring glassy inclusions which contain a fluid with a bubble; but it may be

[1] Poggendorff's Annalen, cxxxvii, 1869, 56, 265.
[2] Proceedings of the Royal Society, xvii, 1869, 291; Monthly Microscopical Journal, 1869, 222.
[3] Transactions of the Royal Society, Edinburgh, x, 1826, 407.

declared, without further proof, that the inclusions of the gneiss-quartz cannot be identified with the latter. In the quartzes of our gneiss, the largest double inclusion of this kind measures 0.0072^{mm} in length and 0.0004^{mm} in breadth at the broadest part. The little gas-bubble in the carbonic acid is in constant spontaneous motion, rolling incessantly through the fluid, in a whirling dance, like a thing of life. Beside these, there occur other liquid inclusions, which do not possess the external zone a, but, when the quick absorption of the bubble is considered, they too are seen to consist of the same remarkable acid. Liquid inclusions of carbonic acid are at present known to occur in the quartzes of the granitic gneiss of the St. Gotthard (very similar in every respect to those which we have been examining), in the quartzes of the gray gneiss from Freiberg in Saxony, and of the granite from Aughrushmore in Ireland; in the topazes from Rio Belmonte in Brazil;[1] in some sapphires;[2] in augites, olivines, and feldspars of basalts from Rhenish Prussia, Hesse, Würtemberg, Hungary;[3] in the greenish apatites from the Pfitsch Valley in Tyrol.[4] If the shortness of this list seems to warrant the conclusion that these highly interesting inclosures are very rarely found in the constituents of rocks, the following lines will prove that they occur in surprising frequency in the quartzes of the gneisses, mica-slates, and granites from the western part of the American continent, and that they are almost a common phenomenon in the rocks of the Fortieth Parallel.

These double inclosures have been observed in the quartzes of many gneiss sections from different localities in Clover Cañon, and in none are they more numerous, distinct or larger than in a variety poor in mica [10]. The quantity of quartz and mica in these gneisses varies considerably, some being poor in quartz, rich in mica [11, 12]; others showing an inverse proportion of these minerals. Apatite is by far more abundant in the gneisses which contain more or less hornblende than in those which bear

---

[1] Vogelsang, loc. cit.   [2] Sorby, loc. cit.
[3] F. Z., Untersuchungen über die mikroskopische Structur und Zusammensetzung der Basaltgesteine, 1870, 21, 33, 60.
[4] Rosenbusch, Mikroskopische Physiographie der petrographisch wichtigsten Mineralien, 1873, 220.

only mica and are free from hornblende. Some of these crystalline schists contain an amount of carbonate of lime which causes the rock to effervesce when wetted with acids, and under the microscope it can sometimes be observed as small colorless particles of calc-spar traversed by oblique-angled fissures.

Another rock from Clover Cañon almost represents a diorite-gneiss [13]. It bears more plagioclase than orthoclase, the former being splendidly striated, considerable quartz, brown mica, much green, excellently cleavable hornblende, with included grains of black magnetite, and interesting phenomena of fracture, the ends of the thick prisms being often totally splintered, and the shivered pieces moved asunder and disjoined, but not so far separated that it is not plain to which individual hornblende they belong. Titanite appears here in pale grayish-yellow, sharp, oblique-angled sections having a rough surface, in all respects similar to those in the hornblende-bearing "Fundamental Gneisses" of the Loch Maree in Scotland, which there form the base upon which rest the Cambrian conglomerates and sandstones. This gneiss is rich in apatite, which is worth mentioning because it contains, in an uncommonly distinct measure, large microscopical fluid-inclusions (see Plate I, fig. 7, representing a similar apatite from a granite). Sometimes they are rounded, sometimes heaped together in cylindrical form, sometimes more isolated and stretched out parallel to the chief axis of the crystal. The fluid here is not liquid carbonic acid, but is probably water, with perhaps a little carbonic acid; for by heating the section up to 110° C. no characteristic absorption of the bubble is discovered. Before now, such fluid-inclusions in apatites have only been observed in those of the hornblende-andesite from the Hemmerich near the Seven Mountains in Rhenish Prussia,[1] and in the up-grown macroscopical crystals from Schlaggenwald in Bohemia and the Pfitsch Valley in Tyrol,[2] where, however, they are not constituents of rocks.

To these interesting rocks of Clover Cañon also belongs a gneiss from the foot-hills north of Secret Pass in the same Humboldt Range [14]. This

---

[1] F. Z., Mikroskopische Beschaffenheit der Mineralien, Gest., 223.
[2] Rosenbusch, Mikroskopische Physiographie, 220.

variety is grained more like granite. While not as slaty as those previously mentioned, it bears many apatites and numerous pale brownish-yellow, little, needle-formed, prismatic crystals, which are widely spread through the crystalline schists of this region. These crystals have a very dazzling lustre and many faces, but their form is not sufficiently distinct to allow of recognizing them. In many cases, they appear to belong to the tetragonal system, and to present the combination of a pyramid, a prism of a different order, and of a ditetragonal pyramid ($P. \infty P \infty . n P n$), a form which suggests the supposition that they may belong to zircon. They are certainly very similar to the microscopical zircon-crystals which occur in the eklogites of the Fichtelgebirge in Germany. The same somewhat obscure crystals are present in great numbers in the Saxon granulites, where it was also impossible to determine their nature with exactness. Zircon possesses the high index of refraction ($n = 1.95$), and beside this the single faces are more difficult to recognize than in other crystallized minerals of the same size. Nevertheless, it is true that Professor Bunsen, of Heidelberg, who kindly consented to analyze one of these gneisses rich in the brown prisms, could find no trace of zirconium. With reference to this analysis, it should be remembered that the prisms are of microscopical fineness, that they constitute only a very small part of the bulk of the whole mass, and that the eminent analyst had at his disposal only a very small quantity of the rock. Beside this, as he says in a letter, the detection of minute quantities of zirconium is one of the most difficult processes in analytical chemistry.[1] Associated with the gneisses and mica-schists in Clover Cañon are some other interstratified rocks which are wont to accompany these crystalline slates.

Among them is a pure hornblende-rock (amphibolite), remarkable for the absence of other microscopical constituents, there being neither quartz, apatite, nor titanite [15], a variety very rarely observed. The contrast is very nice between the long, parallel, fibrous, longitudinal sections and the

---

[1] Mr. R. W. Woodward, the Chemist of the Exploration of the Fortieth Parallel, afterward treated a much larger amount of this same gneiss, and succeeded, by a process of his own, in isolating a sufficient quantity of zirconium to subject to a rigid examination. The details of his process, together with the analysis of several other zirconiferous schists, will be found in the chapter on Archaean Rocks, in Volume I of this series.—C. K.

transverse section of the dark-green hornblende, which shows prismatic cleavage in an unsurpassed manner. Hence it is evident that the individual hornblendes have crystallized into and through each other, and are mutually intertwined in the most complicated manner. Certain isolated fluid-particles, with spontaneously moving bubbles contained in the hornblende, are especially worth mentioning, for they are the first liquid-inclusions which have ever been detected in this mineral. Hornblende must in general be very poor in them, even more so than augite, in which they have been known for a long time to occur occasionally. Perhaps it is allowable to presume that the usual fibrous texture of the hornblende is unfavorable to the incorporation of fluid-particles.

The quartzites from the western slope of the Humboldt Mountains, and from Clover Cañon [16, 17, 18, 19, and 20], contain in the predominant quartz microscopical fluid-inclusions and empty cavities, and besides, laminæ of colorless (never brown) mica, and some feldspar crystals, often light-brown hydrous oxyd of iron in fissures. Here and there long, thin microlites (perhaps belonging to hornblende) lie in the quartzes. These are so narrow that they appear, even under a high magnifying power, merely as fine, short, black lines.

In a quartzite from Clover Cañon [20], long, quite pale-green needles, which very probably are actinolite, are interspersed with crooked and curved ends, and present the most detailed phenomenon of fracture. One of these needles was found broken into not less than fifteen pieces. Rocks somewhat similar to those of the Humboldt Mountains are observed a little farther east, of which the following may be mentioned: a gneissic micaceous slate from Egan Cañon, Egan Range, Nevada, in which the zircon-like mineral, mentioned above, occurs again very abundantly. Two thin, light-brown individual members of this are often grown together in the form of a right-angled joint; nevertheless, it would seem to be improbable that a twin law exists here, for the angle is not always the same, being sometimes sharp and at others obtuse.

A mica-slate from Spruce Mountain, Pequop Range [21], consists of quartz, much deep-green and a little white mica, and the zircon-like mineral. The laminæ of biotite here are likewise filled with fine needles, which sometimes show a hexagonal arrangement (Plate II, fig. 2). It is not impossible that they belong to the zircon-like mineral. They are confined to the magnesian mica, curiously enough, never having been found interposed in the white mica or quartz.

Another mica-slate is observed interstratified in white quartz at Pilot Peak in the Ombe Mountains, the brown mica of which is entirely free from microlites, and the quartz is noticeable by reason of containing almost no fluid-inclusions.

Ogden and Farmington Cañons in the Wahsatch Range, Utah, present an excellent field for the examination of crystalline schists of the Archæan series. Hornblende-gneisses generally predominate in these cañons. There is one specimen from the mouth of Ogden Cañon [22] which is made up of orthoclase, considerable plagioclase, quartz, brown mica, and plenty of hornblende and apatite. It is seen that in the transverse sections of the biotites, sharp and limited layers of a colorless substance are imbedded parallel to the lamination of the individual biotites, or to the chief plane of cleavage. It seems most probable that they belong to white mica, although such a coalescence of the two species, as far as is known, has never been observed either macroscopically or microscopically.

Another hornblende-gneiss from the same cañon [23] is made up of like constituents, but it contains besides, short brown prisms of the zircon-like mineral with a pretty distinct quadratic transverse section. In hand-specimens, the direction of the black prisms of hornblende shows very plainly a linear parallelism; elsewhere it is the mica that presents this phenomenon of macroscopic structure. The quartzes of this variety are very poor in fluid-inclusions.

A characteristic hornblende-gneiss comes from Ogden Point [24], is very coarse-grained, and contains orthoclase, a comparatively large amount of plagioclase, quartz, a little brown mica, and much hornblende, to which nearly all the dark ingredients belong. Apatite is not wanting.

Other gneisses from this point [25, 26] are poor in hornblende, but they possess the zircon-like mineral very well developed and in considerable frequency. Prof. Robert Bunsen, of Heidelberg, has very kindly analyzed this gneiss; he gives the following as the result:

Silica	74. 95
Alumina	9. 42
Sesquioxyd of iron	7.47
Lime	1. 65
Magnesia	0. 13
Potash	2. 02
Soda	4. 05
Water	1. 02
	100. 71

Farmington Cañon in the Wahsatch has a gneiss [27] with grains of garnet more than 1^{mm} thick, which, under the microscope, give intensely red sections and appear perfectly dark between crossed nicols. They are traversed by a net-work of fissures having multitudinous ramifications in which some green matter has settled, running in narrow veins through the garnet in all directions. Without doubt, this epigenetic substance is chlorite, which has been formed at the expense of the garnet bounding the cracks. This is the first step in the development of the true pseudomorphs of chlorite after garnet, which may be seen in the best quality and on the most magnificent scale in the iron-mine of Spurr Mountain in the Lake Superior region.[1] This example again demonstrates molecular alteration to be by the bursting and shivering of a crystal, as has been observed in a corresponding manner in olivine,[2] where it is decomposed into serpentine, and in cordierite,[3] with its numerous pseudomorphous descendants. The substance of the garnets, as such, is quite free from impurities, as is usually the case with the garnets of crystalline schists and granulites. Very small rounded garnets, in form like dew-drops, the largest measuring 0.01^{mm} in diameter, are also interspersed in the feldspars and quartzes of the rock; but there exists no transition in size between these and the macroscopical ones, which are a hundred times larger. In Farmington Cañon, however, the garnets are not confined to hornblende-gneisses.

---

[1] Raphael Pumpelly, Am. Jour. Sci., July, 1875, 17.
[2] Tschermak, Sitzungsber. d. Wiener Akad., LVI, 1867, I. Abth., Juli Heft, 1.
[3] F. Z., Mikroskopische Beschaffenheit der Mineralien und Gesteine, 211.

A mica-gneiss bearing garnet [28] also occurs, composed of alternating light and dark layers, in which there is no hornblende. The light layers are rich in feldspar and quartz, poor in brown mica and deep red garnet (or altogether without them): the dark layers are abundant in brown mica and deep red garnet. The larger garnets lying along fissures are altered into green chlorite. Besides these macroscopical individuals, the rock only contains microscopical garnet grains, which are often found gathered into little heaps. Other beautiful hornblende-gneisses of this cañon are destitute of garnet. One of these rocks [29] which has little mica and feldspar, presents again the yellowish-brown, zircon-like crystals. The quartz of this variety, as is commonly the case with these hornblende-bearing gneisses, is, in a striking measure, poor in fluid-inclusions, if not entirely wanting in them.

This quantitative proportion of the ingredients often re-appears in Farmington Cañon, where gneiss [30], enormously rich in apatite, contains brown prisms and quartzes which are remarkably deficient in the liquid-inclusions that are elsewhere common to them. The peak north of the head of Farmington Cañon is made up of a coarse gneiss, with not very much mica, no hornblende, and no apatite: the feldspars are isabel-colored and decomposed into a rather impellucid substance; the quartzes have numerous fluid-inclusions, and the brown zircon-prisms are wanting.

The hornblende-schists [31] which occur in Farmington Cañon appear under the microscope as splendid mixtures of dark-green, entirely pure and fresh hornblende and colorless quartz, which, like that in the hornblende-gneisses, is generally very poor in fluid-inclusions.

Another metamorphic hornblende-schist [32] from the small cañon on the west slope of Twin Peaks, north of Little Cottonwood Cañon, in the Wahsatch, consists of quartz in the form of a groundmass, penetrated by innumerable small, tender, nearly bluish-green-colored hornblende prisms, which unite inside into pretty bunches and stars: there are also thicker independent hornblende prisms and some brown mica. Sometimes quartzites are found in the neighborhood of the gneisses of Farmington Cañon.

Under the microscope, one of these, having a grayish flesh-color

[33], is seen to be composed only of rounded and evidently worn grains of quartz. The exact age is unknown, its relations to the neighboring gneisses obscure, and is probably referable to the Cambrian and not the Archæan series. The single fragments of quartz show evidence of an amassing by flowing waters, and possess the most diverse structure and behavior. Some of them are rich and others very poor in fluid-inclusions; some are abundant in thin black microlitic hairs, which others entirely lack; in other quartz-grains, a dirty yellowish-gray, dust-like, and very fine-grained matter, never before observed, is interposed in parallel bands, which are often curved or twisted. Its mineralogical nature cannot be distinguished. The grains of quartz are also cemented by penetrating silica, which belongs not to opal, but to quartz, as was proved by examining it in polarized light; but there is only a little of this luting material.

At Twin Peaks Ridge, in the Wahsatch, an unmistakably Archæan quartzite occurs [34] which is filled up with microscopical laminæ of brown mica, and shows numerous fluid-inclusions in the quartzes.

A remarkable garnet rock is found as a member of the Archæan series at the head of Big Cottonwood Cañon in the Wahsatch [35]. It is a quartz-iferous, rather coarse-grained mass, which contains macroscopically in its little hollows a fine, delicate spinning of green epidote. In the thin sections, the garnets have a feeble brownish-yellow color, and present a most excellent layer-structure, owing to the visible enveloping of individual schists during the growth of the crystals. The single zones which surround each other in the sections like concentric shells are only 0.0015^{mm} thick, so that 666 schists come upon 1^{mm}. Pretty contrasts of color are often seen in the different layers and combinations of layers, mostly in darker and lighter tones of the yellowish-brown. Traces of lamellar polarization are in harmony with this structure, the sections showing between crossed nicols, single, colored lines in the dark principal mass. There can be no doubt that this polarization of single layers is produced by pressure. The schistiform structure of garnets has often been macroscopically observed in a rough development (as in the crystals from Cziklowa and Orawicza in Hungary); but as far as is known, it nowhere else appears in such distinct, detailed, and multifarious microscopical development as here. The crystals possessing this structure have grown to their present size by repeated superposition of material, the process being marked by intervals of inactivity, each wrapper-like zone representing the result of a period of formation, and the planes between two of them indicating intermissions in the time of growth. The quartz accompanying these perfectly pure garnets is rich in large fluid-inclusions, which are splendidly formed, sharp, hexagonal pyramids, so that one may look through the pellucid quartz substance and distinctly see even the corners and edges on the farther side of one of these negative crystals containing a liquid. It is but rarely that fluid-inclusions are found which so well represent the exact form of the including crystal. This is, however, as is well known, a phenomenon that often occurs with imbedded glassy particles. Calcite is present in this rock in addition to quartz and garnet.

Other remarkable crystalline schists, belonging also to the old Archæan series, form wide regions of country in Colorado. Here also hornblende-bearing rocks seem in general to predominate, in striking contrast to Germany, where very extensive areas of schists of the same geological position occur in which no hornblende-gneisses are developed.

The fine silvery-white, scaly mica-slate from Red Creek, Uinta Mountains [36], bears such a striking resemblance to the well-known beautiful paragonite slate from Monte Campione, near Faido, at the St. Gotthard, Switzerland, that it is difficult to distinguish one from the other—the more so since it contains excellent large crystals of pale-blue disthene (cyanite). The rock also bears staurolite crystals in the same way that they accompany the disthene in the neighboring darker mica-slate from Airola on the southern declivity of St. Gotthard. Under the microscope, the American occurrence presents merely a mixture of almost wholly colorless, irregularly hexagonal laminæ of paragonite, with ledge-formed transverse sections, which perfectly accords with the appearance of the chief ingredient of the Monte Campione rock. Here, however, the likeness ends, for neither disthene nor staurolite is found in microscopical crystals; these constituents in this case are confined to the large macroscopical individuals. But very few dark oil-green and brownish-green laminæ of mica are scattered through the aggregation of paragonite, and a number of bluish-gray sections of highly dichroitic tourmaline are present, of which the prismatic individuals are often broken into many pieces. The disthene here is like the Swiss,[1] and, like that in the Saxon granulite, totally free from any interposition: it certainly seems that this mineral is one of the purest we know of. It was highly interesting to examine microscopically this new American occurrence of staurolite to prove whether it also belongs to those which are mixed so abundantly with quartz. Chemical analyses of staurolites from various localities, and even of those from one and the same locality, differ very considerably from each other, as has long been known. In general, the amount of silica varies from 27. to 51., that of alumina from 35. to 55., that of oxyd of iron from 13. to 23. per cent., so that it has been impossible to construct a formula suitable to all. The staurolite of St. Gotthard contained the lowest amount of silica of any. Lechartier[2] then pointed out that when the other staurolite occurrences, especially those of Brittany and from Bolivia, are powdered; under the microscope, beside the usual red grains of the staurolite which correspond with the powder of those from St. Gotthard, a great number of unknown colorless grains become visible, which can be extracted by hydro-fluoric acid, leaving the proper staurolite substance unattacked. The chemical composition of the Breton staurolite, originally containing up to 54. per cent. silica, after the removal of those pellucid, water-clear, interposed grains, entirely agrees with that from St. Gotthard in its natural state (with 28.5 per cent. silica). Curiously enough, Lechartier did not express the sufficiently-warranted supposition that the grains belong to quartz. Ascertaining the observations of Lechartier, H. Fischer[3] then demonstrated that the intermixed substance which adds to the natural quantity of silica was really quartz. v. Lasaulx,[4] to whom we owe a careful examination of the different occurrences of staurolite, subsequently corroborated this, and showed that they here and

---

[1] Von Lasaulx has examined these analogous Swiss rocks microscopically—Neues Jahrbuch f. Mineralogie, etc., 1872, 835.

[2] Bulletin de la Soc. chimique (2), III, 1865, 378.

[3] Kritische mikroskopisch mineralogische Studien, erste Fortsetzung, Freiberg i. Br., 1871, 55.

[4] Mineralogische Mittheilungen gesammelt v. G. Tschermak, 1872, III. Heft, 173. See also, on the structure of staurolites, K. Peters, Sitzungsber. d. Wiener Akad., LVII, 1. Abtheil., 646.

there include still other microscopical minerals, such as dark mica, magnetite, garnet, and brookite. The yellowish or reddish brown sections of the new American staurolite (Plate II, fig. 3) microscopically agree in every respect with those of Brittany, the really stereotyped accompaniment of colorless rounded quartz grains being visible even in common light. The quantity of the inclosed quartz is so great that the staurolite would surely, upon a chemical analysis, show silica to an amount between 40. and 50. per cent.

There also exists on Red Creek a beautiful hornblende-rock [37], the spaces between whose broad diverging prisms are filled with colorless quartz and a very few feldspar particles free from apatite.

The granite-gneiss from Rawling's Peak, Wyoming [38], consists of quartz, feldspar (mostly plagioclase), and hornblende. In structure, it is between a granite and a gneiss, not sufficiently grained and without enough direction for the former and not sufficiently slaty for the latter. This hornblende does not form any distinctly featured individuals: it presents membranes instead, which appear, under the microscope, to be composed of innumerable, little, regularly shaped microlites. One may distinctly see how these needles are associated with green grains in such a way as to make what appears macroscopically as an individual of hornblende. In the other constituents of the rock, pale-green, fine prickles, or needles, and grains of hornblende are abundantly scattered, especially in the plagioclase; the quartz has less of them. The latter is, in striking contrast to the former, enormously rich in fluid-inclusions, which contain, with unusual constancy, little cubes of chloride of natrium. These remarkable inclusions have been considered till now as rather rare in the quartzes of some granitic, gneissic, and porphyritic rocks, and in some minerals, but they appear here in considerable frequency, and the following pages will show that they are found widely spread through the analogous rocks of the Fortieth Parallel. These microscopical inclusions (Plate 1, fig. 2) consist of saturated solutions of chloride of sodium, and are characterized by little, included salt cubes in addition to the bubble. The spontaneous motion of the bubbles here visible, as is often the case, prevents any doubt of the liquid nature of the surrounding medium. The small cubical crystals in the liquid look as if made from glass: they are so pellucid that the sharp corners and edges on the farther side appear distinctly through the mass, and all the dimensions of the hexahedric body can be viewed. Sometimes they are extended somewhat rectangularly or are rounded off at the corners. A very fine striation occurs here and there on their quadratic faces, running parallel to the edges, giving the faces something of the drawing of a chess-board, and recalling the same familiar phenomenon which marks cubes of kitchen-salt. Other quartzes inclosing liquid particles, of the same kind, have been found, upon a careful examination, actually to contain chloride of sodium.[1] The water in which such quartz as this has been finely powdered, produces an unexpectedly strong reaction for chlorine when a few drops of nitrate of silver are added. By spectrum-analysis, the presence of sodium in the same quartz may be again demonstrated. If it be held in a flame, at every decrepitation splendid repeated flashings characteristic of the sodium-line are seen, which indicate the moments when the small hollows, one after another, crack, and their contents enter the spectrum-flame of the apparatus. Such inclusions of dissolved chloride of sodium with included salt cubes have thus far been found in the quartzes of the zircon-syenite from Laurvig in Norway, the diorite from Quenast in Belgium, the granite from Johann-Georgenstadt in Saxony, Trevalgan near St. Ives, the Ding-Doug Mine near Penzanse in Cornwall, and the Goatfell in the island of Arran, Scotland; in the felsitic-porphyry (elvan) from Withiel, Cornwall, and from the western coast of Arran; in the post-Liassic syenite-porphyry near the Glamig in the Isle of Skye (Hebrides); in the propylitic rock from Borsa-Bánya in Transylvania; in the gneissic crystalline slates of the Pass Trosachs near Loch Katrine, Scotland. They have also been observed in the calc-spar and nepheline of blocks ejected from Vesuvius, in some smaragde crystals, and in the unaltered cordierite substance of the praseolite from Brakke, near Brevig, in Norway. As mentioned above, the list of these occurrences has been so much amplified by the study of the rocks of the Fortieth Parallel that these remarkable microscopical inclusions must lose a good deal of their rareness and be considered as rather common pheno-

---

[1] F. Z., Neues Jahrbuch f. Mineralogie, etc., 1870, 802.

mena. The inclusions in the quartz of the rock from Rawling's Peak, Wyoming, show besides a property which till now has never been observed except in a very indistinct and doubtful occurrence. In addition to the bubble and little cube in the salt solution, there are small, thin, pale-green microlites of hornblende, which are fixed to the wall of the surrounding quartz and project into the interior of the fluid (Plate I, fig. 3). These microlites are so abundantly interposed in the minerals which constitute rocks that there can be no doubt of this having been mechanically taken up by the liquid-particles. The dimensions of the largest inclusion in the quartzes of this rock are 0.08^{mm} in length and 0.065^{mm} in breadth. Another rock from Rawling's Peak [39] is quite similar to that last described.

At Bruin Peak, Colorado, an excellent mica-slate occurs [40],which consists of quartz containing almost no fluid-inclusions, with dark and white mica. The dark mica, in some places more of a greenish and in others more of a brownish color, includes an abundance of narrow needles, whose parallel border-lines are so near together that it is almost impossible, even with a high magnifying power, to discover whether their substance is or is not colored. These short linear microlites cross each other with curious regularity at an angle under 60°. For one to say to which mineral they belong is difficult; surely not to hornblende, but perhaps to the colorless or white mica, because there are in this rock, beside the laminæ of muscovite, wholly colorless prisms (not transverse sections through laminæ), which can only belong to the latter. It is not surprising that mica appears here in the elsewhere uncommon form of long prisms, for we know by the examinations of Gustave Rose[1] that the very long prismatic crystals which are regularly interposed in the biaxial mica (phlogopite) of South Burgess in Canada and produce the famous asterism of that variety, belong to monaxial mica. In this gneiss, we possibly would have the opposite phenomenon, a regular interposition of biaxial white mica prisms in laminæ of a monaxial, brown one. The same rock contains an exceptionally large amount of magnetite grains whose metallic lustre is shown off to splendid advantage in reflected light. In the larger octahedral crystals are included prisms of colorless mica, which look like

[1]Monatsberichte der Berliner Akad. der Wissenschaften, 1869, 330.

sharp incisions in the black, opaque substance. The mica-slate from Bruin Peak is accompanied by mica-gneiss containing some hornblende [41], and by a hornblende rock [42] strongly resembling that from Red Creek [37], except in possessing less of the quartz-ground and more feldspars, among which also are a few plagioclases. The region of Grand Encampment Creek in the Park Range consists of a similar *suite* of rocks.

On Davis' Mountain, a very typical hornblende-gneiss occurs [43] with thick, alternating, white layers rich in feldspar and dark ones rich in hornblende. Besides the quartz, this rock abounds in plagioclase and beautiful hornblende and apatite; but it bears little orthoclase and almost no mica, and therefore approaches the diorite-gneisses. The quartz displays in great distinctness and beauty double inclusious with liquid carbonic acid in the interior; also very numerous common fluid-inclusions, consisting only of water, with probably a little carbonic acid in solution. Curiously enough, the quartz, in another not less beautiful hornblende-gneiss from Grand Encampment Creek [44], contains hardly any microscopical liquid-inclusions. The Grand Encampment Peak offers a hornblende rock [45] which is, in a rare measure, free from other ingredients. .

Quartzite as white as snow is interstratified in the hornblende-gneisses at the north end of the Park Range [46]. Its chief mass appears in the thin section glass-like and pellucid, but is traversed in all directions by little dull, milky lines, bands, and spots, which, under a higher magnifying power, are seen to be a multitude of aggregated fluid-inclunisons. They belong to two different varieties, some being composed of water with a moving bubble, which does not disappear in a temperature above 100° C, and others being the double inclusions, with carbonic acid in the interior, whose bubble may be driven off by the smoke of a cigar. It is remarkable that these inclusions of different chemical nature are associated also in the quartzes of the accompanying gneisses, a fact which may perhaps prove that the nearest geological connection exists between the two rocks, and that in origin they are the same.

The metamorphic Archæan territory of Colorado presents also the follow-

3 M P

ing rocks worthy of mention: at Mount Zirkel,[1] Park Range, a gneiss [47] with some hornblende; among the feldspars a good many plagioclases; zones with alternating rich bands of feldspar and hornblende, producing distinct layer-structure.

On the south side of Clark's Peak, North Park, is an excellent hornblende-bearing mica-gneiss [48] with an astonishing amount of apatite in quartzes as large as pin-heads; 20 or 30 apatites lying horizontally, pointing in all directions, and showing transverse sections, being often included together; much beautiful plagioclase, also quartz almost free from fluid-inclusions.

In the North Park, one of the best hornblende-gneisses is a decided diorite-gneiss [49], in which the naked eye detects many well-striated plagioclases, while the microscope shows that all the feldspars are triclinic and richly lineated in polarized light; there is also hornblende, quite a little brown biotite, which borders the dark-green hornblende in places, some quartz; in short, a slaty diorite, the hornblende being here filled with a great number of narrow cylindrical hollows drawn out parallel to the fibration.

At French Creek occurs a mica-gneiss rather poor in mica [50], feeling somewhat sandy to the touch, and containing much plagioclase for a rock of this composition. The plagioclases of this latter, show in an eminent degree a combination of the two laws of triclinic twin formation, which was first described by Stelzner in the labradorites.[2] There is one twin composition parallel to the brachypinakoide M ($\infty \breve{P} \infty$), and another parallel to the base P ($O\ P$); so that there the polysynthetic twin striation appears as well upon the face P as upon M, in both cases going parallel to the edge $P\,|\,M$, and the two lamellar systems crossing each other under the angle $P: M = 86° 40'$. So these crystals consist in a certain sense of staff-like individuals in nearly rectangular transverse section, and they present

---

[1] This interesting summit has been named by myself and corps in honor of Professor Zirkel, the author of this memoir; and, without his knowledge, I have introduced the name in these pages.—C. K.

[2] Berg. u. hüttenmännische Zeitung, XXIX, 150; also Schrauf, Sitzungsber. d. Wiener Akad., LX, 1. Abth., Dec. 1869, 19, and F. Z., Mikroskopische Beschaffenh. d. Min. u. Gest., 133.

in the sections a grate-work or lattice, here those of the one and there those of the other twin system prevailing as stronger ledges.

Farther north, at Cherokee Butte [51], there occurs a hornblende-bearing mica-gneiss comparatively rich in titanite, whose brownish-red sections might at first sight, by reason of their unusual color, be mistaken for garnet; they distinctly polarize light, however, and possess besides the characteristic cuneated or sphenoidal figure and one unchanging form of cleavage.

On the slope of Cedar Mountain, south of Cherokee Butte, there is a hornblende-rock [52], in which a colorless groundmass of quartz predominates, filled in every part with large and very fine prismatic or irregularly shaped individual green hornblendes, thousands of which are scattered through the quartz of one small section.

At Deer Mountain, a plagioclase-bearing gneiss [53] was collected, containing hornblende, another green but feebly dichroitic chlorite-like mineral, plenty of titanite in the characteristic sections, some apatite, and the zircon-like crystals.

At Mill Peak Summit, a quartzite was found [54] appearing to the naked eye almost wholly homogeneous, but becoming under the microscope an aggregation of little colorless-edged grains averaging 0.015^{mm} in thickness; they are mixed with exceedingly small granules of calcite, which show very distinctly the well-known characteristic lamellar twin striation after the face $(-\frac{1}{2}R)$, which so often occurs in the crystalline individuals of granular limestones, and which shows in polarized light a variegated parallel lineature:[1] it is rare for calcite to figure in this manner as a constituent of crystalline quartzites.

Long's Peak [55] and the entrance to Big Thompson Cañon, Colorado Range [56], yield two beautiful, dark mica-slates, in which muscovite, unrecognizable to the naked eye and almost colorless, is contained: the first of these is enormously rich in apatite, and its quartz includes innumerable straight and extremely fine colorless prismatic microlites, which, however, belong rather to the muscovite than to apatite.

The differences in mineralogical constitution between the mica-gneisses

---

[1] First detected—one of the oldest microscopical observations on the structure of rocks—by Oschatz, Zeitschr. d. d. geolog. Gesellsch., VII, 1855, 5.

and the hornblende-gneisses in the above-described region may be generally summed up as follows:

MICA-GNEISSES.

Orthoclase largely predominating, but very little plagioclase.
Fluid-inclusions in the quartz more abundant.
Apatite rarer or wanting.
Titanite entirely wanting.
Zircon rare or wanting.

HORNBLENDE-GNEISSES.

Plagioclase frequent, sometimes predominating.
Fluid-inclusions in the quartz more rare.
Apatite generally very abundant, but sometimes wanting.
Titanite sometimes present.
Zircon abundant or wanting.

The apatite is only to be found in those rocks rich in hornblende which also contain feldspar. In the pure hornblende rock, as
well as in the masses composed only of quartz and hornblende, it is extremely rare, even when they are geological equivalents of or regularly
interstratified in hornblende-gneisses, and when the hornblende in both has
an exactly similar structure. There are two other rocks worthy of mention
from the Archæan region of Colorado.

Underlying Medicine Peak, Medicine Bow Range, a black, somewhat
lustrous clay-slate occurs [57], which resembles roofing-slate, and is very
easily fissile. Under the microscope, it is seen to consist of a colorless
ground, which seems to be homogeneous, but polarizes between nicols in
indistinctly outlined, colored spots. But this groundmass disappears by
reason of innumerable black, opaque grains of the very smallest size, which
are scattered through it, here being aggregated in heaps, there woven into
flocks. Where the colorless mass is more or altogether free from these spots
and stripes of dark points, a considerable quantity of small, pale brownish-
yellow laminæ of mica lies in it, and those standing obliquely prove that
they are as well lamellated as those in fine-grained gneisses or mica-slates.
The general composition here, therefore, does not agree very well with that

of the externally and macroscopically similar Silurian and Devonian roofing-slates of the Rhine provinces, Westphalia, Thuringia, Saxony, and Cornwall,[1] especially since the brown microlites, so characteristic of the latter, are here entirely wanting. In the same locality, and in near connection with that last described, is another confused and entangled slate [57], looking more crystalline than the former, and having a dirty green and brown color. It is seen under the microscope to consist for the most part of broad rays of green hornblende, which present transverse sections of very well-formed and beautifully cleavable prismatic crystals. Between the individual hornblendes is a colorless mass, which in this rock must belong to brilliant polarizing quartz. Small heaps of fine black grains, like those seen in the former rock, are interposed in the quartz. Single feldspar crystals, which are wholly wanting in the former, are visible, beside the hornblende, in the latter. The brown spots seen in hand-specimens are produced by a superficial oxydation of the Fe O amount of the hornblende, whose prismatic rays in the thin section are often still green on one end and brown along the fissures of the other. Both rocks bear the closest geological relation to each other, but petrographically it cannot be demonstrated that the second one has ever been like the first, or that it really is a more crystalline development of it. As a supplement to these old crystalline schists may be lastly mentioned a remarkable Jurassic slate from north of Sahwave Mountains.[2] It is very similar to the old Silurian or Devonian roofing-slates, and even possesses a bright lustre upon its fissure-planes. It appears under the microscope to be wholly crystalline, notwithstanding its geological position, and presents nothing which indicates the presence of clastic material. It looks most like a mica-slate whose component parts are extraordinarily fine. Quartz and colorless or light-yellowish tender laminæ of mica, only a few hundredths of a millimeter in size, are its chief components. Through this mixture little black, prickly crystals and minute short needles of an unknown nature, together with some very fine

---

[1] F. Z., Poggendorff's Annalen, CXLIV, 1871, 319.

[2] While from its character and geographical position this slate is judged to be Jurassic, its actual age is unproven, and it may possibly represent a fragment of earlier rocks entangled in the later formations: its remarkable crystalline character may possibly point to a Cambrian or even Huronian origin. The decided probabilities are, however, that it is correctly referred to the Jura.—C. K.

black grains, are scattered; the latter appearing with a low magnifying power like dust, being generally accumulated in small heaps. Without doubt, this Jurassic slate is much more crystalline than the roofing-slates of the Silurian and Devonian formations, in which pronouncedly crystalline elements appear only as an occurrence in the generally prevailing clastic material. This is very unexpected, and the fact is the more striking because the Tertiary roofing-slates (as the excellent and famous ones from Glarus, Switzerland Eocene), which macroscopically cannot be separated, are made up entirely of microclastic ingredients.

The beautiful crystalline-granular marble from Kinsley District, Nevada, should be spoken of before closing this chapter [58]. The grains of calcite in it show the most distinct twin striation (after $-\frac{1}{2}R$), and are remarkable for numerous fluid-inclusions, which, as is known, do not occur at all frequently elsewhere. They attain the size of 0.004^{mm}, and possess a rather mobile bubble, which does not disappear in a temperature of 100° C., and which is doubtless enveloped in water containing some carbonic acid. Then there is, too, a considerably crystalline altered Triassic limestone [59], south of Buffalo Cañon, West Humboldt, which has good fluid-inclusions.

CHAPTER III.

GRANITE AND GRANITE-PORPHYRY.

SECTION I.—GRANITE.
SECTION II.—GRANITE-PORPHYRY.

SECTION I.

GRANITE.

The granites of the Fortieth Parallel are doubtless partly eruptive rocks, which have evidently broken through sedimentary strata of a different geological age, and, in part, dependencies of the old crystalline schists, alternating with gneisses, etc., and showing no sign of eruptive character. Whatever may be the origin of the crystalline schists, that of the accompanying granites must be the same. According to the most favorite theory, these granites that are not eruptive, and are at the same time generally stratified, should be called metamorphic granites. The decidedly eruptive granites may be divided into two classes: one embraces those older rocks that are of ante-Jurassic age; the other, those which have obtruded themselves through the Jurassic strata. For the enormous mass of eruptive granite of the Sierra Nevada, Professor Whitney has demonstrated a Jurassic origin; and, although not definitely proven, a similar age is assumed for a considerable class of granites along the Fortieth Parallel, whose petrographic constitution and habitus are identical with those of the Sierra Nevada. The full details of the reasons of this assignment will be found in the chapter upon granites in Vol. 1 of this series. When, therefore, in this memoir, Jurassic granite is spoken of, the intention is to designate that family of which the Sierra Nevada occurrence is the type in age and constitution. The purpose of this chapter is not only to describe the several occurrences which seem, from a general petrographical point of view, worth mentioning, but also subsequently to develop those macroscopical or microscopical peculiarities which will help to distinguish the single geological granite varieties above classified. The specimens as described are taken from localities ranging regularly from west to east.

An older eruptive granite from Granite Cañon, southeast of Winnemucca Lake, Nevada [60], consists of orthoclase, plagioclase, quartz, biotite, and comparatively little apatite, with no hornblende or titanite. The mica has brownish-green, richly lamellated, pure, homogeneous sections. The quartz is rich in liquid-inclusions; this phenomenon can also be detected in the feldspars, which have a much fresher and clearer substance. The quartz also contains straight or curved needle-like microlites, which are so thin that, even with the highest magnifying power, they look merely like thin, black dashes (see Plate II, fig. 4, representing another variety of granite). They are generally found gathered in large numbers upon a small space or dispersed in all directions through the mass; and it is always easy to distinguish them from cracks or fissures. It has not been determined to which mineral these microlites so widely spread in the granitic quartzes belong.

Going eastward, a series of eruptive granites referred to younger or probable Jurassic series is found. At the north end of the Truckee Range occurs a typical specimen of this rock [61]. It is made up of comparatively little orthoclase, much plagioclase, dark mica, hornblende (easily recognizable even in the hand-specimens, and showing deep-green sections in the slides), much quartz, relatively abundant apatite and magnetite, and the characteristic titanite.[1] The orthoclase shows here and there an excellent zoned structure, which is almost equal to that of the trachytic and rhyolitic sanidins: it is also strikingly clear. The plagioclase, likewise, is not nearly as much decomposed as elsewhere in the granites, but is much more fresh and unaltered. The abundant quartz is conspicuously poor in fluid-inclusions,

---

[1] Clarence King has long since shown that the eruptive Jurassic granites, and only these, are characterized by the presence of macroscopical titanite.

in this respect presenting a remarkable contrast with that of the first-mentioned granite. Apatite is found everywhere in the mass, especially in and about the mica, but also in the feldspar, quartz, and hornblende. A general mutual inclusion and enveloping of the single constituents has taken place on an extended scale. The feldspars and quartzes contain delicate tables of brown mica, needles and lamellæ of hornblende, thin yellowish-red plates of specular iron, hematite, and grains of magnetite, all of which are phenomena seldom found elsewhere in granites. The oxyd of iron, an almost invariable accompaniment of these post-Jurassic eruptive granites, is, moreover, of a twofold nature, appearing sometimes as a very sharp-edged, regular, little, six-sided lamina, ranking among the original constituents of the rock, having nothing to do with fissures, and often included in the compact mass of another mineral, for instance in the midst of quartz; and at others showing a serrated and lobed dendritic formation, lying evidently in cracks and fissures, into which it has evidently been infiltrated in the course of time, being doubtless of secondary origin. The latter probably originates primarily from the decomposition of hornblende (less from that of brown mica), and is therefore wanting in all granites which are free from hornblende, as are most of the older eruptive division. The titanite has brownish-yellow sections, with a rather rough surface, less pellucidity, and generally sharp cuneiform outlines. The titanites are for the most part free from strange inclusions which may perhaps abound in the neighboring constituents of the same rock; and, judging from this fact, a comparatively very early solidification might in all probability be rightly attributed to the titanite. In one instance, there was observed in this granite a crystal of titanite which had made a hole in an individual of mica at its border; it had squeezed and forced its way in, pushing asunder the lamella of the mica, and shivering them like fibrous wood. There is no trace of white mica in this granite, nor is there any in that of the same geological position. Then there is a comparatively large amount of thick, black grains of magnetite. No glass inclusions occur in any of the rock-constituents, nor is there any sign of an amorphous, imperfectly individualized base. The abundance of plagioclase, taken together with the amount of hornblende, removes this rock from the proper granites, to which it is, however, allied by a large quantity of quartz and biotite. It really appears more to belong between granite and hornblende-bearing mica-diorite than between granite and syenite, possessing its true analogy in the series of gneisses.

The hill west of Granite Creek Station, Granite Range, consists of granite [62] similar to the latter, except in being a little poorer in mica and hornblende. The quartzes contain plenty of the thin black needles, which were mentioned as occurring in those of the first old eruptive granite ; so that the microscopical interpositions cannot help to determine the geological age. To these same granites also belong that from the Pah-supp Mountains, Nevada [63], whose quartz is somewhat richer in fluid-inclusions, and that from the summit of the neighboring Sahwave Mountains [64], which is comparatively poor in black mica and hornblende, and whose feldspars are evidently more altered. The larger orthoclases of this latter contain small included particles of beautifully striated plagioclases, and the black needles in the quartz often reach a length of 0.35^{mm}, with a thickness of 0.0015^{mm}; that is, 233 times longer than thick. All these granites belong to the class of possible Jurassic age.

A totally different appearance and composition are seen in the granites next following from the Pah-tson Mountains. One from Granite Ridge [65] bears muscovite, gathered in groups, with concentric radiations like a rosette, which is a very uncommon phenomenon : no hornblende, no dark mica, no titanite, very little magnetite, and considerable apatite. The granite from the dike west of Pahkeah Peak, Pah-tson Mountains [66], has all these peculiarities. In Crusoe Cañon, Pah-tson Mountains, occurs a granite dike [67] which is seen macroscopically to contain garnet and lepidolite (lithia-mica). Under the microscope, no smaller individuals of garnet can be found than those seen with the naked eye. There is also a colorless mica, which often forms, when seen through the microscope, star-like groups similar to the ice-crystals that form on windows. The mass contains neither biotite nor hornblende. When seen on a smaller scale, the lepidolite is found to be exactly like the lithia-bearing " mica-palmée " in the coarse-grained granite from Bagnères de Luchon in the Pyrenees, and that in the pegmatites from the neighborhood of Pressburg in Hungary.

But there occur, in the Pah-tson Mountains, granites which belong geologically to the younger, Jurassic type, and which exactly agree petrographically with that from the Truckee Range, described above, strikingly contrasting with the just-mentioned older, muscovite granites of the same region. Of these, the following may be named: at Granite Ridge, Pah-supp Mountains, a massive hornblende-granite [68], in which quartzes and feldspars are again rendered highly impure by hornblende dust and little biotite plates, and which also contains primary specular iron. On the east side of Pahkeah Peak is a granite [69], having much biotite, but comparatively poor in hornblende. In those very rich in plagioclase, and also abounding in titanite, whose smaller grains are often densely associated in heaps, the titanite seems to search with peculiar persistence for the borders of the magnesian mica. At the head of Grass Cañon, Pah-tson Mountains, is a hornblende-granite [70], with impure constituents, much biotite, doubtless more plagioclase than orthoclase, titanite, specular iron as in former and the following specimens, quartz somewhat richer in fluid-inclusions; hornblende and biotite being here grown together in a peculiar manner, so that as the sections of a green hornblende often show layers of intercalated brown mica, and inversely the brown mica lamels contain hornblende individuals, the limits between the two intimately-connected minerals being so sharp that it is scarcely allowable to explain this new phenomenon upon the supposition of alternating processes.

Granite Peak, Pah-tson Mountains, yields a granite [71] likewise very rich in plagioclase, with somewhat less hornblende but with titanite in the same relative proportion; a large rounded grain of magnetite 0.4^{mm} in diameter was seen bordered with fifteen apatite prisms standing out in every direction; and besides these, which had fastened on the outside, there were three other apatite needles perforating the magnetite, whose colorless sections looked in the black surrounding mass like so many sharp holes.

Still another quite different constitution is represented by two granites from localities not very remote from this, namely, west of Rye Patch, Montezuma Range, Nevada [72], and Montezuma Mine near Oreana [73]. They are somewhat similar to each other, and are much more decomposed than the above-described varieties. This latter is especially true of all the feldspars, which are altered into a granular, mealy, or an indistinctly radiating substance with aggregate polarization. Hornblende and biotite display something of the behavior which is peculiar to these minerals in the gneisses, their flat prisms and laminæ showing undulations and curvatures. They also contain microlites, included in the same way as in corresponding constituents of crystalline slates. Titanite is not present. In general, according to their whole microscopical aspect, neither of these granites have any characteristics in common with the typical titanite-bearing dioritic granites. They belong to the older eruptive family.

The granite from Granite Peak, Pah-Ute Range, Nevada [74], is extremely poor in mica, and *a priori* it is almost in vain to search for hornblende and titanite. The feldspars are somewhat decomposed. The quartzes contain splendid double inclosures of an unusually large size (see page 19). The innermost fluid is here also liquid carbonic acid, the bubble reappearing by a diminution of the raised temperature in all neighboring inclusions of this kind at the same time and at $31°$ C. Sometimes it can be distinctly seen that the outer boundary of the interior carbonic acid runs irregularly or presents a regularly angular form, but no well-rounded line. Judging from this, it would seem highly probable that the outermost zone of these curious double inclusions is not a liquid but rather a solid mass. If this peripheric substance were also a fluid, the included liquid carbonic acid would surely take the form of a globe; but the outer form of the carbonic acid, of course, has the shape of the cavity in the peripheric mass. In addition to these double inclusions, the quartzes of this granite envelop also the more common single inclusions of liquid carbonic acid, and along with these are other cavities filled with a fluid whose bubble does not disappear even at the high temperature of $100°$. Without doubt, the latter is chiefly water, with perhaps a small amount of dissolved carbonic acid. It seldom happens that one has so good an opportunity to observe all together in one quartz grain, these three kinds of liquid-inclusions. This granite doubtless belongs to the metamorphic group.

Those of the Augusta Mountains [75, 76] are rather poor in plagioclase, have here less, and there more biotite, and are somewhat decomposed. Some of these granites contain quite a little hornblende, which is immediately accom-

panied again by apatite, but there is not sufficient to make it at all characteristic, or to warrant separating the rock from the usual biotite-granites, to
which the decidedly prevailing orthoclase also points.

Highly interesting granite rocks occur in the Havallah Range, Nevada,
north of Summit Springs. The predominating variety is a coarse-grained
granite, with somewhat labradorizing feldspars, which are macroscopically
similar to those from Frederiksvarn in South Norway; very rich in
brown mica and hornblende, with a comparatively enormous amount
of apatite, which is often finely porous; but no titanite. Here also the
quartz abounds in the three different sorts of fluid-inclusions: a. aqueous
inclusions, with a bubble which is not condensable within the limits of observation; b. simple inclusions of liquid carbonic acid; c. double inclusions,
whose interior is liquid carbonic acid. The feldspars merit particular attention; a part of them containing many orthoclases show that tender and
fine fibration which is common to the feldspars of the zircon-syenites of
South Norway and to those of the Saxon granulites, a fibration which has
nothing to do with twin formation. These orthoclases are almost free from
strange interpositions. In other feldspars, the orthoclases as well as plagioclases contain in their very clear substance the most diverse microscopical
bodies (Plate III, fig. 1); among them rhombic and six-sided, sharp, yellow,
brown-black, and even gray-violet little plates, real microlitic needles of the
same colors, also seeming needles, which the micrometrical screw proves
to be laminæ standing upon edge; pale-green hornblende-microlites, often
with affixed magnetite grains; in short, interpositions which produce a real
picture of labradorite, in the making of which the external optical effect of
the feldspars has a part. No certain lawful crystallographical grouping of
these included individuals can be discovered. The needles and feldspars
often very nicely present the well-known phenomenon of dissolution into
single grains and ragged bunches. The thin, black, line-like needles sometimes lie parallel and so close to each other, that with a low magnifying power
they give a dark shading to the feldspars. Other parts of the feldspars
have a very remarkable structure: their clear substance is thoroughly
interwoven with a multitude of either colorless or very pale-greenish, long
stripes and bands. These are often a little undulated and contorted, but

they always run in regular parallelism. The transverse sections of the feldspars suggest graphic granite, but it is very improbable that the interpositions belong to quartz. It is more natural to suppose that they are muscovite. Moreover, there are no thin lamellæ extended in two directions, but only, as is seen in the transverse sections, plummet-shaped and vermiform objects having a prevailing direction. In these feldspars, the previously mentioned little tables and microlites are also imbedded, as in the other feldspars which are free from the vermicular interpositions, and they do not at all interfere with the direction of the stripes and bands. Yellowish-red oxyd of iron is plentifully infiltrated into microscopical cracks in the feldspars and quartzes as a secondary product; primary plates of it as a genuine constituent of the rock being wanting.

This coarse-grained granite, from the Havallah Range, is traversed by dikes which represent a wholly different variety [77], namely, one of the hornblende-titanite group, which everywhere are found to be the youngest. Hornblende and biotite often show the previously-mentioned intimate mutual interlacing and interwreathing (Plate II, fig. 4). The quartz is here filled with such a multitude of the black, hair-like microlites so often spoken of, as to surpass any other example of this phenomenon ever seen. They cross each other confusedly, often forming a web, or diverging from one point in all directions, like roots from a stump. The intertwining of the more curved and distorted ones is very beautiful when seen through the water-clear quartz-mass. The thicker hairs are feebly brownish, but transparent. In a quartz grain of one square millimeter lie over 120 of these hairs almost in one plane, so nearly in one, at any rate, that they may be seen without turning the screw; hence, it may be calculated that one cubic millimeter of quartz contains 10,000 of these microlites. Furthermore, the quartz abounds in liquid-inclusions containing the most beautiful cubic crystals of salt. Some of the inclusions contain short black hairs, which proves the simultaneousness of the general act of inclusion. Both salt cubes and minute black microlites can even be detected in one liquid-inclusion (Plate I, fig. 4). Of the fresh feldspars, many belong to the triclinic system. Primary plates of oxyd of iron are present.

The granite from Ravenswood Hills, Shoshone Range [78], is in constitution totally different from the above. It represents a fine-grained variety containing white mica, but no trace of black mica, even under the microscope. Hornblende, therefore, is entirely wanting; and it would be superfluous to say there is no titanite, after having stated the prevalence of white mica. A little apatite appears here. Indeed, this ingredient is a component part of almost every rock, and its quantity rather than its mere presence relates it to hornblende. The quartzes here are exceptionally poor in fluid-inclusions, resembling, in this respect, some of the younger granites.

The granite from the western end of Winnemucca Peak, Nevada [79], is a dark, fine-grained variety, with feldspars that are much decomposed, and considerable magnesian mica. These and hornblende are the only constituents which are distinctly visible to the naked eye. This is one of the older eruptive granites.

At Nannie's Peak, Sectoya Mountains, is another eruptive granite [80], rather fresh, containing biotite but no hornblende, splendidly striated undecomposed plagioclase and little predominating orthoclase, which is more attacked, and shows here and there a distinct zone-structure, resembling the sanidins in trachytes and rhyolites. Some of the orthoclases are fibrated in the lately described manner. The quartzes bear numerous fluid-inclusions, some with beautiful included salt cubes and others with minute black hairs; while some grains are full of very small apatites. A microscopically fine-grained accumulation of pretty well crystallized quartzes, on an average 0.1^{mm}, with less distinct little feldspar crystals, appears in some parts of the rock: a kind of aggregation like that which often forms the groundmass of felsitic porphyries, except that in the latter the component parts are still more minute. Other granites occur on this peak [81] having little particles of hornblende, as it seems, along the borders of the equally small brown mica. They contain quartzes in which every fluid-inclusion bears a salt cube, many of them even having two of these little crystals. Both varieties are entirely free from titanite.

The old eruptive granite from Shoshone Knob, Shoshone Range [82], bears, beside magnesian mica, very much hornblende in prisms up to 5^{mm} long, neither white mica nor titanite, some apatite, and not much plagioclase. That from Woodranch Cañon, Shoshone Range, is similar to this [83], except that it has less mica and hornblende. Titanite is wanting. The clear orthoclases have very distinct fluid-inclusions.

The rock of Agate Pass, Cortez Range, which possibly is a Jurassic eruption, even if the geological evidence is not entirely conclusive, forms an excellent example of the granites holding titanite. The plentiful hornblende is splendidly cleavable: it is accompanied by almost no dark mica. The feldspars are highly altered, so that the comparative proportion of orthoclase and plagioclase is not recognizable. The product of this decomposition is curious, consisting of broader or narrower colorless prismatic rays, which are either massed confusedly together like felt, or are heaped together in the form of stars and bunches, presenting a beautiful aggregate polarization. That such phenomena cannot be well pictured is to be regretted. By this process of alteration, the entire mass of the feldspar crystals has been equally metamorphosed, so that former cracks and channel-ways are not at all preserved. The greater part of the feldspars in the granite of Granite Peak, Pah-Ute Range [84], is in a similar condition. The fresher portions of this constituent prove that it contains numerous liquid-inclusions and empty cavities, both as usual being long and rectangular in shape. The granite is poor in hornblende; there is very little mica, and titanite is not present in the specimens which were examined.

The granites back of Overland Ranch, Humboldt Range, are interesting, both geologically and petrographically [85, 86]. They are intercalated between the Archæan crystalline schists of that region. Much quartz is found in them, also black mica, but they are wanting in white mica. They differ petrographically from most of the eruptive granites previously described in this chapter, the points of difference being the possession by this rock of characteristics in general common to the granites which are members of the stratified crystalline territories and wanting proof of an eruptive nature. A long list of granites of this kind will be mentioned hereafter. The distinguishing characteristics are: a. the mica shows here and there a tendency to form flat plates (*Flasern*), not all its laminæ, it is true, lying parallel, as is the case in crystalline schists, but there often appearing transverse sections of membranes woven together in more or less perfect parallelism, the single accumulations of this kind not being parallel;

b. the small amount of plagioclase, even when compared with the granites, which are without hornblende; *c.* in the quartzes, there are hardly any fluid-inclusions; *d.* the linear apatite prisms are drawn out to an extreme length, are very thin, and often dismembered into numerous pieces, the apatites in massive granites being generally far more broad and short, and not so often or so minutely divided into pieces; *e.* the zircon-like mineral, so widely spread through the crystalline slates, immediately appears here in comparatively large individuals.

The granite from Egan Cañon, Egan Range, Nevada, bears much magnesian mica, considerable plagioclase, a little hornblende (fine green dust of which is plentifully scattered through the other constituents), and very-beautiful titanite in large cuneiform sections [87]. It is surprising to find that the zircon-like mineral also occurs here, for it has never before been observed in any granite. Yet the structure of this rock does not at all remind one of a gneiss, titanite being, besides, extremely rare in this species. There is a rather large number of liquid-inclusions in the quartz.

The granites of Wachoe Mountains, Nevada [88, 89], possess a somewhat porphyritic structure. Their orthoclases are highly metamorphosed. Curiously, the fresher and clearer feldspars all show distinct triclinic striation. Large individuals of hornblende are comparatively numerous, titanite is abundant, and there are many apatites in large, thick, but short, prisms, with terminating pyramidal faces. These apatites are crowded with dash-like, cylindric, narrow pores extended parallel to the chief axis of the crystal, but confined to the middle of the prisms, the outer parts being of a pure substance. This phenomenon may be easily observed in the longitudinal and transverse apatite sections. Sometimes the longer pores are so thin that they look like solid black needles (Plate I, fig. 8). Other apatites are seen containing distinct fluid-inclusions, lying in clusters or bands which run rectangularly to the chief crystal axis (Plate I, fig. 7). In the quartz, whose liquid-inclusions bear little salt cubes, and in the feldspars, characteristic plates of specular iron are enveloped at intervals, and also black hair-like microlites. Biotite is frequent.

In petrographical constitution, a great difference is shown by the

4 M P

granites from Granite Rock, Great Desert, Utah, where three varieties occur. The first [90] bears much dark magnesian mica, no white mica, a dirty-greenish mineral like chlorite, which is also highly dichroitic, but not so absorbing as biotite; hardly any proper hornblende, much titanite, and apatite with gigantic fluid-inclusions 0.03^{mm} in size, long black hairs in the quartz, which is rich in liquid-inclusions; the feldspars also having liquid-particles. The second [91] is a fine-grained granite, with only white mica, a very few microscopical scales of the greenish chloritic mineral, biotite totally wanting, titanite and apatite very rare, an abundance of quartz, and little plagioclase. Here it is pretty certain that the colorless prisms which are so widely spread through quartzes, especially those of granites, which lack the glaring and dazzling sections, and which are not apatite, belong to the white mica or muscovite. The only point which raises any doubt of this is that such microlites also occur in the quartzes of granite which do not have white mica among their proper independent constituents. The third variety [92] contains both black and white mica, the latter predominating. Here it appears that the black hairs in the quartz are exceedingly thin prisms of muscovite, for all the different stages of transition are seen between the most thin, straight, and curved black microlites and the very long colorless prisms, which without doubt belong to white mica.

Little Cottonwood Cañon, Wahsatch Range, presents eminently characteristic types of eruptive granites bearing hornblende and titanite [93, 94]. All their ingredients, including hornblende and titanite, may be seen macroscopically; rather fresh biotite, no muscovite, comparatively much plagioclase, abundant apatite, quartzes strikingly poor in fluid-inclusions as compared with those of the older eruptive granites. In the feldspars, quartzes, and micas, innumerable staff-formed, pale-greenish hornblende microlites are found, often divided by fracture into many single pieces and members, which lie one behind another, like chains of diatoms, associated with the most fine and regularly formed hornblende crystals of only 0.001^{mm} in length, and with roundish particles of hornblende like dew-drops. The little hornblende prisms in the feldspars and quartzes are often thickly covered with a dust of fine magnetite grains. Large individuals of hornblende are built out of single prisms which are not in immediate contact with each other, the spaces between being filled with colorless, beautifully polarizing quartz. In some varieties [94], the amount of titanite is extremely large. Red plates of oxyd of iron are found among the rock-constituents, more frequently in the feldspars, however. Many of the latter also include countless numbers of quartz-grains, the larger of which may be observed even by the naked eye in thin sections.

The granite from Clayton's Peak, Wahsatch, is very similar to the above in the most characteristic points; in the amount of titanite, and the association of hornblende and biotite. The colorless ingredients, such as feldspars (among them many plagioclases) and quartzes, are rendered very impure by foreign microscopical elements. The feldspars particularly contain unusually many violet-brown, red, and black laminæ of specular iron, all the different colors of which depend upon the varying thickness of the plates. So many of these metallic interpositions are accompanied by black hair-like microlites that the sections of the feldspars labradorize more or less distinctly when observed in the sections with oblique reflected light. Here and there parts of the rock show a diverging radiation, like the petals of a flower. Of this it is difficult to say whether it belongs to matter that is not individualized, or whether a product of the alteration of feldspars occurs here. Since this substance is penetrated by the same plates of specular iron, and the same hair-like microlites, as the undecomposed feldspars, the latter supposition seems the most probable; but it must then be acknowledged that the interposed bodies have escaped every alteration. These rocks are for the most part proportionally very rich in magnetite, well-formed crystals of which are also included in the titanite. The apatite crystals, curiously, are pressed flat, so that two opposite prism-faces are often four or five times larger than the four others; but there is no doubt that these sharp and glaring individuals are apatite. Accumulations of minute hornblende grains, biotite plates, and magnetite grains, without any individualized shape, occur among the rock-constituents. Titanite is a darker brown here than in other rocks.

The granite at the mouth of Big Cottonwood Cañon [95] is rich in dull-whitish feldspar, which appears macroscopically in the hand-specimen to form a real homogeneous groundmass; the microscope, however, shows that the crystalline individuals above mentioned are here associated. These feldspars also present an interesting manner of alteration, following most distinctly single, concentric inscribed zones. Within a slide, in the sections of the larger feldspars, three or four inner impellucid lines of a somewhat duller color appear, corresponding in their direction to the external outlines, and separated from each other by a clear unaltered substance. Numerous inclusions that are doubtless fluid can be detected with the microscope in the latter. The quartzes also are rich in liquid-inclusions.

This type of granite extends into Little Cottonwood Cañon [96, 97, 98] with orthoclases which are sometimes a beautiful snowy white, especially in the coarser-grained varieties, excellently cleavable hornblendes, and biotites which are very well lamellated and penetrated by numerous apatite needles. Very small light-brown laminæ of mica are scattered through the quartzes and feldspars. The rocks of this cañon contain the largest titanites that have thus far been observed in the granites of the Fortieth Parallel. When seen under the microscope, they are found also to have a straight and sharply defined contour, while the smaller titanites are often somewhat irregularly rounded. The rough surfaces of their sections are just as characteristic as their dark-shaded border, which depends upon the high index of refraction, according to Des Cloizeaux,[1] in titanite $u = 1.905$.

Different geological characteristics are displayed by the granites next to be mentioned, which are, for the most part, members of the Archæan territory of the crystalline schists, and which at the same time represent other petrographical varieties. That from Bruin Peak, Park Range, Colorado [99], is uncharacteristic, being very poor in quartz and mica and rich in dull impellucid feldspars, traversed by light or dirty green veins of epidote. The granites of Davis' Peak, Park Range, are rather fine-grained [100, 101], and bear macroscopical garnet, black mica, no distinct hornblende, many orthoclases which are fibrous like those in the Saxon metamorphic granulites, and quartzes strikingly poor in fluid-incluisons. The laminæ of mica possess, for the most part, a tendency to parallel grouping; and the pieces of rock knocked off in this direction give slides which present almost nothing

[1] Manuel de minéralogie, part I, 1862, 149.

but the basic sections of the mica plates, of course without the lamellation characteristic of orderless structure, and without dichroism.

Typical Archæan granites are found at Grand Encampment Creek [102, 103, 104]. Their feldspars often have a reddish color, which is produced by infiltrated oxyd of iron deposited in the form of delicate orange-red, and manifoldly dentrically-lobed laminæ upon the faces of microscopical fissures. These granites are partly very poor in mica [102] and partly they contain no real mica at all [104], while in the eruptive granites it is never wanting. They have instead a leek-green or dirty-green, rather strongly dichroitic chlorite, or perhaps mica-like mineral, which is much less cleavable and much more imperfectly lamellated than the proper common biotite, and which also forms only short squames that are confusedly striated. This constituent can be distinguished at first sight from hornblende, which is often similarly colored, by the entirely different cleavage. In some varieties of these granites, it is accompanied by groups of white mica, and in others the brown mica predominates. The quartzes of all specimens from this locality are conspicuously poor in liquid-inclusions.

Very interesting granites occur at North Park. One from Clark's Peak, Medicine Bow Range [105], is an extremely fine variety. It bears considerable fresh plagioclase, black mica of the usual kind, splendidly lamellated, and apatite, but neither hornblende nor titanite. The quartzes are not very poor in liquid-inclusions. A granite from the southern base of Clark's Peak in the North Park is in many respects a remarkable and curious rock [106]. It is very coarse-grained and exceedingly rich in quartz which looks in the thin section like window-glass, and contains the largest number of fluid-inclusions that any rock-constituent has ever been seen to hold. They consist of water: liquid carbonic acid or saturated salt solutions do not occur among them. The bubbles in the single inclusions here are of unusual mobility and restlessness. Beside these fluid particles, the quartz contains innumerable, long, black, hair-like microlites that are extraordinarily thin and scattered without order all through the mass. There is very little of the feldspar, which is powerfully decomposed, and frequently shows well-nigh obliterated vestiges of broad, twin striation. Biotite is present in large laminæ: hornblende and titanite are wanting. A striking occurrence is found in the black bodies, the size of a pea, which show themselves in the slides as perfectly impellucid, even on the thinnest edges, and have in reflected light a distinct metallic lustre, so that they probably belong to magnetite. This seems the more likely because they often present quadrangular outlines, and sometimes little, short, yellowish-red fringes and edgings of oxyd of iron have apparently sweated out of them. It is very remarkable that generally these thick magnetite grains are surrounded in the first place by a nearly continuous margin of a very fine-grained mixture of quartz, feldspar, and colorless mica, the single particles of this aggregation being below 0.1^{mm} thick. This peripheric zone evidently owes its existence and the striking fineness of its structure to the presence of magnetite, and is on an average 0.5^{mm} broad. It is interesting because, a, the proper constituents of this granite are so coarse-grained; b, colorless white mica does not otherwise occur as a constituent of this rock, being limited to the zone which surrounds the magnetite, and perhaps the latter used up in its formation all the contiguous iron, so that in the near neighborhood there was no opportunity for producing dark ferriferous magnesian mica; c, this zonal aggregation does not occur anywhere in the rock independent of the magnetite; d, it is immediately surrounded on its exterior outline by the coarsest granite constituents, most often by thick individuals of quartz, so that no passage or transition in the dimensions of the structure-elements can be discovered.

The granite of Glacier Cañon, south side of Clark's Peak [107], has more of an eruptive appearance than those next following. It is made up of colorless feldspar, considerable quartz, greenish-brown mica beautifully lamellated and penetrated by many apatite needles: besides, there are large reddish grains more than 1^{mm} in size, appearing microscopically, with, on an average, five of these individuals in a common thin section. Neither hornblende nor titanite is present. At the first glance, this ingredient might be supposed to be garnet, but under the microscope the vivid yellowish-red sections intensely polarize the light, and it is most probable that the mineral, which is also pierced by apatite prisms, belongs to zircon. Its peculiar color perfectly corresponds with that of the zircon sections in the syenites of South Norway, and outlines appear which may, without hesitation, be pronounced longitudinal sections of the combined tetragonal prism and pyramid. This mineral is not generally disseminated through the rock in small microscopical individuals, but is limited to the grains which can be observed with the naked eye; a phenomenon which is repeated by the zircon of the Norwegian syenites and by the garnet of the Saxon granulites.

The granite from Cherokee Butte, Medicine Bow Range [108], is doubtless metamorphic. The feldspar is highly decomposed, quite dull and impellucid, the mica brownish and rare, and there is no hornblende or titanite. Curiously, the quartz does not contain liquid-inclusions, and the empty cavities in it are not scattered without order through its whole mass, or gathered into clusters, which send out rays, as is the case in the quartzes of the eruptive granites, but are aggregated into rows, which are often parallel to one another, and, with a low magnifying power, are seen to traverse the quartz-mass in straight black lines, running without deviation to its verge, and there ending abruptly against the adjoining mineral. The behavior of the quartzes in graywackes and sandstones is very similar to this. The course of these lines gives the quartzes something of the appearance of fragments, or even of worn fragments. The quartz-grains are at the same time very much rounded: it is also remarkable that the single particles are very different in size, large and small being associated. This is a phenomenon common to the clastic graywackes; but in the eruptive granites the individuals of quartz do not vary so much, and are nearer of a uniform thickness.

The same characteristics are found in the granites next to be named, which are likewise not eruptive; and this tends to support the theory that these rocks are altered clastic sedimentary depositions.

Other metamorphic granites are found at Bellevue Peak, Medicine Bow Range, very poor in mica, and bearing decomposed feldspars, containing also rounded grains of garnet the size of a pea, rich in macroscopical cracks and fissures, but not in microscopical ones [109].

Further, at Elk Mountain is a very fine-grained variety [110], which bears hardly any true mica, but instead that greenish, chloritic ingredient, already described, in the granite from Grand Encampment, Park Range.

That from Long's Peak, Colorado Range [111], differs somewhat from the most characteristic metamorphic ones. In the hand-specimens, indeed, the feldspars are arranged with a certain degree of parallelism; but the rock contains beautiful brown mica richly lamellated, and quartzes with irregularly disseminated liquid-inclusions and black microlitic hairs. In the quartzes and feldspars, a long prismatic mineral that is colorless and glaring is interposed, whose innumerable individuals look at first sight like apatite; but a closer examination shows that the dazzling transverse six-sided sections are neither regular nor compressed hexagons of 120°, but belong to obtuse prisms, with the faces truncating the acute angle. Obtuse quadrangular prisms also occur, and here it becomes distinct that the angle of the prism is about 124°. Such sections have a splendid transverse striation, the infallible sign of twin formation, visible in common light, and between crossed nicols it causes variegated color-lines. Without much doubt, these crystals belong to grammatite or tremolite ($\propto P . \propto \breve{P} \propto$), a variety of hornblende free from iron and alumina, which may replace here the usual hornblende. The crystallographical dimensions of the occurrence point to this conclusion as much as does the twin formation so characteristic of hornblende and actinolite; so also the observation that these colorless prisms (which reach a thickness of 0.01^{mm}) exhibit on their surfaces numerous longitudinal ribs and furrows parallel to the chief axis; a system of striation that often occurs in actinolite, but never in apatite; and the twin formation (parallel $\propto \breve{P} \propto$) mentioned is, of course, also impossible to apatite. Notwithstanding this, apatite is doubtless present in the rock.

A number of granites next follow, which are inseparable members of the stratified territory of the crystalline schists. They are wanting in all geological evidence of eruptive character. The stratified granites of Granite Cañon, Laramie Hills [112 113], show transitions into crystalline schists. The reddish color of these rocks is secondary, having been produced by the abundance of yellowish-red oxyd of iron, which has entered the numerous capillary fissures in the form of dendritic lobes. There is biotite, and also a macroscopical ingredient of a dark substance, a little transparent on the edges, only having a feeble brownish or dark-green color and irregular shapes, and which seems to be a kind of mica similar to lepidomelane. The quartz here contains an enormous quantity of pale-brown, grayish-yellow, sharp, little laminæ of mica, scarcely larger than 0.005^{mm}, placed in all directions, horizontally and obliquely, and standing on their edges. In a quadratic surface of quartz 0.2^{mm} in length, there were on one plane 60 laminæ of mica to be seen, which would be 1,500 mica plates to a surface of one square millimeter. In the large quartzes are also some liquid-inclusions, among them several consisting of a saturated salt solution with cubic crystals. The feldspars of this granite include a very large quantity of quartzes presenting rounded or rough hexagonal sections, and showing in polarized light splendidly variegated spots upon the equally colored feldspar-ground. Mica, too, is dispersed through the feldspars, so that they often actually swarm with foreign interpositions.

Virginia Dale, Laramie Hills, produces a very coarse-grained metamorphic granite [114]. It contains no characteristic biotite, but only that dark substance just now mentioned, whose feebly green transparent borders show here strong dichroism, and whose lamellated structure occasionally becomes distinct. The quartz is very poor in fluid-inclusions, and there is no hornblende and hardly any plagioclase.

In the metamorphic granite from Signal Peak, Laramie Hills, we find again, very characteristically, the dark-green, chlorite-like mineral in place of real mica. Limited to the aggregations of its laminæ, and mixed with them, are very numerous, rounded, yellowish-red, or reddish-yellow grains up to 0.08^{mm} in thickness, which distinctly polarize; they are not garnet, but they may possibly be zircon. There is much plagioclase. The quartz is just as poor as the above in liquid-inclusions, and all the constituents here are very fresh and unaltered.

A red metamorphic granite [115] is found on the west side of Laramie Hills, northwest from Sherman. It is very rich in quartz (with very few liquid-inclusions but more empty cavities), and contains, besides, fine fibrous orthoclase, considerable plagioclase, no characteristic mica; and the green chloritic mineral is very rare. All the fissures and cracks in and between the rock-constituents are filled with blood-red, reddish-brown, and brownish-black oxyd, and hydrous oxyd of iron.

The gray metamorphic granite from Iron Mountain, Laramie Hills. however, bears richly lamellated real brown biotite. In the metamorphic granites from the six last-mentioned localities, microscopical apatite could not be detected.

By generalizing the foregoing observations of this chapter, we find that the several geological varieties of granite in the examined territory are generally characterized by the following petrographical features:

I.—METAMORPHIC GRANITES.

Rocks often colored reddish by secondarily infiltrated oxyd of iron.

Frequent replacement of the usual biotite by a dark-greenish chloritic mineral.

Rareness of hornblende and apatite.

Absence of titanite and of primary specular iron.

Frequent poorness of the quartz in fluid-inclusions.

Quartz grains often rounded with fluid-inclusions arranged in lines, which end in such a manner at the limits of the grains that it makes them appear like worn clastic ingredients.

II.—OLDER ERUPTIVE GRANITES.

Orthoclase generally predominating, no titanite, no primary specular iron, less magnetite, constituents not rendered very impure by strange, solid, microscopical, crystalline interpositions. There are two chief divisions:

a. With white mica.—The rarer variety, hardly ever containing dark mica, always free from hornblende, and free from, or very poor in, apatite.

b. With dark magnesian mica.—The more frequent variety:

1. Without hornblende.

2. With a hornblende that is very coarse-grained, and generally bearing comparatively much apatite.

III.—YOUNGER ERUPTIVE GRANITES.

Richer in constituent minerals, which are generally more fresh.

Characterized by titanite, dark mica, and hornblende.

Orthoclase, accompanied by proportionally a great deal of plagioclase. Feldspar never of a reddish color, but always white.

Quartzes and feldspars rendered highly impure by microscopical dust like hornblende and biotite material.

Never white mica.

Generally rich in apatite.

Frequently microscopical primary plates of specular iron.

Proportionally richer in magnetite.

Quartzes more often relatively rich than relatively poor in fluid-inclusions.

It should be particularly stated that the described contrasts are valid only for the examined rocks of the Fortieth Parallel, and that it is not allowable to generalize from them for other countries.

SECTION II.

GRANITE-PORPHYRY.

Under this name, porphyritic rocks are collected which present the usual contrast between a groundmass and larger imbedded crystals of orthoclase alone, or orthoclase and quartz. This groundmass looks to the unaided eye too fine-grained to allow of placing the rock among the porphyritic granites, and, on the other hand, it seems not to be homogeneous enough to permit of assigning it to the proper felsite-porphyries. These rocks stand petrographically between porphyritic granites and felsite-porphyries. Those occurrences which are rich in macroscopically prominent hornblende may be named syenitic granite-porphyry. Typical examples of this division are found in the German rocks from Beucha and Wurzen, near Leipsic, from Frauenstein and Altenberg, in the Saxon Erzgebirge, lately examined microscopically and described by J. Baranowski;[1] also in the rocks from Aschaffenburg, in Bavaria. Along the Fortieth Parallel, these rocks, elsewhere not very frequent, are developed in many places and in an eminently well-characterized degree. Sometimes they manifestly stand in close geological connection with the other granites of a given locality, presenting the same rock-mass in merely a somewhat petrographically different relation.

Beginning at the west, and going east, the first member of this series found, is not very characteristic. It occurs in Granite Hills, Nevada, west of Spanish Spring Valley [116], and is a light yellowish-gray rock with whitish feldspars and black hornblende points in an almost homogeneous groundmass. Under the microscope, the presence of quartz is detected, and almost all these quartzes are yet only roughly crystallized, their sections most frequently showing the rhombic outlines of the longitudinally-cut, hexagonal pyramid. The groundmass is an aggregation of such quartzes whose crystallized forms are notoriously strange to the granites, and of feldspar individuals; between them being a substance of a light grayish-yellow color that is not individualized, and which polarizes between the nicols but feebly and indis-

[1] Über die mineralogische und chemische Zusammensetzung der Granitporphyre, Inaugural-Dissertation, Leipzig, 1873; see Zeitschrift d. d. geolog. Gesellsch., 1874, XXVI, 522.

tinctly, and is full of numerous aculeate, prickly microlites. The same mass, occurring here in only a few spots, sometimes fills an important part in the composition of the felsitic groundmass of the real porphyries. There is some biotite and apatite besides the hornblende. The larger quartzes are almost free from fluid-inclusions. Whether some very small inclusions with an extremely delicate outline and a dark-bordered bubble are glass particles cannot, on account of their minuteness, be determined.

Rocks from Nannie's Peak, Sectoya Range [117], connected with the granites occurring there, strongly resemble some from Maggie's Peak [118, 119]. Both belong to that class of granites which are almost felsite-porphyries. In the very fine-grained, yellowish-gray groundmass, feldspars and sharp, six-sided plates of dark mica, up to 2^{mm} in size, are abundant. Quartzes are less frequent. The groundmass of the rocks of Maggie's Peak is, curiously, an extremely fine-grained mixture of quartz and feld-spar, in which the larger quartzes again show pretty well-developed crystal-lized forms. Polarized light proves that this aggregation, at one position of the nicols, mostly resolves into colored, double-refracting particles, and the little spots which had appeared dark, become colored by turning the ana-lyzer, or the specimen section around its vertical axis. There is nothing, or extremely little, of amorphous, unindividualized, micro-felsitic matter in this aggregation. A noticeable formation of sphærolites occurs in the rock from Nannie's Peak, the process of formation often being far advanced. They have an evident centre and well-developed concentric rays, which consist either of indistinct crystalline grains arranged in linear form (granosphærites) or of bunch-like felsitic fibres. The effect is pretty where these felsitic fibres are conglobated into sphærolitic balls, entirely encircling many of the little quartzes, and having the appearance of a radiating garland. This same phenomenon has been observed with the quartzes in the rhyolite from Mount Baula in Iceland. The larger fresh feldspars of these rocks are for the most part plagioclases, or sanidin-resembling orthoclases, with imbedded ledges of striated triclinic feldspar. The thicker and most nearly macroscopical quartzes do not contain any glass particles, but a few liquid-inclusions, among which are some with included cubes of salt. Biotite, though a very rare ingredient in the corresponding German rocks, is here defined with surprising sharpness, and is as remarkably regular in lamellation: it is pierced by many colorless apatite prisms. Green hornblende occurs infrequently. One light-gray variety of these rocks from Maggie's Peak, Scotoyn Range [118], appears alto-gether homogeneous, being almost deprived of all larger crystals, and is easily mistaken for rhyolite; its felsitic groundmass, however, has pre-cisely the same structure as the described varieties, and the quartzes are very full of fluid-inclusions.

A rock from Clover Cañon, Humboldt Range, is exactly similar to those above mentioned, the groundmass being distinctly grained without amorphous portions [120]. Nevertheless, quartzes the size of a pea here contain double inclusions, with liquid carbonic acid, in such abundance as is seldom seen. The many hundred inclusions which one field of view presents in one plane, and which look under a low magnifying power like a dust arranged in stripes, heaps, and bands, are all of this remarkable nature. Mica is also present here.

Characteristic occurrences of the granite-porphyries, or rather of the syenitic granite-porphyries, are found at the Franklin Buttes, Nevada [121, 122, 123, 124, 125, 126, 127, 128]. They are generally greenish or flesh-colored rocks, first one and then the other tinge predominating, and consist of an extremely fine-grained groundmass, which often passes into the fel-sitic, seemingly homogeneous state, and through which a comparatively large number of whitish feldspars, dark-green hornblende, gray quartzes, and sharp, black plates of biotite are disseminated. Under the microscope, a long series of hand-specimens of these rocks show considerable resem-blance in their respective behavior. Their groundmass, though as yet only in some varieties macroscopically crystalline, is, nevertheless, a crys-talline-granular aggregation without an amorphous unindividualized base, or, at any rate, without one appearing. Microscopically, this mixture is comparatively coarse-grained (the thickness of the single grains averaging 0.03^{mm}); and it presents in extraordinary completeness, the contrast between dull-gray, and poorly translucent little feldspars, often presenting rectangu-lar shapes and water-clear quartzes that are sometimes roughly crystallized. The minute feldspars of this groundmass have a good many little spherical

or oval hollows. Sphærolitic formations, and even indications of a tendency
to form them, are generally rare here. The larger porphyritical quartzes
are always entirely free from glassy particles, but they contain in some
places, very many, and in others, strikingly few fluid-inclusions. These
latter here consist for the most part of a saturated solution of chloride
of sodium with minute salt cubes [124, 122, 127]. Sometimes these fluid-
inclusions contain two beautiful cubic crystals; and, again, the larger of
them are remarkable by reason of including a great quantity of foreign
substances, which have no doubt been partly taken up mechanically;
inclosures 0.024^{mm} in length and 0.008^{mm} in width, often containing
colorless salt cubes, pale-green round grains, and thin needles (most probably hornblende), and even plates of blood-red oxyd of iron (Plate I,
fig. 5). Sometimes there are so many of these foreign objects in the fluid-
particles that the bubble cannot have its usual round shape, but appears
bent or drawn out and bag-like; and in some of the inclosures there is a
confusion of actually undeterminable objects. Moreover, the larger quartzes
of these granite-porphyries contain distinct " stone cavities " (Sorby); i. e.,
amorphous inclosures of a microfelsitically devitrified substance, often
having a good hexagonal shape, like those which so often occur in the
quartzes of genuine felsite-porphyries. There exists also another similarity with felsite-porphyries in the phenomenon where arms of the groundmass penetrate into the quartzes in the form of wedges and bags. In a few
varieties of these rocks, the larger feldspars in the groundmass are altered
into a substance which is fibrous or confusedly radiating [128]. The
amount of hornblende in some specimens is proportionally large, and apatite occurs in most of them. The presence of well-characterized titanite is
remarkable; the mineral is scattered in microscopical crystals through many
of these rocks, and in some places it is even visible macroscopically
[124]. It is curious that in this series, lying as close together as they do,
one occurs [129] which every petrographer would, from its macroscopical
aspect, prefer to place among the genuine felsite-porphyries, and that the
quartzes of this rock are seen under the microscope to contain very good
glass-inclusions, which are entirely wanting in those of the granite-porphyries of this region, and which prove that the macro-petrographical percep-

tion that discerned this occurrence from the accompanying ones was not mistaken.

To this same group also belong those from Marble Hill, Kinsly District, Nevada [130, 131, 132, 133, 134]. Macroscopically, they are middle members, being less between granites and felsite-porphyries than between granite-porphyries and felsite-porphyries. They are very rich in crystals, but the groundmass looks macroscopically rather homogeneous and compact. Its color is a feebly greenish gray. The microscopical structure is again distinctly crystalline. Among the secreted crystals, beside quartz and feldspars, hornblende and black mica are to be found. The quartzes contain inclusions of the groundmass of such size that the larger ones can be seen in the sections with the naked eye. They bear also many empty cavities and fluid-inclusions, among the latter some double ones with liquid carbonic acid. Here also there are no glassy particles. The thin sections show that a part of the feldspars, are in the interior, still quite fresh and pellucid, while alteration has only surrounded them with a thin, milky-whitish exterior; but in other individuals decomposition has progressed farther toward the centre, and only a small kernel of fresh primary feldspar-substance is left; at last the whole feldspar section is found to be metamorphosed into the usual impellucid kaolinic mass. All these interesting stages of transition may be seen in one section. Some varieties of these rocks bear excellently striated plagioclase [133]. The larger hornblendes in the groundmass often have a fibrous appearance, produced by their being built up of innumerable acicular microlites, whose bunch-like ends spread out like sheaves of wheat. Hornblende of this construction seems sooner to undergo molecular alteration than the common form. Those rocks from this locality (Marble Hill) which are rich in secreted crystals, contain comparatively very many large plates of deep-black mica, which, under the microscope, are richly lamellated and frequently pierced by sharp needles of apatite. The apatite needles, however, occur quite plentifully independent of the biotite. A substance which is doubtless titanite has been observed microscopically in some varieties [132, 133], whose groundmasses are proportionally coarser-grained. Magnetite is sometimes found in extraordinarily numerous and well-shaped crystals. The brownish spots which appear in some parts of the groundmass are hydrous oxyd of iron, produced by the decomposition of hornblende, which has entered as a liquid between the feldspar and quartz grains of the groundmass. One interesting variety of these granite-porphyries from Marble Hill resembles the others in every respect, except that the entire groundmass is not a microscopical aggregation of individualized quartz and feldspar, part of these substances having contributed to the formation of fine felsitic sphærolites. There are not only evident tendencies to this process and elementary stages of it, but splendid complete sections through well-rounded radiating sphærolites which feebly polarize, and bunches of their fibres are found fastened rectangularly upon the outlines of quartzes. This variety contains biotite plates up to the size of 4^{mm}. It is simply a sphærolite-bearing modification of the former rocks. Beautiful titanites are disseminated through it, and its green hornblende sections do not show a fibrous structure, but a compact mass having splendid cleavage-directions. The association of titanite with hornblende in these rocks has a particular significance, if we remember that the first mineral is so nearly an exclusive characteristic of the later eruptive granites. Perhaps the presence of titanite would be sufficient to warrant the belief that the granite-porphyries of Marble Hill, as a petrographical modification of granite, belong also to a relatively late geological epoch.

In the Goose Creek Hills, Nevada, granite-porphyries occur [135, 136], with very little or else with considerable hornblende, white orthoclase, some plagioclase, and quartz in a genuine, excellently fine-grained groundmass, in which the microscope detects, beside grayish feldspar particles and quartzes, rough elementary stages in the formation of sphærolites, sometimes in the shape of rather distinctly fibrous bunches. The larger feldspars are altered into an entirely dull, impellucid mass, in some places with feeble vestiges of a former triclinic striation. Some of these decomposed feldspars contain a large quantity of colorless, acicular and prismatic crystals, three or four being usually joined together in the form of a star, which may possibly belong to muscovite. A remarkable microscopical structure is developed in the larger individuals of hornblende: the characteristic outlines are perfectly preserved, but the original mass is totally altered into

5 M P

leek-green fibres, which form single independent systems and bunches, following one upon another at sharp or obtuse angles. Often these fiber-systems are undulating and curved, and sometimes parallel bands and strings appear in place of the fibers. Inside the hornblende, these substances are accompanied by opaque, black, angular grains, which are surely magnetite, and as surely a product of decomposition, because they do not occur in the fresh hornblende prisms of analogous rocks. Dathe has shown that the development of magnetite out of the altering augites of diabases can be followed with certainty under the microscope;[1] and Gustav Bischof long ago determined that this process was probable upon chemical grounds.[2] But in addition to these two products of alteration, the hornblende sections include dark greenish-yellow grains, and little accumulations of such grains, most probably belonging to newly formed epidote. It is further remarkable that while hornblende which has undergone so active a process of metamorphism, has changed into not less than three easily distinguishable epigenetic minerals, the old apatite prisms which pierce it in all directions have been conserved without the slightest touch of alteration; a fact which may always be observed where apatite is included in highly decomposed minerals, and which leads to the conclusion that the water holding carbonic acid, which is generally regarded as the chief chemical agency in the decomposition of silicates, has no effect upon phosphate of lime, notwithstanding it is so easily dissolved by hydrochloric acid.

The syenitic granite-porphyry from the divide between Bingham and Tooelle Cañons, Oquirrh Mountains, Utah [137], belongs to this same series. It resembles those above described in the most characteristic points. Here the alteration of the hornblende has gone still further (Plate III, fig. 2). Its outlines have been as well preserved as in the last described specimen, but much colorless calcite having distinctly rhombohedral cleavage-fissures has settled in the sections of the primary mineral. The leek-green matter mentioned above, is reduced to single undulating strings and bands separated from the calcite by a botryoidal or bud-like boundary-line, which appears with a high magnifying power to be very delicately crenated. It

[1] Zeitschrift d. d. geolog. Gesellsch., XXVI, 1874, 29.
[2] Lehrbuch der chemisch. u. physikal. Geologie, 2. Aufl., II, 913, 944.

is remarkable that the general direction of the green stripes and bands plainly corresponds with the cleavage of the hornblende. The outermost zone of these sections usually consists of the green matter, while with the interior portions are again mixed black magnetite and dark-yellowish epidote grains, the latter often presenting regular crystalline forms which are not unlike those of epidote. Sharp prisms of apatite are also present. These altered crystals are the most complex in composition, and, with reference to the history and destiny of hornblende, are the most instructive of any that have ever been studied, and may not hereafter be easily surpassed.

At the foot-hills between Tooelle and Stockton, Oquirrh Mountains, a granite-porphyry occurs [138], with little felsitic groundmass, much quartz, orthoclase, very beautiful hornblende, and macroscopical titanite. A crystal of yellowish-brown titanite reaching a length of 1.5^{mm} was found included in an orthoclase.

A curious granite-porphyry forms a dike in the northern ridge of Twin Peaks, Wahsatch Range [139]. It contains, in an extremely fine-grained groundmass, large biotite plates, but neither macroscopical quartz nor feldspar. The minute elements of the groundmass, which is entirely crystalline, are well-shaped, dull feldspars, grains of quartz filling up the spaces between these and the brown biotite laminæ which lie in all directions; the horizontal ones appearing darker, those transversely cut lighter brown, and the smallest ones sharply hexagonal. There is also a comparatively enormous quantity of apatite, but there is no hornblende, and therefore no titanite.

A macroscopical appearance similar to the last described is seen in a dike in the limestones of Big Cottonwood Cañon, Wahsatch Range [140], but the groundmass is somewhat coarser-grained and poorer in mica, though it has some very fresh feldspars, among them fine plagioclases, visible to the naked eye. The rock is extraordinarily rich in iron pyrites, which forms in transmitted light fine black macroscopical grains, appearing even with a low magnifying power as thick lumps, entirely opaque of a yellowish color, and having a metallic lustre in reflected light. It is curious that this mineral forms real veins through the quartz grains, the phenomenon suggesting fissures in the grains that have been filled up. The larger quartzes, proved by polarized light to be one individual, are traversed by such a mineral-net, which divides the quartz into isolated, single grains. Ramifications of the iron pyrites in the form of thin, delicate lines, also traverse the feldspars, always giving proof of its later injection. There is also an indistinct, green constituent in the rock, probably belonging in part to half-weathered hornblende and in part to epidote.

A beautiful granite-porphyry is found north of Clayton's Peak, Wahsatch Range [141]. It has a greenish-gray groundmass, rich in plagioclase and iron pyrites, and formerly in hornblende, which, however, as proved already by the macroscopical aspect of the hand-specimens, is now for the most part often altered into coarse, radiated epidote, and occasionally into quartz. The pale-reddish, flesh-colored feldspars seem from the beginning to have been rendered impure by much dust of oxyd of iron. Dirty reddish-brown spots, with contours similar to the magnesian mica, as shown in the corresponding fresh rock, seem to be the product of the alteration of this constituent.

At Good Pass, east of Parkview Peak, between North and Middle Parks, Colorado [142], and on Parkview Peak [143], occur rocks belonging petrographically to the granite-porphyries, and bearing considerable resemblance to the Saxon rocks of that name from Beucha and Wurzen, and still more to that from Altenberg in the Erzgebirge. The groundmass is a dirty yellowish-gray, and to the naked eye its place seems to be between the extremely fine-grained and the nearly homogeneous state. The rock from Good Pass is remarkable on account of its large and most excellent, roundly formed crystals of orthoclase. They have the most characteristic shape, resembling the perfect individuals in the fine-grained porphyritic granites from Thuringia and from Neubau near Hof in the Fichtelgebirge, Germany. They present the faces:

$$
\begin{aligned}
T \text{ and } l &= \infty\, P = \dot{I} \\
M &= \infty\, \mathcal{R}\, \infty = i - i \\
P &= O\, P = O \\
s &= \infty\, \mathcal{R}\, 3 = i - 3 \\
\cdot y &= 2\, \mathcal{P}\, \infty = 2 - i \\
n &= 2\, \mathcal{R}\, \infty = 2 - i
\end{aligned}
$$

These feldspars, sometimes an inch long, are generally of an adularia-like clearness in the interior, and on the outside milky, dull, and impellucid. Plagioclases also occur, but they are wanting in that extraordinary morphological individualization. Macroscopically, both rocks contain some hornblende and quartz grains, but they have no glass and only a few liquid-inclusions. Fluid-particles are also observable in the fresher portions of the feldspars, and in greater frequency and distinctness than usual. The rock from Good Pass also bears brownish mica. That from Parkview Peak possesses a lighter color, and has more green, strongly fibrous hornblende, in which bunches of finely radiated, pale-brownish, crystalline needles, probably epidote, are often interposed. Both rocks are rich in apatite and in beautiful titanite, and they also contain magnetite and splendid sharp cubes of iron pyrites, which have the color of brass in reflected light. The groundmass is almost entirely crystalline here, as is generally the case through all these granite-porphyries. It may be mentioned that, in a locality not very far from this, Steve's Ridge, Elkhead Mountains, an undoubted Tertiary sanidin-trachyte exists, in which orthoclase-feldspars are developed, presenting in rich profusion precisely the same list of crystallographical faces as the above orthoclase. The geological evidences of the age of the Good Pass rock are insufficient to warrant any determination from them, though it might be supposed from the great superficial resemblance of the feldspars that it belongs also to the eruptive rocks of the Tertiary epoch. But a number of petrographical circumstances combine to contradict this theory, founded only on the analogous form of the feldspars, and tend to prove a probable older origin. These petrographical facts are: a, their feldspar crystals in the above-described porphyry have the antique behavior which is characteristic of the orthoclases of the old granites, the crystals in the trachyte referred to presenting that really modern type which has received the proper name of sanidin; b, the well-developed form, rich in rare faces, is certainly far less remarkable in orthoclases of older granitic than in sanidins of younger trachytic rocks; c, the microscopical structure of the sanidins in question differs in many points from that of our orthoclases; d, the hornblende in the rocks from Good Pass and Parkview Peak, give green-colored sections, characteristic of the older, granitic rocks, the hornblende sections in the Tertiary trachytes being always brown here; e, the quartzes of these two rocks contain only fluid-inclusions, those of the trachyte only glass-particles; f, iron pyrites would be extraordinary as a secondary constituent in younger rocks; g, the presence of titanite is just as usual in granitic rocks as it is highly rare in trachytic ones. So the theory that these two granite-porphyries belong to the Jurassic eruptive rocks, i. e., to the youngest division of the older ones, is generally strengthened.

CHAPTER IV.

FELSITE-PORPHYRY AND SYENITE.

SECTION I.—FELSITE-PORPHYRY.
SECTION II.—SYENITE.

SECTION I.

FELSITE-PORPHYRY.

There are few questions in petrography which are of such importance and which have been so differently answered as that concerning the microscopical behavior of the groundmass of felsite-porphyries, which appears to the naked eye to be compact and homogeneous, or at least mineralogically indeterminable. Abstractions founded upon analogies and interpretations of chemical analyses, were early formulated with a view of elucidating the subject, but none of these has ever risen above the rank of a more or less satisfying hypothesis. It is evident that a question of this kind can only be accurately solved by close microscopical examinations, and this branch of research and investigation is the most difficult of any that has been undertaken with this instrument.

For a long time, two contradictory opinions on the point have confronted each other. Most of the earlier petrographers believed with Leopold v. Buch[1] that the groundmass of felsite-porphyries is an intimate aggregation of extraordinarily minute crystalline particles, especially of feldspar and quartz in microgranitic structure. Delesse, on the other hand,

[1] Reise durch Norwegen u. Lappland, 1808, i, 139.

pleaded for the opinion[1] that the seeming homogeneous paste which includes
the porphyritical crystals was to be compared with a mother-water, presenting in a certain respect the residuum of crystallization, and was not composed
of individualized mineral particles, but a half-crystalline mass; an indefinite
silicate consisting of silica and all bases which occur in the porphyritical
crystals. This important conflict was even mooted after the microscope
began to take an active part in the investigation of the question by the examination of thin sections. But it should be remembered that the first studies in
this new field were made without first-class instruments, with insufficient
material, on sections which were not reduced to the extreme thinness necessary, and without exhausting all the resources of polarized light. In 1862,
F. Z. arrived at the conclusion that the groundmass of half a dozen felsite-
porphyries which he had examined microscopically had an entirely crystalline structure, composed of little particles of impellucid feldspar and clear
quartz.[2] H. Laspeyres[3] and E. Weiss[4] corroborated this testimony after a
microscopical study of the felsite-porphyry from Halle in Prussia. Vogelsang's[5] microscopical interpretation of the groundmass, however, approaches
very nearly to that of Delesse. The groundmass proper, independent of
the secreted crystals, is not resolved under the microscope into single minute
crystalline particles, but appears in an unindividualized, half-crystalline
state. Some groundmasses are even really amorphous and simple-refract-
ing. Then Stelzner came to the front[6] as an opponent of the theory of his
predecessor, and reasserted the conclusions of the earlier investigators,
namely, that the groundmass is, under the microscope, a fine crystalline
aggregation, all of whose elements become colored in polarized light, and
therefore cannot be amorphous. E. Cohen,[7] after examining the typical
felsite-porphyries of Odenwald, Germany, was the first to suggest that
their groundmass is not generally the same, but in the several occurrences

---

[1] Bulletin de la Soc. géolog. (2 sér.), VI, 629.

[2] Sitzungsber. d. Wiener Akademie, 1863, XLVII, 239.

[3] Zeitschrift d. d. geolog. Gesellseb., XVI, 1864, 402.

[4] Beiträge zur Kenntniss der Feldspathbildung, Haarlem, 1866, 146.

[5] Philosophie der Geologie u. mikroskop. Gesteinsstudien, 1866, 133.

[6] Petrograph. Bemerkungen über Gesteine des Altai, 1871, 22.

[7] Die zur Dyas gehörigen Gesteine des südlichen Odenwaldes, 1871, 37.

of a different microscopical constitution. Some of them, indeed, are crystalline-grained, while others contain a predominating glassy, amorphous mass (base).

The more all these theories as to the microscopical constitution of the felsitic groundmass differed, the more necessary became a thorough examination of larger numbers of specimens, in the light of the experience which had meanwhile been accumulating. F. Z. therefore undertook, in 1873, a new series of investigations of the subject,[1] the general result of which is that the microstructure of the groundmass is not at all equally constituted in each case, as it was believed to be before Cohen, and that the masses which are most similar macroscopically are found when viewed microscopically to be entirely different. There are, indeed, groundmasses which possess wholly, or almost wholly, a granitic, crystalline structure, being resolved by polarized light into double-refracting particles; but there are, on the other hand, some which consist in a largely predominating measure of an indistinctly or wholly unindividualized substance, entirely, or almost entirely, indifferent to polarized light. Between these two extreme formations appear middle members, having some of the characteristics of both. And thus it appears that the earlier theories, notwithstanding their difference, were not so very far out of the way, except that it was not permissible to generalize the single result gained by so few examinations.

Genuine felsite-porphyries are not very frequent along the Fortieth Parallel, as compared with other countries; for instance, Germany or France. It almost seems as if the granite-porphyries here, elsewhere rather rare in this behavior, play the geological and petrographical part which in France and Germany is assumed by the felsite-porphyries. In the first place, it may be said that the porphyries of the West generally possess a felsitic groundmass of an extremely pronounced micrographitic structure, made up almost wholly of crystalline particles; and that the unindividualized, glassy, indistinctly devitrified, or microfelsitic substance is rare.

The rock from Miner's Cañon, Truckee Range, Nevada [144], is a felsite-porphyry, intercalated in beds referred to the Triassic formation, presenting that variety which, on account of its splintery fracture, is known as

[1] Mikroskopische Beschaffenheit d. Mineralien u. Gesteine, 1873, 324.

hornstone-porphyry, although the real constitution of its groundmass is related neither chemically nor mineralogically to that of the compact micro-crystalline quartz. The rock looks like certain *hälleflintas* from Sweden, and in color it is a light greenish gray. Little dirty-green spots and quartz grains, up to the size of 2^{mm}, are its only prominent secretions that can be distinguished. The predominating groundmass appears extremely compact, but under the microscope it is entirely crystalline, though, even for a felsite-porphyry, unusually fine-grained; no particle or little point appearing dark in polarized light by turning the analyzer or thin section. It nevertheless seems as if its single constituent (probably quartz and feldspar) had, in the form of extremely minute particles, balled together into very small lumps; for in polarized light roundish spots are visible, which are really glittering little points, but which present as a total impression the same tinge of color; for instance, yellowish or bluish. The macroscopical quartzes show pretty well-defined crystal-outlines, and contain some fluid-inclusions and beautiful, imbedded, isolated particles of the groundmass, with evidently the same structure, but no glassy grains. There is green hornblende in perfect little crystals and partly obliterated spots; no larger feldspars.

To the south of Willow Spring, Montezuma Range, just north of French Cañon, a rock occurs [145] which might be taken at first sight for a rhyolite, but which surely belongs to the geologically older felsite-por-phyries. The orthoclases in the thin sections are quite milky-white and impellucid; they seem highly altered, but certainly a part at least of the dust, which is usually found in connection with kaolinization, appears in a very high magnifying power with sufficient distinctness as very minute fluid-inclusions. The quartzes, which appear macroscopically the size of a pepper-corn, are, besides the feldspars, remarkably rich in large liquid-inclusions, which are superior in dimensions even to those of the granitic quartzes, and are, for the most part well-shaped hexagonal pyramids, with rather sharp edges. Glassy inclusions are wholly wanting. The light groundmass, probably entirely crystalline-grained, is made up of nearly colorless con-stituents, the feldspar-particles being only a little less pellucid than the clear quartz, and containing as coloring materials only some very light yellowish-green little grains of an undeterminable nature, which are of so pale a tinge that they evidently do not belong to hornblende. An analogous case to this is found at Ravenswood Peak, Shoshone Range, Nevada. Here, in a rhyolite country, a rock occurs [146] which a superficial examination would lead one to think was united with the predominating occurrence; but its macroscopic habitus shows some petrographical differences from the rhyolites. Through a gray groundmass unusual to the latter, milky impellucid feldspars, which have no similarity with rhyolitic sanidins, and large quartzes are distributed. With this antique behavior of the feldspars (nearly all of which belong to orthoclase), the abundance of fluid-inclusions in the quartzes agrees. Glassy inclusions are to be found very rarely (see the remarks on these objects at the end of this chapter on felsite-porphyries). The groundmass is for the most part crystalline, consisting of feldspar and quartz grains. Upon first viewing it between crossed nicols, one is inclined to believe that a thin, amorphous, single-refracting substance, which appears black, predominates; but the greater part of these dark little spots show chromatic polarization when the section is turned around its vertical axis. Some amorphous unindividualized base is present, however, in the form of a yellowish-gray, granular, globulitically devitrified mass, and the behavior of this hidden base is entirely unusual in rhyolites. Larger sections of altered hornblende are to be observed macroscopically; and dispersed through the groundmass are many pale-green, little needles and grains, which most probably also belong to hornblende. The feldspars include distinct prisms of apatite. This is remarkable for two reasons; first, because generally apatite does not occur in feldspars, even if other rock-constituents are plentifully pierced by it; secondly, because apatite has never been noted among the macroscopical accessory ingredients of felsite-porphyries, although it has often been subsequently detected by microscopical examinations.

Of the same geological age as the described granite from Granite Peak, Pah-Ute Range, Nevada, is the excellent felsite-porphyry [147, 148]. It shows macroscopically feldspars and quartzes, and also some little plates of white mica. The feldspars are altered into an impellucid substance, and the quartzes are full of fluid-inclusions, but contain no glassy ones. Here, also, the groundmass is distinctly microgranitic, consisting of grayish-yellow, granular feldspar and colorless quartz, which produce a sharp contrast and give a spotted appearance in polarized light, the single individuals wanting in distinct outlines. Even in the smallest microscopical quartz grains of the groundmass, scarcely 0.01^{mm} in size, fluid-inclusions are found interposed. Among the granite-porphyries of the Franklin Buttes, Nevada, described on page 64, there is one which is built up of a genuine, interesting felsite-porphyry, with a yellowish-gray groundmass that appears homogeneous, little quartz, feldspar, and laminæ of biotite. The mica individuals can be seen with the naked eye, and the use of the microscope does not increase their number, this ingredient not being present in smaller plates. The sections have an extremely fine lamellation, are highly dichroitic and transversely perforated by colorless apatite needles. The groundmass appears under the microscope to be an entirely crystalline-grained aggregation, which resembles more than any other felsite-porphyries that of the Cornish elvan; and yet in the smaller quartzes of the groundmass occur the most distinct little glass-inclusions, with the usual included, dark-bordered, fixed bubble. There are rounded quartz sections of only 0.04^{mm} in diameter, which contain in one plane six or eight glass-particles very similar to those which are held in the quartzes of the famous rhyolite from Mount Baula in Iceland. All the glass-inclusions in the quartzes of this rock are not of like importance. Bodies of this kind are usually entirely wanting in the constituents, where the rock has proved to possess a crystalline structure throughout, and they occur, on the other hand, where a part of the original rock magma has passed into the glassy or otherwise amorphous, unindividualized state. Here the very rare phenomenon is presented[1] of glass-inclusions in the quartzes of a wholly crystalline rock, proving that arguments for a once molten state and for a crystalline rock structure do not necessarily exclude each other, as till now there has been reason to believe. This fact is invested with additional interest if we consider that the rock in question, composed of feldspar, quartz, and mica, is really nothing else but an

[1] Baranowski has observed glass-inclusions in the feldspars of the likewise-crystalline granite-porphyries from Beucha in Saxony. Inaugural-Dissertation, Leipsic, 1873.

extremely fine-grained granite, and that therefore the objections made to the theory of the igneous origin of granite, on the ground of its crystalline structure and of the absence of glass-inclusions in its constituents, are very weak.

The limestone of the Waehoo Mountains is traversed by dikes of a typical felsite-porphyry [149], a crystalline aggregation being again presented in its groundmass. The large feldspars show to the naked eye, in the thin sections better than in the hand-specimens, that they are composed of a dim and dull exterior zone of a milky, impellucid condition, with a rather adularia-like, clear, interior substance, the passage from one to the other at the boundary being soft and gradual. The larger secreted quartzes are distinguished by their entirely rounded dihexahedral shape, and by their containing the most beautiful liquid-inclusions, with salt cubes. One of these inclusions of saturated salt solution was 0.015^{mm} long and 0.004^{mm} broad, the contained salt cube measuring 0.0017^{mm} in length on one of its edges. Most of the cubes are very clear and sharply defined, but some are rounded at the edges and even pass into real grains, yet all are connected by easily observable transitions. In some quartzes, these inclusions are extremely abundant, and perhaps in their nearest neighbors they will be found to be very rare or altogether wanting. It is remarkable that microscopical objects so identical in nature as these are interposed in the quartzes of genetically different rocks, namely, gneisses, granites, felsite-porphyries, and diorites. Long arms and short, obtuse wedges of the groundmass penetrate far into the water-clear quartzes, which, beside these, include a lot of *isolated* particles of the groundmass, whose behavior is entirely like that of the surrounding or main mass, and which in outline, copy the rough pyramidal form of the quartz itself. The presence of such characteristic inclusions is of importance in the discussion of a genetic question. Vogelsang was inclined to think that the present crystalline or half-crystalline constitution of the porphyritic groundmass was not original, but rather the result of a secondary, molecular devitrification, which, in the wet way, had happened to a primary, glassy substance of the nature of the hyaline pitchstones.[1] This theory is, in truth, supported by the fact that

[1] Philosophie der Geologie u. s. w., 144, 153, 194; see also Kalkowski, Mineralog. Mittheilungen, gesammelt von Tschermak, 1874, 52.

the glass mass of pitchstones is traversed by fractures along which a really felsitic devitrification has taken place, producing a mass which cannot generally be distinguished in either ordinary or polarized light from the groundmass of felsite-porphyries. But it is doubtful whether this devitrification is indeed a secondary hydro-metamorphic one, developed in the lapse of time, or whether it was not originally connected with the solidification of the pitchstone mass, as is doubtless the case in felsitic rhyolites. As against this, however, is the fact of the presence of genuine isolated particles of groundmass in the midst of compact quartzes and the absence of any microscopical fissures leading to them, circumstances which prove that *these* mechanically included little bodies can by no means be a product of a secondary devitrification of glass-inclusions; and as in constitution they entirely agree with the general groundmass of the rock, the burden of their testimony is that at the time when the quartz crystals became solid, a felsitic substance of the behavior now exhibited was, as such, already present around them.

In the neighboring limestones of Spruce Mountain, Peoquop Range, occurs an interesting felsite-porphyry [150] which presents macroscopically only small quartzes and no feldspars. Under the microscope, the groundmass appears to be principally an aggregation of extremely nice, concentrically radiating sphærolites up to the size of 0.3^{mm} in diameter, and feebly polarizing without showing the colored cross. The globules have neither a different interior structure nor a defined peripheric zone, and no foreign centre. Some feldspars are dispersed between them. This sphærolitic structure cannot be distinguished in hand-specimens, nor is it visible in the thin sections, even to the naked eye. Perhaps this characteristic rock is in some way connected with the granite-porphyries from Marble Hill, Kinsley District, some of which also bear sphærolites (see page 65), but the rock in question is entirely free from hornblende. In later times, much attention was paid to these felsite-porphyries in which portions of the groundmass have undergone a process of aggregation and radial arrangement into globular masses, on account of the striking and genetically important analogy between them and their later Tertiary successors, the rhyolites, in which the development of sphærolites is much greater, and which also have the natural, and artificial, glassy masses of which the secretion of such globules is so characteristic. Stelzner has microscopically examined and described the sphærolitic felsite-porphyries from the Korgon and the Tscharisch in the Altai;[1] E. Cohen those from Apfelskopf and the Edelstein in Southern Odenwald, Germany;[2] and Samuel Allport that from Corriegills on the island of Arran, Scotland,[3] which forms a dike near the well-known pitchstone. Other sphærolitic porphyries, which have not yet been examined, occur in Thüringer Wald, Germany, at the Schneekopf, Regenstein, Meisenstein, at the Hauskopf near Oppenau, and at Ganzenbach near Baden in the Schwarzwald.

Another felsite-porphyry forms a dike in the granite of Long's Peak, Colorado Range [151]. It is one of those varieties which is as rich in hornblende as most others are very poor. The groundmass is probably entirely crystalline. Many liquid-inclusions appear in the quartzes, and it is remarkable that numerous large and distinct specimens of them with a spontaneously moving bubble are also found imbedded in the orthoclases, where their substance is pellucid enough to admit of seeing through. The contrasts in the shape of the liquid-inclusions here are very striking, those of the feldspars having a very irregular form and those of the quartzes being oval or nearly globular. The farther our studies of the structure of feldspar proceed the more it becomes probable that the microscopical dust-like material which is so often interposed in the clear unaltered individuals consists, for the most part, of extremely minute fluid particles. Hornblende occurs in the form of little, fresh, green prisms, abundantly scattered through the groundmass; and the thin and delicate, almost colorless, and often broken microlites, which are taken up by the quartz, belong with certainty to hornblende.

If we compare the American felsite-porphyries of the Fortieth Parallel with those from other regions which have been examined microscopically, principally German occurrences, the chief contrast, all other relations being strikingly similar, seems to exist in the fact that the quartzes of

[1] Petrographische Bemerkungen über Gesteine des Altai, 1871, 31.
[2] Die zur Dyas gehörigen Gesteine des südlichen Odenwaldes, 1871, 89.
[3] Geological Magazine, 1872, IX, No. 12.

the former are generally remarkably poor in glass-inclusions, or wholly devoid of them, containing only liquid ones. The typical felsite-porphyries of Europe, for instance on the other side of Halle, from the Odenwald, certain localities in Westphalia, and from Northern Saxony (Rochlitzer Berg, etc.), for the most part show in their quartzes some excellent glass-grains, beside the predominating fluid-inclusions. The rocks of the two continents are strikingly similar in all other points. Perhaps this difference warrants the conclusion that the above-described porphyries are generally of an older geological age, equivalent to that of the older eruptive granites, while those of Germany are chiefly younger than most of the granites occurring there. In accord with this theory of older origin is the fact of the total absence of titanite in the felsite-porphyries of the Fortieth Parallel, the significance of which is that these rocks probably are not petrographical modifications of the younger granites, if indeed the latter are as recent as has been supposed.

SECTION II.

SYENITE.

Among the examined rocks of the Fortieth Parallel, genuine characteristic syenites resembling the classic German ones from the Plauenscher
Ground near Dresden and from Weinheim on the Bergstrasse are extremely
rare. Properly, there is only one really old syenite in this region. It
forms the main mass of Clure Hills, Cortez Range, Nevada [152]. Macroscopically, it consists of prevailing flesh-red, monoclinic feldspar and
greenish hornblende, which are not fresh in appearance. Under the microscope, the feldspar is seen to possess the same behavior as the orthoclase of
granites; but it is remarkable that some of its individuals are altered, their
exterior outline only being preserved, into an accumulation of short, radiated,
gray, fascicular and radially arranged needles, which give an excellent
aggregate polarization. The hornblende sections prove not to be homogeneous individuals, every one being made up of an aggregation of light-green,
broad rays, or narrower prisms, which are in one place straight and parallel, and in another curved and diverging, like sheaves or ice-flowers. On
the outside, these polysynthetical hornblende crystals are often colored
brownish-yellow by oxidation; but their present structure is probably original and not the result of alteration, because in the quartzes of the rock the
same component bodies, rays and prismatic needles, are found to be included,
in precisely the same manner as they build up the hornblende. Here and
there some of the feldspars present half-obliterated remains of a twin-striation. This fact is interesting as showing that even this remote syenite is
not free from plagioclase. It was believed formerly that syenite was only
a combination of orthoclase and hornblende; but even the famous rock
from the Plauenscher Ground near Dresden, always considered to be the
most typical syenite, and the first to receive this name from Werner, has
been found, in polarized light, to contain some triclinic feldspar. It is most
probable that there is no syenite at all free from plagioclase, just as a
trachyte is not likely to exist, which does not contain this associated feldspar. The rock also bears microscopical but very distinct grains of quartz,
with many fluid-inclusions; another ingredient which was not formerly sup-

G M P

posed to exist in the German syenites, but which can be detected in most of them by the microscope.

Amorphous matter does not exist between the crystalline ingredients, a characteristic of all genuine syenites. A rock from the south of Palisade Cañon, Cortez Range, Nevada, should be mentioned [153], which seems macroscopically to be a porphyritic modification of the foregoing syenite. This syenite-porphyry contains, in a seemingly homogeneous, greenish-gray, felsitic groundmass, flesh-colored feldspars, altered green hornblendes, and small quartzes. Under the microscope, the felsitic mass is seen to be composed entirely of crystalline grains of feldspar, quartz, and altered hornblende. Many of the larger feldspars are triclinic. The hornblende is decomposed into a green, earthy substance, and has caused the production of the yellowish-brown ochre-masses which surround its metamorphosed sections, and are accumulated elsewhere through the rock; for example, on the fissures of quartz grains. All the feldspars are evidently fragments.

CHAPTER V.

DIORITE, HORNBLENDE-PORPHYRY, DIABASE, MELAPHYRE, GABBRO.

SECTION I.

DIORITE.

The Virginia Range is traversed by the cañons of the Walker, Carson, and Truckee Rivers, and full eight-tenths of its mass is made up of younger volcanic rocks. Only at rare intervals, where deep erosion in the cañons has laid bare the original range, or where its hard summits have been lifted above the volcanic flows, is there any clue to the materials or position of the ancient chain. Mount Davidson (7827 ft.) is one of the few remaining vestiges, being composed of diorite and forming the central mass of a bold outburst of this rock rising above the city of Virginia. This dioritic body is bounded upon the north by propylite, which forms the northern slope of Ophir Ravine. Crown Point Ravine marks its southwestern limit. It is really an insular mass, one of the ancient original summits, which is completely surrounded by the subsequent propylite. The overflow of propylite has also failed to cover two narrow insular ridges, which still outcrop on the slope of Cedar Hill; and in the bottoms of ravines, eroded in the volcanic material, it is shown that these diorites have obtruded through considerable masses of metamorphic rocks, schists, limestones, graphitic shales, and slates, whose folds date from the period of Jurassic upheaval.[1] The diorites of Mount Davidson [154, 155] sometimes contain coarse-grained secretions and traversing light zones rich in feldspars. The plagioclases are still partly fresh, having fluid-inclusions, are beautifully striated, and partly metamorphosed into dull milky spots. There is considerable quartz: no orthoclase is visible. Distinct hornblende appears in very fibrous individuals of a dark-green color, but none quite unaltered. Epidote often occurs macroscopically, and under the microscope a great quantity of the very thinnest veins of this mineral, colored an intense greenish-yellow, is seen traversing the rock in all directions. The same capillary fissure is sometimes filled in one part with epidote and in another with calcite. It is plainly visible how the epidote enters into the hornblende. Where microscopical cracks are found in the hornblende individuals, their walls are discovered to have been altered for a wide extent into epidote, and often the borders of the hornblende consist partly of the yellowish products of alteration. Magnetic and titanic iron occur together. This diorite, made up chiefly of plagioclase and hornblende, and possessing an entirely crystalline structure, is as regards the absence of orthoclase a very typical one, and a member of the quartziferous division. In the plagioclase rocks, the presence or absence of quartz is not of so much importance as in the orthoclase series; in the former, it often happens that the same deposition is in one place free from, in another poor, and again rich in quartz; a phenomenon which does not occur in the orthoclase rocks.

A small obscure outcrop of diorite in Basalt Cañon, Washoe [156], contains, beside the hornblende, dark reddish-gray feldspars, almost all of which are triclinic. On the south side of Ophir Ravine are portions of the diorite which have become microcrystalline, and look quite homogeneous. The coarser varieties of this locality [157] bear, beside plagioclase and a little pale hornblende, some orthoclase and quartz. The plagioclase includes many foreign particles, among them excellent fluid-inclusions,

---

[1] See vol. III, Geology of the Washoe Mining District, by Clarence King, 13, 21.

some of which are 0.003^{mm} in diameter, with distinctly moving bubbles. In larger fluid-inclusions, whose bubbles are usually immovable, small, short, greenish hornblende-microlites are seen.

Very similar to these Washoe diorites are some fresh occurrences from Bevel-hyma Ledge, Peavine Mountain, Nevada [158, 159]. They are rather poor in hornblende, with proportionally much orthoclase. The hornblende principally forms irregular aggregations of grains, but all the feldspars are at intervals actually overladen with fine, light-green hornblende dust, as is the case also with the German diorites. In the larger and more compact hornblende individuals, the development of intensely greenish-yellow epidote may be easily followed. The rock is very poor in quartz, or free from it.

The diorites of the railroad-cut in Truckee Cañon vary somewhat from each other. One of them [160] has a highly distinct crystalline texture, containing plagioclase with fluid-inclusions, almost no orthoclase, splendid sections of dark-green hornblende, showing that the crystals possess also the faces ($\infty P \infty$); biotite often partially encircling the hornblende or included in it, without being a product of alteration, some quartz, apatite, magnetic iron; in short, a most typical diorite, having all the ingredients possible to this rock, like the classic ones from Ilmenau in the Thüringer Wald. Another [161] is also crystalline; but it is poor in hornblende and biotite, rich in quartz and apatite, and contains, besides, the zircon-like mineral. Still another variety [162] is a diorite-porphyry, consisting of a ground-mass with imbedded crystals, which distinctly appear only in the thin sections; feldspars rather strongly altered, often having an aggregate polarization and a fibration which is visible in ordinary light. The characteristic sections of the almost wholly decomposed hornblende consist on the outside, of a black, impellucid border, in the interior, of a nearly aquamarine-colored mass, sprinkled throughout with black grains, and showing fibrous aggregate polarization between crossed nicols. The yellowish-gray ground-mass is half granular, devitrified, and indistinctly polarizing; yet small feld-spar-microlites appear in this insufficiently individualized base. Diorite bearing the same relation to the ancient series of metamorphic rocks, is found in different localities throughout the whole basin. Wherever observed, its manner of occurrence is always the same: it invariably accompanies the mountain-fractures presumably of middle geological age, and is always assumed to be later than the granite and earlier than the propylite.[1]

In the Kawsoh Mountains, a diorite forms a part of the region through which the basalts protrude: it contains hornblende, which has been attacked by decomposition, and biotite, but almost no quartz.

On Nache's Peak, Truckee Range, is found an old rock [163] similar to that from Quenast in Belgium: it is highly decomposed and indistinct in texture, yet there is no doubt that it is a plagioclase-hornblende rock, with some quartz.

The hills south of Rabbit Hole Spring in the Kamma Mountains, Nevada, are composed of a dirty-green rock, which appears under the microscope as an excellent, fine-grained diorite [164]. Notwithstanding the cleavage of the green hornblende is well conserved, it contains small light-brownish grains, which are probably epidote. The plagioclases are rather fresh, and include much finely distributed, pale hornblende material, together with spots of a light brownish-gray dust, consisting of grains so minute as to be undeterminable even with the highest magnifying power. No quartz is visible.

The diorites of the Pah-Ute Range are, for the most part, distinctly coarse-grained, and, like most of the above, crystalline throughout, without any amorphous substance. These rocks are made interesting by the wide difference in the amount of quartz and by the replacement of hornblende by biotite, which produces the group of mica-diorites. The beautifully crystalline diorite from the Hot Spring Hills, Pah-Ute Range [165], is almost wholly composed of plagioclase, traversed by dull opaque veins and spots and splendid fresh hornblende and magnetite. It is almost totally free from quartz. Another coarse-grained diorite from this range [166] shows white, porcelain-like, decomposed feldspar, whose twin striation is entirely obliterated; pretty hornblende, which is arranged with some degree of parallelism, making the rock somewhat slaty; biotite, little quartz, and much apatite. The black and very much broken mineral seems to be titanic iron. Another variety [167] is a fine-grained, light greenish-gray rock, with highly altered

---

[1] See vol. III, Geology of the Washoe Mining District, by Clarence King, 21.

plagioclase, and rich in quartz. But, in this neighborhood, a diorite also occurs, which is midway between the coarse and fine grained varieties [168]. The largest part of the feldspar in this rock has remained pellucid, and presents the most brilliant variegated lineature, so that there is no doubt of the triclinic nature of the above-mentioned decomposed feldspars. The rock has no mica. It can be easily seen how yellowish-brown hornblende has been metamorphosed on the borders into a parallel fibrous green mass, which sometimes spreads over the whole individual, in which appear dots and spots of brownish hornblende, showing a soft, pleasant blending of the colors. On the other hand, the most typical mica equivalent of the above-described hornblende-diorites occurs in the Pah-Ute Range. The feldspars in these mica-diorites [169, 170] are not in any respect different; but biotite in brown laminæ, half an inch in length, by far outweighs the hornblende. Apatite is more abundant here and quartz is wanting. Similar mica-diorites are known in Europe, at the Muhlberg near Dreihacken in the Bohemian Forest, between Schönfeld and Schlaggenwald in Bohemia, at the Kyffhaüser in Thuringia, at Clefcy near Fraize, Vosges, at Vaugneray, Département du Rhône, at Plemeuf, and Pont-des-Îles in Brittany.

Very coarse-grained diorites are found at the west foot of Augusta Mountains, north of Shoshone Springs [171], containing well-striated plagioclase, very cleavable brown hornblende, apatite in proportionally large prisms, and titanite. There is, beside these, a mineral in dark-brown sections without any cleavage, and seeming to be nearly homogeneous and compact. By these features, and by its outlines differing at first sight from the hornblende, the individuals appear pretty strongly dichroitic, and it seems most probable that they belong to tourmaline, notwithstanding the fact that this mineral has never till now been observed as a macroscopical, accessory constituent of diorites.

The Jurassic diorite which occurs as country-rock in the New-Pass Mines is a remarkable product [172, 173]. It contains large milky feldspars 4^{mm} in length, and green, fibrous crystals of hornblende 6^{mm} in length. The greater part of the feldspar shows vestiges of a former twin striation, and is filled up with a multitude of the most fine and delicate prickles, awns, needles, and grains of light-green hornblende. The larger hornblende sections, which look to the naked eye like homogeneous individuals, are really built up of aggregated fine microlites in as interesting and instructive a manner as may be seen anywhere. (Plate I, fig. 11). Thin needles and delicate prisms of greater or less length have a parallel arrangement and are in immediate contact; the effect of this accumulation and joining being to represent roughly or distinctly the contours of a crystal. The larger crystals have been welded together of thousands or tens of thousands of minute hornblende staffs. This structure is the more evident because the borders of the sections are not sharply defined like those of really homogeneous individuals. Here some of the larger needles or bunches project out beyond an even line; there the outline curves inward, where the needles are not long enough to reach and help to form an even external section-line to the crystal. Hence the margins of these aggregations often look corroded or gnawed. Sometimes these accumulations of microlites, imitating crystals, with their surrounding mass, have been solidified before the single needles employed in their construction had taken their place, so that some appear near the external borders of the crystals as if they had been stopped in the act of approaching. The fine hornblende-microlites are also heaped together in the form of pretty stars and irregular fascicles. Traversing the feldspars, and also more or less the whole rock, are lines of small, greenish-yellow, closely-crowded grains, whose secondary origin is evident, and whose epidotic nature is certain. The same substance is also found in the hornblende, forming, beside the vein-lines, patches and spots which can be easily distinguished from the fibrous hornblende by their granular composition and color. The rock also contains colorless prisms, which have a rhombic section, with an angle which is even more obtuse than 120°. When considered with reference to other occurrences, there is scarcely any doubt that this, in some places very abundant mineral, is tremolite. Beside all these, magnetite is found in the rock, together with long, black, opaque staffs, which probably belong to it, because they often have smaller appendages, of the same nature as themselves, fastened rectangularly to a strong, thick shaft.

In Dale Cañon, Havallah Range, Nevada, a dike is formed by an old greenish-gray rock with thick quartz grains. It belongs to the diorites, but is a very peculiar variety [174]. Pale short needles and laminæ of green fibrous hornblende, often aggregated into stars and bunches, are in contact with totally decomposed feldspars, whose features are not easily distinguishable, and with quartz grains and apatite, in a yellowish-gray, granulated, amorphous, and indistinctly polarizing base, in which a tendency to confused fibrous structure is often evident.

In the cañon south of Ravenswood Peak, Shoshone Range, another similar diorite is found, except that it is more crystalline and more altered and bears considerable biotite [175].

Characteristic diorites were collected at Winnemucca Peak, Nevada. The porphyritic variety from the southwest end of the peak [176] has a gray groundmass, with feldspars, more prominent hornblende, and some quartzes. The green hornblendes (some reaching a size of 2^{mm} in length) appear very distinctly, especially in the slides, possessing a peculiar structure. They are not fresh, but in a stage of alteration into epidote, whose greenish-gray radiated or fibrous substance forms parts of the border and wholly replaces the smaller hornblende individuals. The larger hornblendes (Plate III, fig. 3) contain, beside thick rounded nests of epidote, smaller grains of it united into long bands, or stripes, which are curved like a paragraph-mark. The fibration of the hornblende, which is evidently secondary, and probably causes the development of the epidote, often runs in twisted lines resembling the curves of the letter S. The hornblendes also include newly formed geode-like particles of calcite somewhat resembling eyes. Moreover, compact brown spots belonging to the original crystal substance of the hornblende are visible in its interior. Occasionally in one section all these stages of alteration may be seen surrounding each other in right order: a. brown hornblende; b. green fibrous hornblende (viridite); c. epidote with calcite. The rock from the eastern end of Winnemucca Peak [177] is very similar to that from the southwestern, except that dull feldspar is more prominent in the groundmass. The vividly greenish-yellow aggregation of concentric-radiating epidote having the outline of hornblende is very beautiful (Plate III, fig. 4). One frequent feature of these pseudomorphs shows several centra of little irregular balls, to which the epidote needles have been united. Titanic iron is found here, which has undergone the same curious alteration as that usually met with in diabases, except that the secondary mass is here a more dirty yellowish-gray. Black strokes run through it, cutting each other under 60° and 120°, which probably belong to the more resisting lamellæ. In the German diabases, this metamorphic product covers the individuals of titanic iron as a whitish opaque crust. Its mineralogical and chemical nature is wholly unknown.[1] The diorite from the southern slope of Winnemucca Peak is more granular than porphyritic, having fresher plagioclases than both former rocks [178]; very rich in quartz, which contains innumerable fluid-inclusions that are mostly dihexahedral, and a part of them envelop little salt cubes like those in the quartzes of the famous Belgian diorite from Quenast, the pavement-stone of Paris. The abundant hornblende shows all the phenomena of alteration just mentioned, more or less advanced stages of which are indeed found pretty generally spread through all diorites, but seldom with all the stages as distinct as they are here.

Other diorites are found on the divide between Grass and Cortez Valleys, Nevada. One [179] is a fine-grained quartziferous rock, somewhat decomposed and without biotite.

In Trout Creek Cañon, Shoshone Range, a beautiful porphyritic rock occurs [180–81], which has a greenish-gray groundmass, containing quartzes nearly the size of a pea, with numerous fluid-inclusions, attacked hornblende, striated feldspars, and some orthoclases, among others a crystal an inch long. Under the microscope, the groundmass shows itself as entirely crystalline, consisting of decomposed feldspar, little quartz, much titanic iron metamorphosed in the same manner as in a recently described variety, small apatites, and some leek-green mica, in which are very thin brownish bunches of extremely delicate needles crossing each other under 60°.

A fine-grained diorite occurs at Ravenswood Peak, Shoshone Range [182]. Wherever the feldspar is fresher, it proves to be evidently striated, which throws light upon the nature of the more decomposed feldspars found in previously mentioned varieties.

---

[1] See Senfter, Neues Jahrb. f. Mineralogie, 1872, 673; F. Z., Mikroskop. Beschaffenh. d. Mineral. u. Gesteine, 409; Dathe, Zeitschr. d. d. geol. Gesellsch., XXVI, 26.

The diorite from Mill Creek Cañon, Cortez Range, is very peculiar [183]. Large plagioclases and short black prisms of hornblende appear macroscopically in a seemingly very fine-grained groundmass. The thin sections prove that the larger part of the feldspars are triclinic; they are accompanied by a little orthoclase and considerable microscopic brown biotite. The fine crystalline groundmass, curiously, is found under the microscope to be enormously rich in quartz, whose colorless grains give out brilliant variegated colors between crossed nicols; moreover, the ground-mass is composed almost wholly of quartz and hornblende. There is, indeed, almost too much quartz in it for a diorite, for this quantitative pro-portion of constituents is extremely rare. The rock is a plagioclase-bearing quartz-hornblende variety. It is remarkable that in some places the plagio-clases have precisely the structure of the well-known labradorite from Paul's Island on the Labrador coast.[1] They contain the same black needles, grains, and brown laminæ, in exactly the same arrangement. The presence of such an abundance of quartz becomes the more curious because this behavior of plagioclase has never before been observed save in the very basic gabbros and hypersthenites, which are absolutely free from quartz.

A typical diorite without any trace of an amorphous mass, rich in quartz and in brown biotite, beside the hornblende, is found near the mouth of Agate Pass, Cortez Range [184]. The feldspars are not yet so far decom-posed as to make their striation very indistinct.

In Bingham Cañon, Oquirrh Mountains, is a diorite which contains quartz, biotite, and apatite [185]. The laminæ of mica, as is shown by the micro-scope, are broken and shivered, and the larger ones may be seen glancing on the fracture-planes of the rock.

A remarkable member of the metamorphic Archæan series is a rock which has the composition of diorite, found at the mouth of Ogden Cañon, Wahsatch Range. Pale-red feldspar, hornblende, and quartz, in a wholly crystalline mixture, may be seen with the naked eye. At first sight, it would seem that the feldspar is orthoclase, and that the rock belongs to the syenites,

---

[1]Vogelsang, Sur le labradorite coloré, Archives Néerlandaises, 1868, tome III; see also Scheerer, Poggendorff's Annalen, 1845, LXIV, 162, and Schrauf, Sitzungsber. d. Wiener Akad., LX, 1. Abth., Dec. 1869, 1.

but under the microscope it becomes plain that with but rare exceptions all the feldspars, which are unusually fresh, bear a splendid twin-striation. On the borders of these plagioclases are variously crenated laminæ of blood-red specular iron, appearing as dendrites on capillary fissures, and causing the pink color of the feldspar. The substance of the plagioclases is not much less impellucid than that of the quartzes, a dust-like material being interposed in them, usually accumulated into stripes. A high magnifying power (immersion-objective No. 10 of Hartnack) shows that this matter is composed of very fine pale-green grains, which are probably hornblende; very small, hollow, rounded, or funnel-like pores; and, an extremely rare phenomenon in the plagioclases of diorites, fluid-inclusions with distinctly moving bubbles. The fresh hornblende has a very detailed cleavage, which makes the single transverse sections seem to be composed of innumerable oblique-angled rhombs. Quartz is rather abundant; and, beside this, there appear under the microscope a comparatively very great quantity of apatite prisms included in all three of the chief constituents, and single titanites, which are elsewhere by no means frequent in diorites. In another variety from this locality [186], short and thick brown prisms of the zircon-like mineral are found. These diorites pass geologically into hornblende-schists.

A dike on the divide between American Fork and Little Cottonwood Cañon, Wahsatch Range, is made up of a greenish-gray and seemingly nearly homogeneous groundmass, with crystals of hornblende and plagioclase. The smaller and fresher individuals of hornblende are plentifully mixed with opaque, black magnetite; nevertheless, alteration has already progressed in them, and the larger ones especially have become totally fibrous. Indeed, there are no parallel fibres developed here, but in their stead, bunches having a cross and transverse direction, like the crystals of frost on a window. Plagioclase is rendered very impure by a fine dust of hornblende. The groundmass appears to contain some glassy base between the net-work of microlites.

One of the most beautiful diorites in this region is that from the west side of the Medicine Bow Range, between French and Brush Creeks [187], consisting, in the section, of interwreathed, prevailing dark-green, and colorless patches, whose alternations give the effect of mosaic work. The dark-green spots are hornblende, or rather an irregular but intimate aggregation of grains and prisms of strongly dichroitic hornblende. The patches have no proper limits, but are irregularly rounded or angular. The borders are armed with beautiful delicate and bristly hornblende crystals, stretching into the colorless places which fill up in a certain sense the holes between the green hornblende. It is also noticeable that the borders of the hornblende are a darker green than the interior parts. Under the microscope, it is seen to be impregnated with finely-distributed hornblende dust, and to consist very largely of splendidly striated plagioclase, accompanied by some few orthoclases in the form of Carlsbad twins. There is no vestige of an amorphous or microcrystalline groundmass, no quartz, and no apatite; in short, a typical diorite made up of the characteristic ingredients, but arranged in a singular manner.

At the close of these pages on diorites, a hornblende rock may be mentioned, which forms a dike in the granite of the low hills northeast of Havallah Range [188]. It consists of quartz and hornblende in needles and prisms (Plate IV, fig. 1). The quartz constitutes a kind of colorless groundmass in which the hornblende individuals are distributed. Here and there occur larger hornblende members, irregularly shaped but showing an evident tendency to the characteristic hornblende features: their borders distinctly prove that they are built up of single needles and rays, yet they have in the interior the uninterrupted, oblique-angled cleavage of hornblende. Larger quartz members also exist, in which the rarer hornblende needles are aggregated into the most delicate, looser, or denser bunches. Some of these places microscopically resemble the prasem from Breitenbrunn in Saxony, the more because the quartz contains fluid-inclusions: there is also brown mica.

SECTION II.

HORNBLENDE-PORPHYRY.

Some rocks of the Augusta Mountains [189, 190] bear a striking macroscopical and microscopical likeness to the well-known hornblende-porphyry from Potschappel in Saxony, belonging to the porphyritic tract which runs southwest from Dresden to Potschappel. They are dark-gray rocks, with a tinge of green, showing to the naked eye as porphyritical constituents, only small black hornblende prisms. The porphyry from Potschappel, which has been until the present referred to the rocks characterized by the preponderance of plagioclase, curiously contains, when examined microscopically, decidedly more orthoclase in single individuals and Carlsbad twins than striated feldspar; and it is a striking analogy that the rock from Augusta Mountains, so similar also in its external aspect, likewise bears at least as much orthoclase as plagioclase, although the smaller crystals seem chiefly to be triclinic. Under the microscope, the groundmass is seen to consist of a yellowish-gray, amorphous, somewhat indistinctly globulitic, devitrified substance, including small feldspar prisms, which are sometimes aggregated into larger forms, and, beside these, numerous black, point-like grains, which are often gathered into heaps or spread out into lines or chains. Hornblende does not seem to fill much of a place in the composition of the groundmass. It forms chiefly large crystals, the number of which is not much augmented by observations through the microscope. The larger hornblende sections having a darker or lighter brownish-yellow color, in both the American and the Saxon porphyries, are in a surprisingly similar, peculiar condition (Plate IV, fig. 2). Provided with an excellent cleavage, they exhibit, according to the direction of the sections, either a longitudinal fibration or two systems of cracks cutting under an obtuse angle; but none of them have a regular crystallographical shape, and often even lack straight outlines, having instead rounded ones: moreover, they are mostly fragments. All are encircled by a border of black grains, which, really belonging to hornblende, limits them externally. This is the same granular zone that plays so important a *rôle* around the hornblende of andesites and trachytes. The breadth of this black border varies. Sometimes it is so broad that it preponderates, and only a small spot of the hornblende individual appears in the interior; again it is narrower, and the individual is larger and better shaped. Hornblende presenting this behavior has long been known in other, peculiarly basaltic, and andesitic rocks. With reference to the presence and origin of this remarkable black border, it was formerly explained as a peripheric aggregation of attracted magnetite grains, which had been more or less forced by the crystallizing power of the hornblende to follow its own form, in exactly the same manner as in the so-called sandstone from Fontainebleau, grains of sand are mechanically forced into the rhombohedral form of calcite, some carbonate of lime crystallizing between them. A careful study of the phenomenon, however, leads to another and more satisfying supposition. There is no proof that the black grains composing the border are really magnetite, and they may therefore be called by the non-committal name of opacite (page 13). The porphyries seem to support the view that the hornblende crystals, upon first becoming solidified bodies, were superficially altered by the still molten surrounding rock-mass, and that the border of opacite grains is the relic of this conflict. With the chemical reaction and change, the mechanical tendency present went hand in hand, and from this results the decidedly fragmentary nature of so many of the individuals, as does also the phenomenon where at the ends of sections the black border is dilacerated or torn, and the groundmass has penetrated into the hornblende substance. Both actions confirm and explain each other. The deeper the process of caustic alteration advanced, the more the form of the attacked crystal became obliterated. This supposition also makes it easy to conceive how it happens that the black border of opacite often grows gradually looser on the surface, and becomes dismembered into single isolated grains; and it may not be impossible that many of the dark grains which are scattered through such rocks, and are generally taken for magnetite, are really finely-distributed, powder-like particles of the pyrogenous alteration-product of hornblende.

In one of these rocks from the cañon south of Granite Point, Augusta Mountains [190], the black-bordered hornblende has undergone a later, secondary process of decomposition in the wet way, the result being a vivid green substance which appears macroscopically in many hornblende individuals of the rock. This viridite substance, which is probably green-earth, penetrates the fissures of the crystals in the most distinct manner; and so it comes that the brown hornblende, with its dark outline, shows first, narrow, green alteration-lines along all the parallel or obliquely crossing cracks. Gradually they become broader, and form a green net-work, including small, brown kernels of the original substance. The black border does not seem to be much attacked by this kind of decomposition. When it does happen, however, calcite must be formed, for it may be found macroscopically deposited in the form of small veins in the larger fissures of the rock. The larger feldspars, often built up zonally in great distinctness, are somewhat fresh, and bear beautiful glass-inclusions, which are sometimes found arranged in regular concentric bands. The small rectangular ledges of orthoclase even contain a large, rectangular, compact kernel of light-brownish glass. There is some dirty apatite, but no augite. This would be expected on account of the close analogy between this rock and hornblende-andesite, of which it represents a real ante-Tertiary precursor.

SECTION III.

DIABASE.

Some macroscopically indistinctly characterized rocks occur in Miner's Cañon, Truckee Range. It is uncertain whether they belong to diorites, diabases, or syenites, neither the nature of the feldspars being recognizable, nor is discrimination between hornblende and augite possible. A microscopical examination, however, discovers them to be diabases [191, 192, 193, 194, 195]. These rocks are made up of plagioclase, augite, with its products of alteration, little quartz, magnetite, and sometimes apatite. The feldspars are still pretty fresh and well striated, in some places richly and brilliantly so; and they contain numerous strange interpositions, which seem to vary in the different specimens. In some cases, these interpositions consist of fine grains and crippled microlites of augite, accompanied by amorphous particles of the groundmass; in others, of more or less distinct fluid-inclusions, associated with empty cavities. In general, these plagioclases are much less decomposed than is common in the German diabases. The augite often forms sections of a yellowish-brown color, with the characteristic generally eight-sided ($\infty P . \infty P \infty . \infty P \infty$) features, of feeble or wanting dichroism,[1] and the typical directions of easy cleavage, crossing each other nearly rectangularly. Beautiful variegated parallel lines sometimes appear in polarized light, which proves the existence of the well-known twin lamellation parallel to ($\infty P \infty$). This augite substance is altered along the borders and fissures into a fine, dark-green, parallel and fibrous mass, which might easily be taken for the uralite-like hornblende, so often occurring as a secondary product of augite, until it is examined with the under nicol; but this process demonstrates that it is not at all dichroitic. It must be, therefore, another of the numerous but indistinctly characterized epigenetic substances of augite which have

---

[1] Tschermak was, as is known, the first to point out that hornblende and augite can be easily distinguished by their optical behavior if the polarizer be put into the microscope : the sections of the very strongly dichroitic hornblende very plainly change their color upon turning around that nicol; the sections of augite then keep their color entirely, or almost entirely, being almost totally undichroitic.—Sitzungsber. d. Wien Akademie, LIX (I), May, 1869.

7 M P

been recently collected under the general name of viridite (page 14). Perhaps it belongs to chlorite. Some of the crystals have been entirely metamorphosed, and yet have preserved very exactly their original outlines as augites. But the same green fibrous mass also forms many irregularly-shaped individuals found in the rock which have doubtless been augites, but whose features have been partly or totally obliterated by the alteration. Considered by themselves, these green spots would hardly be taken for decomposed augites, but the presence of all the members of transition between them and fresh augite crystals, puts the question of origin beyond doubt. Through this product of alteration, numerous fine black opaque grains of magnetite are scattered, which must have been taken up during the time of alteration, for they are not found in the unattacked augite. This is a process the chemical possibility of which was stated a long time since by Gustav Bischof,[1] and subsequently corroborated by Dathe in his excellent memoir on the microscopical constitution and structure of (German) diabases[2] (see page 67). In certain specimens from Miner's Cañon [195], the product of the augitic alteration is a light green in color, not fibrous, and evidently isotrope, showing no colors at all between crossed nicols. Although many black magnetite grains have developed, it must belong to some other substance than the above-mentioned dark-green fibres, which present a vivid chromatic polarization. Fischer has shown that the seladonite of Fassa Valley, Tyrol, is unaffected by polarized light,[3] and it is not impossible that the light-green substance in question may stand in close relation to it. These diabases contain quartz in single colorless grains. This ingredient was never formerly supposed to exist in these basic rocks with augites and plagioclases poor in silica. The first diabases in which quartzes were observed as original constituents are those trap-rocks which form layers and dikes in the Lower Carboniferous sandstones in the island of Arran, Scotland.[4] And Dathe has proved that quartz is also frequent in the German diabases, especially in those of the Voigtland and of the Lausitz in Saxony, which had never before been

---

[1] Lehrbuch d. chemisch. u. physikal. Geologie, 2, edit. II, 913.

[2] Zeitschrift d. d. geolog. Gesellsch., XXVI, 1874, 30.

[3] Kritische mikroskopisch mineralogische Studien, 1869, 24.

[4] F. Z., Zeitschrift d. d. geol. Gesellschaft, XXIII, 1871, 28.

examined microscopically. Quartz also occurs in a diabase from the neighborhood of Torquay, England, and in those splendid fresh diabase rocks (traps) which form intercalated contemporaneous layers and eruptive dikes in the Triassic sandstones near New Haven, Conn.[1] Titanic iron, which so frequently appears in the German diabases from Saxony and the Fichtelgebirge, Nassau, as the accompaniment of magnetite or replacing it, cannot be detected in these rocks from Miner's Cañon. An amorphous yellowish-gray base fills up the spaces between the crystalline ingredients. It is devitrified in a globulitic manner (page 2), and is penetrated by thin colorless feldspar-microlites.

At Diabase Hills, Truckee Range, is another region of old diabases [196, 197, 198], where they have been overflowed by the younger Tertiary basalts. The more beautiful ones present under the microscope fresh striated plagioclase, but no orthoclase, brownish-green augite, often in a comparatively rather small quantity; olivine, which is mostly altered in the interior into a brownish-yellow, and on the borders into a darker yellowish-brown serpentineous matter; and a little black ore, which, according to its form, belongs rather to magnetite than to titanic iron. Beside these constituents, there are numerous, long, colorless, prismatic microlites, a part of which belong to apatite, while another part are probably of a feldspathic nature. Search for quartz here is in vain. The structure is entirely crystalline, without any trace of an amorphous, unindividualized base. This feature causes a considerable difference between the basalts and the diabases of the same region, although in the nature of their crystalline constituents there is the closest analogy between them, the basalt also containing olivine. The latter are here rich in a well-developed, half-glassy base. The decomposed olivines can be seen in the sections as small brown spots. These rocks strongly resemble some of the above-mentioned Scotch Sub-carboniferous traps, in the abundance of olivine they contain and the absence of titanic iron; but they are nearly as unlike the German diabases, as they are similar to the Scotch; for the German generally contain titanic iron, although they have no olivine. The general petrographical rule that olivine-bearing diabases are

---

[1] E. S. Dana has made a very valuable microscopical study of these rocks, in which, however, he does not mention quartz.—Amer. Jour. of Sci. and Arts (3), VII, 390.

free from quartz, and that quartziferous ones are free from olivine, has been proved as well by the Scotch as by the German varieties, and it is further corroborated by the study of the American occurrences. Some diabases present a singular microcrystalline structure, which reappears in the younger basalts, but not in those of this country. Between the usually not very widely diverging rays and ledges of colorless, well-striated plagioclase are crowded dark-yellow, angular and rounded augite grains, up to the size of 0.01^{mm}, and black particles of magnetite. In this so-constituted aggregation, which figures as a microscopical groundmass, larger brownish-red, altered olivines are distributed in a porphyritical manner. The olivines very often form the most characteristic rhombic sections, being very sharp-featured, like those in the basalts. Larger augites do not occur, but the feldspars sometimes attain dimensions equal to those of the olivine. This structure becomes especially characteristic when the ledges of feldspar are crowded close together and the narrow spaces between them are filled up with grains of augite and magnetite, ranged behind one another lineally. Quartz is wanting in this rock also, but it contains some sanidin-like orthoclase. A few sharp rectangular sections are seen, which would at first sight be taken for nepheline, but in polarized light they become neither monochromatic nor polysynthetically striated, but are divided by a longitudinal middle suture into differently-colored halves, and belong to orthoclase twins, after the manner of the Carlsbad law.

To this series of diabases also belongs one from the high peak at the south end of the Truckee Range [199]. It is rich in olivine, but richer in augite. There is both orthoclase and plagioclase, the latter of which shows a most excellent schistiform composition of very numerous water-clear and conformable layers surrounding each other. In a strict sense, it is rather difficult to understand how this structure, distributed regularly through the whole crystal, can exist together with so pronounced a polysynthetical lamellation. The rock also contains a little globulitic, half-glassy base. Secondary oxyd of iron has infiltrated into small fissures, and formed delicate, yellowish-red, dendritic lobes.

In the quartzites of Humboldt Cañon, West Humboldt Mountains, a dike of a dark, very fresh, and distinctly-grained rock occurs [200], which so closely resembles macroscopically, as well in the hand-specimens as in the prepared slides, a Tertiary dolerite, that one is inclined to consider it as a dependence or a variety of the neighboring basalts, although its geological relations do not favor this conclusion, but instead betoken a greater age of eruption. It is remarkable that the rock numbers among its constituents, beside quite_clear and splendidly linear plagioclase and entirely unaltered augite, beautiful characteristic grains of quartz, with moving fluid-inclusions, an ingredient which has never been observed in any dolerite or basalt in the world. So the microscopical quartz pronounces the true nature of the dike-rock to be akin to that of the older diabases, which agrees with its geological circumstances but differs from the suggestions of its macroscopical aspect. Between the individualized minerals, a little of an amorphous mass of felsite is distributed, but it does not at all partake of a globulitic, glassy nature, as is the case in the neighboring basalts. It is locally transformed into a dirty brownish-yellow substance. The black ore may be partly titanic iron. The large plagioclases contain glass-inclusions, with dark, fixed bubbles, which is rarely a distinguishable phenomenon in either diabases or dolerites.

Another old diabase dike breaks through at Granite Peak, Pah-Ute Range, Nevada [201]. This is a distinctly grained rock, consisting of plagioclase in a somewhat more advanced state of alteration than in the diabases of Diabase Hills, Truckee Range; considerable augite, some apatite sections, and a black mineral, which in this case is magnetite. Both olivine and quartz are wanting, and no amorphous base is visible. The augites contain glass-inclusions, and in some places a multitude of long and narrow, fine, cylindrical, empty cavities, placed in parallel arrangement near each other.

The rhyolite from Owyhee Bluffs, Rock Creek, includes foreign fragments [202], which belong to an excellent fresh diabase, closely resembling that from the Truckee Range. It bears plagioclase, much pale-brown augite nicely crystallized, half-metamorphosed olivine, and small quantities of a globulitic base. The black mineral here seems to be titanic iron, which, however, is not connected with that curious and unexplained product of alteration which so often appears in the German diabases.

The limestone at Seetoya Peak, Nevada, is traversed by a dike of rock which probably must also be placed among the diabases. It is entirely decomposed, and of a dirty grayish-green color, and it contains calcite, mica, and a green product of alteration, which, judging from its features, should be referred to augite rather than to hornblende.

In general, these diabases of the Fortieth Parallel are characterized by the relatively fresh condition of their augites, by the feeble development of a chloritic or viriditic secondary substance, and by the frequent occurrence of olivine; and they therefore much more closely resemble the Scotch than the German diabases.

SECTION IV.

MELAPHYRE.

Some other rocks from the Fortieth Parallel, which the German geologists would place among the melaphyres, could, by reason of their close affinity to the diabases, be classified as such. Most of these rocks are characterized by the absence of easily distinguishable macroscopical ingredients, by their seemingly homogeneous mass of a dirty greenish-gray or brownish color, and by the presence of amygdaloidal calcite or green-earth (delessite). Self-existing amygdules of quartz or of other silicious matter seem not to be frequent. Such secretions, which here often reach the dimensions of a hazel-nut, are, as is well known, derived primarily from the decomposition of the augitic constituent. These macro-petrographical points give the rock a certain degree of difference from common diabases, and stamp it with some peculiarity, which is the only apology for using the unfortunate name, melaphyre to classify them. Careful microscopical examination of a large number of the so-called rocks from Germany and Transylvania[1] shows that the single occurrences differ widely from each other, and that they are not much alike in general composition. This is not very astonishing when it is remembered that this class of rocks has been established merely upon their exterior aspect, without any certain knowledge of their real constitution, and without their exhibiting a normal occurrence which could be made a basis of comparison. So it has happened that for half a century all rocks whose constituents it has been found impracticable to determine macroscopically, have been named melaphyre.

A series of specimens from Berkshire Cañon, Virginia Range, belongs to these melaphyres [203, 204, 205, 206, 207, 208]. For the most part, the feldspars of these rocks are in a somewhat decomposed state, but here and there the triclinic lamellation is doubtless still visible. In one variety [205], the larger plagioclases, having a somewhat parallel arrangement in the hand-specimens, appear under the microscope to be partly altered into calcite: the mass

---

[1] G. Haarmann, Zeitschr. d. d. geol. Gesellsch., XXV, 1873; F. Z., Basaltgesteine, 1869, 198; C. Dölter, Jahrbuch d. geolog. Reichsanstalt, XXIV, 1874, 1.

of the crystals is traversed by broad veins, all of which present in polarized light the characteristic picture, with delicately changing and playing colors, which is characteristic of calcite in very fine-grained aggregations. Ortho-clastic feldspars cannot with certainty be said to be present. These Western Nevada varieties bear a striking likeness to the melaphyres from Germany and Transylvania, in that they contain under the microscope poorly distinct augite. Augites are sometimes totally wanting here, and generally rather rare, but the rocks are rich in a greenish ingredient which seems to be a product of the decomposition of that mineral. The presence of olivine in these melaphyres is an interesting fact, for it has been by degrees discovered in a large number of macroscopically more or less similar European rocks, in which it was formerly supposed never to exist. Tschermak[1] found the first olivines in melaphyres from Breitenbrunn, between Kuchel and Smolenitz in the small Carpathians, from Falgendorf in the Lower Bohemian Dyas formation. Haarmann observed microscopical olivines in the melaphyres from Oberstein and Weiler at the Nahe (Rhine), from Ilmenau, Thuringia, from Würschnitz near Stollberg, from Wildenfels, Kainsdorf near Zwickau, Saxony, from the Mummel near Landshut, Silesia; and Doelter recognized this mineral in some melaphyres from Western Transylvania. The olivines are generally somewhat decomposed into ser-pentineous products, at least on the borders and along fissures. The pre-vailing color of this product of alteration is a deep reddish brown, and it is very slightly pellucid. The nearly colorless original substance of the olivines remaining unattacked, appears as kernels in the dark net-work of metamorphosed crack-walls. Some of the olivines have a dirty-green color, and it would seem that this hue is the symbol of an earlier stage of altera-tion. In the basaltic olivines, it is often observable that the reddish-brown colors follow upon the green. Thus brown veins here traverse the greenish, decomposed olivines, marking the ways by which the oxydation and hydra-tion of the protoxyd of iron have penetrated. In some of these old mela-phyres, the crystals of olivine can even be detected macroscopically, either in the hand-specimens or in the slides [205]. Another, but uncommon, ingredient is apatite, which here shows in the middle of its colorless sub-

---

[1] Sitzungsber. d. Wiener Akad., LII, 1865, 1. Abth., 265.

stance the thin, black, nail-like, longitudinal prism so often occurring in those of the basalts, but which is entirely wanting in the thousands of apatites of crystalline slates that have been examined. Here and there between the diverging ledges of plagioclase some of a yellowish-gray, amorphous, half-devitrified base is squeezed in, in the form of little spots. The amygdaloids in these melaphyres, some of a size of 5^{mm} (Plate IV, fig. 3), but the general mass of them being smaller, consist in the transverse section of a prevailing grass-green, and of a colorless substance. In view of its compact mass, its pellucidity, and its vivid chromatic polarization, the latter of these is surely quartz. The green material is probably greenearth; in one place entirely structureless and unaffected by polarized light, and in another a fine fibrous mass producing a feeble aggregate polarization. The outermost zone of the amygdaloids usually consists of a narrow schist of pure quartz: in the interior, the green matter predominates, forming radially fibrous globules, heaped together into botryoidal and lenticular aggregations. The section running through these little balls presents concentric rings varying from a lighter to a darker color, so that one of the thin fibres possesses several tones of green, at different distances from the centre. The green material also forms peculiar, feebly fibrated, horseshoe-like semi-circles and three-quarter rings, like those which have been observed in the analogous amygdaloids of English toadstones occurring as contemporaneous layers in the Carboniferous limestones of Derbyshire. The spaces and gaps between the single spots and aggregations of the green-earth are filled with a little pellucid quartz.

There is a melaphyre in Berkshire Cañon [208], seemingly an almost homogeneous, dirty, yellowish-gray mass, which belongs geologically to the above-described rocks, but differs from them in its structure and composition. It appears in ordinary light under the microscope to be a colorless mass containing innumerable, angular, dark-yellow grains, some of which are 0.02^{mm} in length, most probably belonging to augite. In polarized light, the colorless substance is not homogeneous, but an aggregation of doubly refracting particles: these are possibly feldspar, but they are without distinguishable twin-striation. The yellowish grains for the most part lie irregularly and without order, though very equally distributed through the mass; but they are found in numerous places densely accumulated, and grouped into exact rings, which of course correspond to sections of balls. The interiors of these circles are filled with the structureless chief mass of the rock, which seems here, however, to be poorer in the yellow grains, or to contain smaller ones; as if a part of those in the middle had been used for the construction of the outer rings. Sometimes smaller concentric rings are placed within the main ones: these are formed of very densely accumulated yellow grains, and in some places they are disturbed and pressed out of shape, or else two or more of them run into each other at the peripheries. All these phenomena surely prove a peculiar mode of solidification, but it is remarkable that no centre can be found from which the spherical arrangement of the grains could have been governed. The circles appear in the slides with a lens as little rings, from the size of 1^{mm} downward; but in the hand-specimens hardly anything can be seen of them.

There is another entirely decomposed melaphyre, with secretions of calcite and green-earth [209]. The microscope shows that the calcite has also settled in the interior of the rock in small portions. Larger crystals which have been wholly altered into a pale-green, secondary matter, are surrounded on the outside by a very distinct series of blackish-brown grains, and these features seem to point toward augite. Pulverulent, brownish-black grains, probably a product of decomposition, are scattered through the whole rock, and are often found aggregated into loose heaps.

SECTION V.

GABBRO.

A remarkable gabbro [210] forms a hilly dome in the gray metamorphic granite east of Iron Mountain, Laramie Hills. It is composed almost entirely of bluish-gray plagioclases, which have a somewhat feeble play of colors, and whose broad faces M are, for the most part, nearly parallel in direction, so that the excellent polysynthetic twin-striation only appears in the transverse fracture. Thin sections show that another grayish or yellowish-green mineral takes part in the composition of the rock: this is far less distinct in the hand-specimens. The plagioclase shows in polarized light, where it lies obliquely, a splendid variegated lineature; and, under the microscope, it is seen to have exactly the structure of the other gabbro-plagioclase, which is altogether similar to that of the genuine labradorite from Paul's Island, on the coast of Labrador. It contains a multitude of characteristic interpositions of little, sharp, dark, linear needles, which cause the grayish color of the crystals. These microlites are in part entirely black and opaque and partly brownish and transparent: their maximum length is 0.06^{mm}, but they decrease in size to the most minute proportions. In one section of a plagioclase crystal, they have for by far the most part a strictly parallel arrangement; but there are some which traverse the same system without any visible regularity. Small grains of the same nature accompany these needles; but the well-known, little, flat laminæ included in the labradorite are here, as is often the case in gabbro-plagioclases, comparatively rare. Some sections seem, with a low magnifying power, to be filled with a dark dust, which, with a higher power, turns out to be needles and fine grains. All these impregnations are, as is usually the case in such feldspars, abundantly gathered together into straight, dark, parallel lines or bands which correspond to the lamellation of the triclinic feldspars, or else thicker grains and stronger needles are interposed along such lines. No liquid-inclusions were found. In short, these plagioclases have the same characteristic microscopical structure that has been observed in the European gab-bros from Volpersdorf, Buchau, Ebersdorf, Schlegeler Mountains, in Silesia; from Harzburg, in the Harz; from La Prese, in the Veltlin, Northern Italy; from Valeberg, near Krageröe, Norway, and from the islands of Mull and Skye, off the western coast of Scotland.[1] It is very remarkable that wherever the plagioclase possesses this peculiar structure, it is accompanied by diallage or hypersthene; the triclinic feldspars associated with common augite or with hornblende never being filled with such interpositions as far as known. The American gabbro strikingly corroborates the conclusions reached by study of the European occurrences. Sometimes these pla-gioclases also show the lamellar structure, resembling a grate or lattice-work, which is mentioned on page 34. The rather obscure grayish or yellowish-green ingredient of these rocks is diallage, with one prevailing cleavage, not the double prismatic one of augite, and having here and there small lamellar interpositions that are not dichroitic, but are sometimes altered on the borders into fibrous, green hornblende; a phenomenon comparable with the uralite originating from augite, well known in all European gabbros. No olivine can be detected in the American gabbro, although it has been recently discovered in many European specimens where it was formerly never suspected. Titanic iron appears in long, irregularly shaped members, wrapped in the whitish-gray crust produced by decomposition, which is so often seen covering it in diabases. The general structure of the rock is purely granular, without any trace of an amorphous, unindividualized mass. This also is a peculiarity common to all diallage-bearing gabbros without exception, and it is in contrast with the greater part of those rocks which are characterized by augite. This rock, with its strongly predominating amount of plagioclase (labradorite) seems not very far removed from the Norwegian norites, as described by Scheerer and Kjerulf.[2] A chemical

---

[1] R. Hagge, Mikroskopische Untersuchungen über Gabbro u. verwandte Gesteine, Kiel, 1871; F. Z., Zeitschr. d. d. geol. Gesellsch., 1871, XXIII, 59, 94; Karl Urba, Gabbro from the entrance of Lichtenau Fjord, Greenland, showing all the above-mentioned peculiarities, Sitzungsber. d. Wiener Akademie, LXIX, 26th February, 1874.

[2] Scheerer, Gaea Norvegica, II, 313, Neues Jahrb. f. Mineralogie, 1843, 668; Kjerulf, Bulletin de la Soc. géolog., XXIX, 1862, 413.

analysis of this rock made in the laboratory of Wiedemann in Leipsic gave the following result:

Silica	52.14	Oxygen ratio	27.80
Alumina	29.17	Do	13.60
Protoxyd of iron	3.26	Do	0.72
Lime	10.81	Do	3.09
Magnesia	0.76	Do	0.32
Potassa	0.98	Do	0.16
Soda	3.02	Do	0.80
Loss by ignition	0.58		
	100.72		

The composition of the rock so much resembles that of the so-called labradorite that only a very small amount of diallage can be present. The oxygen ratio of $Si\,O^2 : Al^2\,O^3 : RO = 27.8 : 13.6 : 5.09 = 6.13 : 3 : 1.12$, is nearly the same as that of a pure labradorite. There is also the closest resemblance in chemical respects between this rock and the norite from Tronfield, Oesterthal, and the labradorite rock from Zaerdals Oeren in Bergenstift (both in Norway), which were once analyzed by Kjerulf.

CHAPTER VI.

PROPYLITE, QUARTZ-PROPYLITE, HORN-BLENDE-ANDESITE, DACITE.

SECTION I.

PROPYLITE.

With the exception of the diorite summit of Mount Davidson [211], the entire Virginia range in the Washoe district was formerly covered by an outflow of propylite, the first eruptive rock of the Tertiary age. On the north and south, propylite occupies the summit up to the boundary of the diorite mass, and descends to the plain on either side. In Ophir and Crown Point Ravines, propylite is found superimposed upon the older diorite, and penetrating it in well-defined dikes. The rock continues in a southeasterly direction to Carson Plain. In its course thither, it is uninterrupted, except by occasional dikes of andesite, which cut it in north and south lines and overflow limited areas. Over all the upper portion, the propylite was a sub-aërial ejection, but as it approached the lowlands it outpoured below the level of the great fresh-water lake which formerly skirted the range. Evidence of this is afforded by the tufacious form of the propylite, which shows all the phenomena of aqueous arrangement and stratification. Leaves of Tertiary plants are found in the tufa at a height of about seven hundred feet above the present bed of Carson River. Following the propylite, but after a lapse of time which permitted a considerable erosion, three parallel fissures were broken through the propylite, and large volumes of andesite were thrown out.[1] The propylite in these regions has also an important connection with silver-veins, as in the Carpathian Mountains and in some parts of Mexico, where prominent silver districts occur either upon it or associated with it. It forms one of the walls of the famous Comstock Lode along some of its most productive portions. Moreover, it is connected with several of the veins in the Aurora District, with some of those in Silver Mountain, and with the Moss Lode of Arizona. Propylite is everywhere the oldest eruptive rock of the Tertiary formation, and it consists of the same ingredients as the always-younger hornblende-andesite, but has the characteristic older external habitus of the ante-Tertiary dioritic porphyries. Propylites are either free from quartz (proper propylites), or they contain it (quartz-propylites): both rocks present the same contrasts as (quartzless) andesite and quartz-andesite or dacite. The quartziferous modification of propylite is in reality its dacite, or, in an inverse sense, the propylite of the dacite. Some geologically well-defined occurrences of quartzless propylite will be first described.

In Crown Point Ravine, Washoe, excellent propylites are found [212, 213, 214, 215, 216]. They have a seemingly almost homogeneous, light greenish-gray groundmass, in which larger plagioclastic feldspars, measuring some millimetres, and often of a pale-greenish color, are imbedded. In the interior, these feldspars are still rather fresh; but, on the outside, they show a dull product of alteration, and a net of the same decomposed material, indicating former capillary fissures traversing them inwards. All these crystals, as well as the microscopical ones of the rock, are closely impregnated with fine particles and a quite pale-greenish dust of hornblende, as is often the case with the feldspars of older diorites and porphyries, but hardly ever happening in those of the younger andesites. This causes the characteristic color here. Where the green hornblende is still in some degree fresh, it presents a pretty good cleavage; but it is for the most part already decomposed, and the vivid yellowish-green product of alteration, which is

---

[1] Clarence King's Geology of the Washoe Mining District, vol. III, p. 17-25.

evidently developed out of it, and which already fills narrow cracks, and
has settled in the groundmass as grains arranged one after another, like
beads on a string, seems surely to be epidote. The brown hornblende
of andesites never produces secondary epidote. The formation of epidote has even taken place in the interior of the feldspars, where it originates from the decomposition of the imbedded hornblende material; and
it seems very probable that the so-called pseudomorphs of epidote after
feldspars, which have been described by G. Bischof,[1] Blum,[2] and I. Lem-
berg,[3] and which are chemically so very difficult to explain, do not depend
upon an alteration of feldspar into epidote, but upon a development of
epidote out of hornblende particles originally inclosed in the feldspars.
This supposition is strengthened by the fact that all such pseudomorphs
are porphyritical crystals in hornblende-bearing rocks. The crystals of
hornblende in this propylite reach the size of 0.1^{mm}. Its groundmass
also is very rich in hornblende in the form of pale-green grains and fine
needles, like that of porphyritic diorites; for instance, those from the vicinity
of Quenast, Belgium. Such an abundant presence of hornblende in the
groundmass never occurs in andesites. Some excellently fissile, light-
yellowish augite sections and apatites (pure and dirty brown ones curiously
intermingled) are present in single varieties, all containing proportionally
thick crystals of magnetite.

The propylite from Gold Hill Peak, Washoe, is an interesting one [217].
It has a greenish-gray groundmass, which contains plagioclases the size of
a pea, externally decomposed but pellucid in the middle. The groundmass includes some worn and washed fragments of dark-bordered, brown
hornblende, the substance of which is pretty well preserved and fresh; some
pale augites; and a larger quantity of a darker or lighter green, somewhat
fibrous substance, showing a splendid aggregate polarization, whose outlines
prove beyond a doubt that it is the product of the alteration of hornblende.
This seems to be the proper hornblende of the rock which has never
possessed a black border. The fresh hornblende, with the dark, crumbled

---

[1] Lehrb. d. chem. u. physik. Geologie. II, 549.
[2] Die Pseudomorphosen Mineralreichs, dritter Nachtrag, 1863, 118.
[3] Die Gebirgsarten der Insel Hochland. Dorpat, 1867.

margin, has, at the first sight, nothing to do with the other, possessing the appearance of a strange, erratic body, which is much less easily decomposed than the other. In the groundmass, rich in feldspar-microlites, the product of altered hornblende (which does not here seem to belong to real epidote) takes an important part. Large, dirty black apatites are present.

In the typical propylites from Ophir Ravine, Washoe [218, 219], the feldspars also are completely filled with hornblende material, and the larger hornblende crystals are entirely altered into vivid-yellow epidote, slightly tinged with pale-green. The forms of the hornblende, nevertheless, have been conserved in the most exact manner. Section-lines corresponding to the combination ($\infty P . \infty \not P \infty$) bound a space which is an aggregation of broad, radiated, and confusedly fascicular epidote, often showing colors of varying intensity. Beside these long forms, rounded grains of epidote have been developed in the interior of the hornblende: these are of a somewhat deeper color, and are often strung out into curved lines which traverse the radiated aggregations. These epidote grains were formerly the external outlines of the hornblende sections, and the contours become evident, in especial distinctness, when two concentric series of darker grains form the border. Surely nobody would, from petrographical reasons, refer such rocks to the andesites, but would, without hesitation, place them among the old dioritic porphyries. Geologically, however, they are decidedly Tertiary eruptive rocks. Quartz grains are scattered here and there, but they are too small and rare to allow of considering the rock to be a quartziferous propylite. Apatite forms curious, short and thick, rounded prisms, which sometimes have a pyramidal termination at one end. It is rendered impure by an intensely brown, dust-like material, which is confined to an inscribed hexagonal prism surrounded by a water-clear zone of pure and pellucid apatite, so that the transverse sections bear a close resemblance to noséan. These rounded hexagons might the more easily be mistaken for noséan because the dust is sometimes arranged in black cross-lines; but, at the same time, the entirely unaltered condition of these seeming noséans would be inexplicable in a rock in which even the new formation of parasitic epidote is so far advanced, and the prisms lying horizontally give abundant proof that the mineral is double-refracting.

S M P

A totally altered propylite of a deep yellowish-brown color occurs in the hill east of Steamboat Valley, Virginia Range [220].

In Sheep Corral Cañon, Virginia Range, a gray propylite occurs [221], which is geologically of a decidedly older age than the neighboring andesites and trachytes. The feldspars of the rock are rather fresh; but the hornblende is metamorphosed, its form being preserved, into an excellent radial aggregation of dirty-green fibres. Judging from its color, this secondary product is not epidote. Thick magnetite grains, slightly dusty apatites, and many hornblende particles are in the groundmass.

The Truckee and Montezuma Ranges are connected by low hills of typical yellowish-green-gray propylite, consisting of triclinic feldspar and the product of the alteration of hornblende, which is here for the most part epidote, although the alteration did not happen in a proper pseudomorphosing manner, since the contours of the hornblende are almost entirely obliterated and no longer recognizable. The substance of such changed and irregularly shaped spots would scarcely be supposed to have any genetic relation to hornblende, if different sections did not present the various stages of passage between this mineral and epidote, showing how the secondary material gradually comes entirely to occupy the place of the old hornblende.

Some hills north of Storm Cañon, Fish Creek Mountains, Nevada, are made up of a splendid propylite [222], which bears large feldspars. The hornblende is here and there rather fresh, and it has been built up out of thin, staff-like, green microlites, the accumulation being plentifully impregnated with little, black grains. These hornblende individuals are decomposed, their outlines being preserved, into an aggregation of, a, calcite, with a rhombohedral cleavage; b, the usual epidote; c, a dirty-green mineral like viridite, which is not epidote. The rock also bears augite in very distinct, pale-yellow sections, but in far less abundance than hornblende; brown mica, often with somewhat curved, tender laminæ (all propylites previously described were entirely free from biotite); and pure (not dusty) apatites. There are many hornblende particles of extreme minuteness in the microlitic groundmass.

The pale-yellowish or reddish-gray propylite from Storm Cañon, Fish Creek Mountains [223], also shows green hornblende crystals, which are here beautifully constructed of prismatic staffs joined in long, parallel grouping. Longer and shorter ones enter into the composition, and so the ends of the polysynthetic crystals appear fringed and notched, and the side-lines do not run in one direction, but show prominent curves outward and inward. Hornblende of such a structure as this never occurs in andesite; but it is, on the other hand, a striking repetition of that in the older dioritic porphyries, in which the mineral is so abundantly scattered. Apatites often lie rectangularly against the microlitic fibration. Hornblende is also plentifully distributed through the groundmass. Moreover, the secondary formation of epidote has begun here. There is neither augite nor biotite in this variety.

A good greenish-gray propylite, with characteristic groundmass [224], occurs at Tuscarora (Plate IV, fig. 4), Cortez Range. It is worth mentioning that it contains two kinds of hornblende; first, a predominating green variety, characteristic of propylite, which is somewhat fibrous, not very distinctly fissile in the transverse sections, always without a black border, and sometimes in an early stage of alteration into epidote; and it is this kind of hornblende which is found in smaller particles in the groundmass and thicker microlites and grains of which are imbedded in the feldspars; secondly, a dark-brown, much more strongly dichroitic, hornblende, having a black border; it is prismatically cleavable, never metamorphosed, and always pretty fresh; in short, a hornblende very similar to that in andesites. The individuals of the latter are much the rarer of the two, and are present only as an accessory: they may be a foreign ingredient. There is no augite or biotite.

At Wagon Cañon, Cortez Range, a propylite occurs [225], with distinct macroscopical but dirty-greenish, and somewhat earthy, decomposed hornblende, and large dull plagioclases, measuring 5^{mm} in length, in a reddish-gray groundmass. Larger apatites and some biotites are discernible with the microscope. The groundmass is no longer fresh, and the hornblende particles in it especially seem to be secondary and brownish. All of the described propylites also contain small quantities of monoclinic feldspar.

The typical quartzless propylite from Sheep Corral Cañon mentioned above was subjected to a quantitative chemical analysis in the laboratory of Professor Wiedemann in Leipsic, and was found to have the following composition:

Silica	64. 62
Alumina	11. 70
Protoxyd of iron	8. 39
Lime	8. 96
Magnesia	1. 18
Potassa	1. 95
Soda	3. 13
Phosphoric acid	trace.
Loss by ignition	1. 02
	100. 95

A relatively high amount of silica is here unquestionable; for another test for this constituent gave 64.60 per cent., and a third one gave even 65.05 per cent. The quantity of silica in this propylite, therefore, is much higher than in the diorites and diorite-porphyries (50. to 60. per cent.), to which in other respects the rock bears the closest mineralogical resemblance. It seems also to have more silica than the European hornblende-andesites, which on an average possess 58. to 62. per cent. The newly analysed andesite of the Fortieth Parallel likewise gave only 61.12 per cent. of silica; and the Hungarian greenstone-trachytes (propylites), besides, are somewhat more basic. An analysis of the propylite from the Comstock Lode, made by W. G. Mixter,[1] gives of silica 58.68 per cent.; but the enormous amount of water (6.53 per cent.) in the rock proves that it is no longer in its original state.

---

[1] Vol. III, page 90.

SECTION II.

QUARTZ-PROPYLITE.

To facilitate the description, and better to explain the significant peculiarities of these rocks, they will not be arranged geographically; but the most typical will be mentioned first. One of the best examples of this group forms the hills next east of Golconda [226]. It is a dark yellowish-gray rock, in which the unaided eye can only distinguish single, clear quartzes the size of a pepper-corn, and dull, whitish feldspars. The ground-mass has been attacked by decomposition, and is therefore not so easy of microscopical analysis. For the most part, it is an intimate mixture of isabel-colored, more or less impellucid, feldspar, the small individuals of which are sometimes distinctly defined, and of pale-green, granular and acicular hornblende-particles. Some amorphous base may perhaps be interspersed in the mass; but, even in polarized light, it can scarcely be distinguished from the decomposing feldspar. Here and there, an abortive tendency to sphærolitic formations appears. Decomposition has also begun upon the larger feldspars, which appear, in polarized light, to be covered with a glittering dust belonging to the products of alteration, which is surely, in this first stage, carbonate of lime (see the chemical analyses later). In the beginning, like those in the quartzless propylites, they were rendered exceedingly impure by hornblende particles, and in most of them traces of the former triclinic striation are still distinctly visible. The quartzes in this Tertiary eruptive rock are very remarkable, in that they do not contain glass, but fluid-inclusions, in great profusion, the best specimens of which contain briskly moving bubbles; and in some double liquid-inclusions were observed, the interior consisting of liquid carbonic acid. As respects this point, indeed, the quartz of this Tertiary propylite, and, without an exception, that of all which follow, behaves exactly like that of the ante-Tertiary dioritic porphyries, and differently from that of all other Tertiary quartziferous rocks, dacites and rhyolites, which only contain glass-inclusions. Microscopical quartz does not seem to be disseminated through the ground-mass. Hornblende crystals, which are indistinguishable in the hand-specimens, become evident in the sections. They are decomposed, half fibrous, inclined to develop epidote, and most resemble hornblende of the old syenitic granite-porphyries. Black magnetite grains are present and apatites are comparatively very abundant. A chemical analysis of this rock has been made by Dr. Walter Kormann in Leipsic, with the following result:

Silica	66.336
Alumina	14.803
Sesquioxyd of iron	4.068
Lime	2.991
Magnesia	0.920
Potassa	3.190
Soda	5.160
Loss by ignition	3.341
	100.809

In the heavy loss by ignition, showing the far advanced stage of alteration of the rock, 1.034 per cent. of carbonic acid is included. The iron was determined as sesquioxyd because, at the ignition, the browning which happens if the protoxyd be present was not observed.

The quartziferous propylite from West Gate, Augusta Mountains, is very similar to the above [227]. It contains hornblende in larger individuals, which are in part highly, and in part altogether, decomposed and altered into a greenish substance resembling epidote. The feldspars, plentifully filled with the dust of fresh or altered hornblende, look in every respect like those in the old diorites. The quartz has fluid but no glass inclusions, and many apatites are present.

Other excellent quartziferous propylites occur at and in the vicinity of Cortez Peak, Cortez Range [228, 229]. These rocks have a light-greenish or brownish-gray groundmass, in which are macroscopical, dull feldspars and hornblendes that look as if decomposed. The groundmass presents an entirely crystalline aggregation of, a, dark, isabel-colored, very slightly pellucid feldspar, resembling that of granites; b, half-altered hornblende particles; c, quartz which cannot be distinguished macroscopically, the maximum length of its grains being only 0.1^{mm}. The presence of such an abundance of minute quartz grains has the effect of giving to the thin sections in transmitted light, when viewed with the naked eye, the appearance of being perforated with innumerable pin-holes. The quartzes have no glass-grains, but fluid-inclusions (among which some with salt cubes) could be detected, making stronger its resemblance to the old dioritic quartzes. The large feldspar crystals are dull; but they still show that they have once been triclinic, the dimming lines, densely crowded together, crossing each other like lattice-work or the bars of a grate, and leaving small, somewhat clearer, fields between them. The best-preserved porphyritical hornblendes are splendidly built up of long prismatic staffs, therein repeating the peculiarity which is shown as well in the quartzless propylites as in the older diorites. No dacitic hornblende has ever grown in such a manner. There is apatite and also some characteristic titanite. An incomplete analysis of the quartz-propylite from Cortez Peak, executed in the laboratory of Professor Wiedemann, Leipsic, showed the following:

Silica	67.79
Alumina	16.13
Protoxyd of iron	3.64
Lime	2.30
Magnesia	0.53
Loss by ignition	1.70

Both quartz-propylites present a larger amount of silica than the quartzless variety. In composition, they very closely resemble the dacites (see the analyses on page 136), and there does not seem to be a sustained chemical difference between them.

Another quartziferous propylite makes its appearance in Wagon Cañon, Cortez Range [230]. It contains somewhat clearer feldspars, green hornblende, and large, macroscopical, fresh laminæ of brown biotite, which contain, curiously, in the direction of their cleavage, interposed layers of pellucid calcite (Plate V, fig. 1), in one place being lamellated with twin-formation, and in another riven with distinct rhombohedral cracks. Very minute fluid-inclusions are found in the quartzes. The groundmass seems to contain some globulitic glass of a brownish-yellow color. There are quite a good many apatites in the groundmass and biotites.

The propylite [231] from Cross Spur, below Virginia City, shows the beginning of the introduction of carbonate of lime in those feldspars which are as large as peas, yet they are fresh enough to permit of determining that they are chiefly plagioclase accompanied by a little sanidin. Hornblende of a beautiful green color, and partly composed of aggregated microlites, occurs. The only microscopical quartzes bear extremely small interpositions, which, under a high magnifying power, prove to be fluid-inclusions. Apatites are present.

One of the finest members of this group of propylites occurs at Berkshire Cañon, Virginia Range [232]. The gray groundmass, rich in macroscopical, dark-green hornblende, is seen under the microscope to be composed of colorless plagioclase and light green hornblende. An extraordinary quantity of the hornblende in the form of small, dust-like grains, short needles, thin laminæ, and especially beautiful, long, acicular microlites, is disseminated through the larger feldspars. These foreign corpuscles are so thickly distributed in the feldspars, appearing under crossed nicols and in a low magnifying power like a glittering powder, that even the fresh feldspars sometimes show only faint rudimentary twin-striation. The way in which the hornblende needles are attracted to different centres and group themselves into crystals is not often as clearly seen as here. Hornblende needles growing together in crystals, the attracted microlites pushing and bending together from all sides, is rarely so distinctly observed; and those stages are very interesting where only half a dozen needles are tending to form an individual, which, as yet, presents merely a bunch-like figure. The cleavage of the hornblende can be distinctly seen in the interior of the larger products, while their ends and borders still consist of disunited fibres. Single prisms are not yet, on their own part, cleavable, and it almost seems as if the cleavage was solely produced by aggregation. Some quite small grains of quartz are present. The quartz-propylites of Washoe overflow the propylites and the metamorphic rocks of American Cañon with their accompanying granite, and are in turn capped by basalt. That they succeed the propylite is evident, since they are found cutting it in dikes above the American Flat Road. Generally, they are of a very great variety of nature and constitution, and the quantity of quartz they hold differs widely, some specimens containing only here and there a grain and others being thickly studded with the mineral.

SECTION III.

HORNBLENDE-ANDESITE.

In the Washoe district were formed three zones of fissures, through which penetrated to the surface and outpoured thin, table-like masses of hornblende-andesitic[1] rocks.[2] Some of these fissures cut through the diorites of Mount Davidson, as well as the propylites, on both the north and the south of the peak.   On the heights above Ophir Grade considerable fields of andesite cover the summit, and pour downward over the propylite to the north of the road.   In ascending Crown Point Ravine, two of these dikes are passed whose outcrops show a thickness of one hundred feet.   Another zone of andesites traverses American Flat and the plateau in front of Virginia, but its outcrops disappear to the northward under the later outpourings of sanidin-trachyte.   A third, and by far the most important, lies about two miles to the eastward, where an almost continuous overflow of andesite covers the country from near Devil's Gate in Gold Cañon, and a large part of Silver Terrace Spur, reappearing in the Roman Catholic burying-ground.[3]   The andesite from the first hill north of Gold Hill Peak, Washoe, is in many respects a thoroughly characteristic occurrence.   Nearly all the feldspars are fresh plagioclases: there are only very rare individuals and Carlsbad twins of sanidin, in which this variety is like the Siebengebirge andesites.   Nevertheless, the included hornblende is decomposed into a light-green substance, surrounded by a black border, which preserves the old contours.   The composition of this rock is remarkably simple; neither augite, biotite, quartz, tridymite, nor olivine being found.   Apatite is present, but it is very rare.   The groundmass is of a dark-gray color, and is simply an aggregation of small ledge-formed feldspars and feldspathic microlites, presenting distinct fluidal lines, and of dark, opaque grains, which are mostly magnetite.   Between these constituents, however, there is more or less of an isabel-colored, half-glassy base, although (as in the andesites of the Siebengebirge)

---

[1] The members of this group are in the following lines named simply andesites.
[2] See King's Geology of the Washoe Mining District, vol. III, page 28.
[3] Ibid., page 30.

smaller hornblende grains and microlites are almost entirely wanting; a remarkable contrast with the groundmass of the propylites.

The rock from the second hill-top north of Gold Hill Peak [233], with its splendid brown hornblende, is not a propylite, as might be supposed, but an andesite.

Other hornblende-andesites having a dark-gray groundmass, and containing beautiful brown hornblende, occur west of Quartz-porphyry (dacite) Peak [234].

East of Gold Hill Cemetery are varieties [235] bearing large triclinic feldspars; and at the Gould and Curry Road some quartzless members are found in the company of quartz-bearing dacites. Still another member, which was discovered at Silver Terrace, contains dirty-greenish, fibrous hornblende, and some quite pale-greenish, fresh augite, but no biotite. It is evident that the green color of the hornblende here is not primary (as in the propylites), but a result of the alteration which has begun to take place. At the Cross Spur near the burying-ground, an andesite is found [236] which has a brownish-gray groundmass, and contains excellently striated plagioclases the size of a millimetre; and indistinct hornblende, which seems to have been largely replaced by an abundant, dirty-yellowish, somewhat globulitic, base.

A specimen of the andesite from the first hill north of Gold Hill Peak has undergone a quantitative chemical analysis at the hands of Dr. Walter Kormann, of Leipsic, who announces the following results:

Silica	61.12
Alumina	11.61
Sesquioxyd of iron	11.64
Lime	4.33
Magnesia	0.61
Potassa	3.52
Soda	3.85
Loss by ignition	4.35
	101.03

The loss by ignition included 1.51 per cent. of carbonic acid. A part

of the iron discovered must be in the form of protoxyd, as shown by the
change of color during calcination. In composition, this rock generally
agrees with that of European andesites, as may be seen by the appended
table of analyses, except that the amount of alumina present is comparatively small. No. 1 is an andesite from the Walkenburg, Siebengebirge,
Rhine, examined by G. Bischof;[1] No. 2 is from Macska, Hungary, analyzed by K. v. Hauer;[2] No. 3 is from Schemnitz Kremnitzer Stock, Cziffar,
analyzed by K. v. Hauer;[3] No. 4 is from the railway-station at Tokaj,
Hungary, analyzed by K. v. Hauer;[4] No. 5 is from Monte Sieva, Euganean
Hills, Italy, examined by G. von Rath;[5] No. 6 is from Gunung Patna,
Java.[6]

	1	2	3	4	5	6
Silica	62.38	61.70	60.10	62.67	62.21	58.84
Alumina	16.88	14.00	17.62	14.94	12.49	17.09
Sesquioxyd of iron	7.33	6.15	....	....	....	....
Protoxyd of iron	....	....	7.03	6.95	9.32	10.61
Lime	3.49	6.47	2.24	5.07	3.02	7.03
Magnesia	0.82	2.65	1.85	0.71	1.30	3.90
Potassa	2.94	1.45	3.82	3.80	2.57	0.83
Soda	4.42	6.10	4.01	5.18	7.51	2.12
Loss by ignition	0.87	2.09	2.11	2.00	2.79	....
	99.13	100.61	98.78	101.32	101.21	100.42

A large and interesting group of varieties of andesite occurs on the
south flank of the entrance to Truckee Cañon [237, 238, 239, 240, 241, 242,
243, 244, 245, 246]. They generally possess a gray groundmass, which passes
into the pale-yellowish or reddish sort. Being rather porous and somewhat
loose, they look rough and trachytic; but, in polarized light, all the distinctly
observable feldspars are beautifully and thickly striated. Viewed macroscopically, these large feldspars are seen to have a dull, opaque border. A

---

[1] Lehrb. d. chem. Geol., 1854, II.
[2] Verh. geol. Reichsanst., 1870, 338.
[3] Ibid., 1869, 81, 59.
[4] Ibid, 1869, 146.
[5] Zeitschr. d. d. geol. Ges., 1864, 502.
[6] Prölss, N. Jahrb. f. Mineral., 1864, 432.

high magnifying power shows that this is not, as is often the case, produced by molecular alteration, but by the presence of an enormous number of imbedded glassy and half-glassy particles and grains. Smaller feldspars of the same rock sometimes contain, inversely, a kernel which is rendered impure by the same inclusions, and with a clear border. The splendid zonal structure of most of the feldspars is not at all disturbed by these foreign interpositions. The relation between the hornblende and augite in these geologically inseparable rocks is curious. There are specimens which are rich in excellent, dark-brown hornblende sections, with a broad, black border, but free from discernible augite; and in some of the same specimens, where a very small quantity of the pale-green augite accompanies the largely prevailing hornblende, the augites are always without a black border, but rich in glass-inclusions, which, on the contrary, are invariably wanting in the brown hornblende. The contrast here in color between hornblende and augite, and also in general behavior, is precisely the same as it is in the andesites of the Siebengebirge and of Hungary. Specimens with rather many augite and rather few hornblende individuals are in the *suite;* and at last some are found presenting only a very small quantity of augites and no large hornblendes at all. It should be especially mentioned that there occur, in the groundmass of these rocks, feebly transparent, dark-brown, undichroitic, needle-formed microlites, generally about 0.015^{mm} long, which cannot be unhesitatingly referred to hornblende, but which seem to be hornblende when their relation to the larger hornblende individuals of the rocks is noted. They are very rare or wanting when the latter are numerous, and are found in great abundance in the groundmass when the others are scarce; one seeming, as it were, to fill the place of the other. The augite along the fissures of some specimens of these andesites is curiously accompanied by a fibrous product of alteration, small denticles or teeth of which project into the augite, a point of behavior similar to that of the serpentine in olivine. This substance polarizes with different colors, and its mode of growth is easily observed between nicols. There are other specimens in which this alteration of augite, and the clouding or dimming which results therefrom, are further advanced. Some sections in places strongly remind one of fibrous diallage or enstatite, although the cleavage is still parallel to the prismatic faces. Ultimately, the augites become quite dull, retaining but slight traces of pellucidity. The groundmass of all these andesites contains, beside the above-mentioned brown needles (supposed to be hornblende), colorless, triclinic feldspar microlites, often producing splendid fluidal lines, black grains of opacite, and often yellowish-gray or pale-brownish, pure, or somewhat globulitic, glass.

Some reddish-brown rocks occur in this same part of Truckee Cañon whose color is not caused by secondary alteration, but by the presence of a primary, brown, half-glassy, amorphous material in the groundmass, whose long but irregularly formed fragments streak the feldspars, often being found in an enormous quantity. These varieties are for the most part finely porous, and they are comparatively rich in green augites. No biotite, tridymite, or olivine could be detected in any of them.

A perhaps more typical andesite occurs in Berkshire Cañon [247]. The plagioclase predominates and also forms the largest crystals; but there is beside not a little sanidin, beautiful brown hornblende without a black border, and some biotite. There is, however, no augite. A neighboring andesite [248] cannot be separated geologically from this, but the sanidin in it either really or apparently predominates.

A brownish, half-glassy rock from the west shore of Pyramid Lake, Nevada [249], also belongs to the andesites. Feldspar of both kinds is present in individuals up to the size of 3^{mm}; yet plagioclase decidedly predominates: all the larger individuals bear striation. The rock is exceedingly impure, but the strange glassy inclusions are arranged in several zones, which are sharply separated by pure feldspar substance. It contains also strongly dichroitic, brown hornblende, with a broad, black border, which externally decomposes into opacite grains and tail-formed aggregations of the same grains without any trace of hornblende in the interior; but having the form of those bodies which consist for the most part of a central mass of hornblende. Some good augite crystals are also found. The groundmass is made up of colorless (feldspar) and light-brownish (augite?) microlites, with much brown glass between them, and considerable magnetite.

Another sanidin-bearing andesite is found near Lander Spring, Kamma Mountains, Nevada [250].

In the Kamma Mountains other andesites occur. Those found at the Honey Lake Road Pass [251, 252], and to the southward [253], somewhat resemble each other. The feldspars, nearly all plagioclases, and most of the larger hornblendes, are somewhat decomposed. No augites could be detected. The groundmass is almost free from hornblende. It is chiefly feldspathic, but contains a great quantity of brownish-black grains and irregularly-formed particles, which are mostly opacite, but a small part of which belong to magnetite, and these are accompanied by some dark yellowish-brown grains of ferrite, the mass becoming slightly pellucid under a high magnifying power. Apatite is present in all these specimens in the form of dusty, dismembered prisms, with hydrous oxyd of iron between the horizontal cracks. Sometimes the strange, dust-like material in the apatites is arranged in short lines, which are gathered into broom-like and tuft-like forms (Plate I, fig. 9).

A typical andesite occurs in the first cañon north of Wright's Cañon, West Humboldt. Macroscopically, it is almost a homogeneous, gray mass, without any crystalline secretions. The feldspar is, with very few exceptions, triclinic. Beautiful, brown, strongly dichroitic and absorbing hornblende, surrounded by a narrow, black border, with a splendid cleavage, is present. Brownish microlites of hornblende are more frequent in the groundmass here than in that of any former andesite.

The Augusta Mountains, Nevada, yield other characteristic andesites. In the dark specimen from the south head of Augusta Cañon [254], the hornblende is for the most part altered into an extremely fine, fibrous substance, almost the color of green malachite, while its outlines and even its black and occasionally brownish border are preserved; or in other words, the place of the hornblende, as exactly marked out by the border, is occupied by a texture of pale-green fibres and a compact colorless substance seeming to be homogeneous, which, judging from its general behavior and its vivid chromatic polarization, is nothing else than quartz (not calcite). The effect is very pretty where the thin and delicate greenish needles penetrate into the colorless substance. The groundmass is very rich in the most minute, brown ferrite grains, by no means to be mistaken for the dark, similar globulites, which are products of a simple devitrification of a glassy mass. The feldspar-microlites of the groundmass show excellent fluidal lines. The aggregation is colored more or less brownish by microscopical spots. Here also, curiously, the apatite sections are not colorless, but a light brownish-yellow. There is no augite.

One of the most interesting andesites of Augusta Cañon [255] macroscopically resembles that from the Wolkenburg in the Siebengebirge. Its dark-gray groundmass contains some hornblende crystals a millimetre in length which present the most wonderful phenomenon of rupture, being partly visible even with a loupe in the sections (Plate V, fig. 2). The crystals, generally brown, but here and there found with greenish or reddish tinges, and environed by the well-known dark border, are divided by countless fractures. The lines of rupture of a single individual can be followed among the fragments of a neighborhood, and the broken crystals may be ideally reconstructed in their exact original form. Sometimes a real breccia of hornblende fragments and splinters, cemented by groundmass, appears. Many splinters are again broken, and the diverging particles hang together only at one end. Often one of the larger individuals is fractured into thirty or forty pieces. It is very remarkable that around the broken crystals, and winding among their fragments, bodies of the groundmass, plainly visible in polarized light, are found curving; showing how the stream of the half-plastic magma produced the fractures. Since these traces of movement remain, it follows that the rock-mass was solidified in a moment. Many angular, cuneiform splinters are disseminated through the rock which cannot be traced to a broken crystal, and which originated in some other place than where they occur, being in a certain sense erratic. They are, almost without exception, entirely surrounded by the black border, which proves that they had nothing to do with the *original* formation of the crystals, but have been added to the hornblende since the fracture. So this phenomenon strongly supports the theory that the dark border is the product of a chemical reaction between the already solidified hornblende and the still half-molten, environing magma (see page 95). It is in no sense a contradiction of this theory where splinters are found which have the dark zone only on those contours which correspond to the original faces of the crystal, and not on the lines of rupture as well; for such are fragments of already peripherically metamorphosed crystals which were not afterward altered superficially. Bodies of the groundmass are frequently found which have broken through the black border and indented the crystals in the form of deep and broad inlets and bays; and the most distinct fluidal streams penetrate even into the middle of the hornblendes. It is very significant that the black outline is in such cases found on the limit between the hornblende substance and the intrusive groundmass. The penetrating groundmass is an aggregation of largely predominating, minute, colorless feldspar ledges and a few brown hornblende-microlites and black grains.

A very similar rock occurs at the head of Clan Alpine Cañon, Augusta Mountains [256].

The andesite from the head of Crescent Cañon, Augusta Mountains [257], is rich in feldspar, poor in hornblende, and contains not a little quite pale-greenish augite. An amorphous base is present in the groundmass.

An andesite from above Tuscarora, Cortez Range [258], is a peculiar one. It has a brownish-gray felsitic groundmass, seldom found in these rocks, and contains many large, macroscopical feldspars and some dark hornblende prisms. Under the microscope, feldspars are found to be, for the most part, well-striated plagioclases. In the sections, the hornblende has a vivid, dark grass-green color, and is fibrous and exceedingly dichroitic, changing from a light bluish-green into a deep, dark blackish-green. The black border of the hornblende is here lacking, but numerous angular grains which are doubtless magnetite are disseminated through its substance. Seen under the microscope, the groundmass between these crystalline ingredients is a light yellowish-brown in color, with a multitude of the finest and most delicate black hairs and grains strung together in lines, really trichite-like, short bodies. These minute bodies (measuring only 0.003^{mm} in length) are densely aggregated, and accompanied by thicker black grains, which are probably of the same nature, and they produce the most splendid, waving, fluidal phenomena. The direction of these trichite swarms makes it evident that the groundmass has really flowed among the large feldspar and hornblende crystals. The trichitic hairs are at intervals also grouped radially,

9 M P

and form dark, radiated sphærolites. The mass in which these hairs are imbedded, and which is thickly filled with them where it occurs in the pure state, has a simple refraction, and is isotrope glass. There is neither augite, biotite, nor tridymite. Some apatite prisms perforate the groundmass. The unusual green color which the hornblende has here, certainly seems to. be original; green products of its alteration being far less dichroitic. Perhaps it was the amount of iron in the glass base which prevented the hornblende from taking that deep-brown color which is most common to the andesites. Occasionally, a thicker, black, club-formed body is found lying in the groundmass, looking like a stout trichite, and surrounded by a remarkably pale glass zone.

A neighboring andesite from the foot-hills at Tuscarora [259] does not possess the same structure. It is somewhat decomposed, and its hornblende, surrounded by a narrow black border of grains, has been in a measure altered into epidote, which appears in the form of grains arranged in lines and gathered into heaps. This is an extremely rare phenomenon in andesites. Feldspars are also attacked, and have produced carbonate of lime. There is also much somewhat dusty apatite.

Brown andesite occurs in the Cortez Range south of Palisade Cañon [260]. It does not, however, contain any good hornblende.

A peculiar variety is found in the rock from Wachoe Mountains [261]. It is a dark-gray rock, in which a great quantity of laminæ of brown biotite can be seen macroscopically. Seen in section under the microscope, the number of these laminæ is largely increased. The feldspars, arranged in splendid zones, are partly sanidins, but plagioclases predominate. They are without doubt very fresh; for they are entirely water-clear and comparatively very pure, containing only extremely few remarkably small foreign inclusions of an undeterminable nature. Beside the predominating biotite, there is only a little hornblende, mostly in the form of aggregations of small, brown grains. There is no augite. This rock is therefore the mica equivalent of the hornblende-andesites; the former standing in the same relation to the latter as mica-gneiss to hornblende-gneiss. A few microscopical quartzes are present in the form of compact grains, having hexagonal and rhombic sections, and which show a strong chromatic polarization.

Another remarkable andesite occurs at the head of Annie Creek, Cortez Range [262], whose dark-gray groundmass has that microstructure which will be subsequently mentioned as characteristic of the augite-andesites, a dense felt composed of the smallest microlites and having more or less glass distributed through it. There are some light yellowish-brown, sharp augites, beside so many deep, dark-brown hornblendes, that these latter, no doubt, predominate. Both minerals are easily distinguishable by the cleavage, which is never lacking here. The schistiform feldspars are largely monoclinic, but plagioclases surely prevail among the larger individuals. This point also places the rock in a certain relation with the augite-andesites. The feldspars (Plate V, fig. 3) contain remarkably good glass-inclusions (indeed, the best which have ever been observed); being of a yellow color, having a thick bubble, and sometimes including short, black needles which are very distinctly imbedded conformably with the directions of the zones of growth. There are even frame-like layers in the feldspar sections, consisting of a dust of glass grains less than 0.001^{mm} in diameter, densely crowded together into blackish lines. Signs of thicker and more yellowish glass-particles appear in the feldspar between these lines or bands. Some apatite is found.

Emigrant Road, north of Palisade Cañon, Cortez Range [263], gives a beautiful andesite, which in general resembles that last described. Here again the plagioclases contain an enormous quantity of a foreign substance: rounded glass-inclusions are less numerous; long strips and shreds of light-brownish glass, growing alternately wider and narrower, predominating; a perfect net-work of glass, the holes in which are filled with feldspar. Sanidin is also present. Hornblende is plentiful, and largely predominates, seeming to consist chiefly of larger or smaller macroscopical crystals, although there is a good deal of microlitic felt in the dark-gray, somewhat glass-bearing, groundmass. Its deep-brown individuals have a very broad, black border: some of them are almost all border, having only an extremely small and faint spot of the original hornblende substance in the interior. Ultimately, the individual is totally transformed into the same material as that which first appears merely as a border, and is simply a product of alteration, possessing the same rounded and often tail-formed outlines as in the original body. Some pale brownish-yellow augites, with sharp, well-defined crystal outlines, and lacking the black external zone, are also found. This and the last-mentioned rock present a good example of the phenomenon of a waving, fluidal groundmass.

To this same variety (which curiously does not occur among the western andesites of Washoe and Nevada), the andesite from Traverse Mountains, Utah, also belongs [264]. It bears plagioclase, a little sanidin, abundant dark-brown hornblende in crystals reaching 2^{mm} in size, which are without, or possess only the rudiments of, a black border, and a small quantity of excellent augite. The groundmass is a microlitic felt rich in gray glass. By comparing these andesites from the Fortieth Parallel with the European specimens from Siebengebirge, Rhenish Prussia, Nassau, and Hungary, we find that in general structure there is the closest analogy between them, and it is therefore curious that the American rocks have proved, in nearly all cases, to be free from biotite and invariably to be without tridymite; two minerals which are seldom lacking as accessory ingredients in the corresponding European occurrences. Some sanidin and some augite, beside the prevailing plagioclase and hornblende, seem to be common to all the andesites of both hemispheres.

The general question now presents itself, By what points may propylites and andesites be distinguished and separated petrographically? Their chief constituents are the same, and they belong to different epochs of the same Tertiary age. But this slight difference in geological time is of sufficient value to express itself in some characteristic petrographical peculiarities, which, in their combination, always indicate the distinction between propylites and andesites. Perhaps it may not be superfluous to insist that all the rocks described in the foregoing pages as propylites and andesites were first referred to one or the other group by geological observations in the field, and that the petrographical diagnosis and the classification of them have not been influenced by any artificial point of view or preconceived opinion. The examinations have proved that in every rock the geological and petrographical differences perfectly accord. The diagnostic differences between the two rock's may be summed up as follows:

    a. The general color of the propylitic groundmass has more of a greenish-gray, while the andesitic groundmass has more of a pure gray or brown tinge.

b. In structure and in the behavior of its constituents, the propylite still resembles the older ante-Tertiary diorite-porphyries.

c. The groundmass of the propylites is rich in minute particles of horn-blende, while in that of the andesites this mineral appears only in the larger individuals, fine hornblende dust being wanting.

d. The propylitic feldspars are usually filled with a considerable quantity of hornblende dust, while the andesitic feldspars are entirely without it: the latter not infrequently containing glass-inclusions, which do do not seem to occur in the propylitic plagioclases.

e. The color of the proper hornblende sections in propylite is always green (never brown), while the color of those in andesites is almost without exception brown; and the propylitic hornblende never shows the curious black border which is so common to that of andesites; and again, propylite in some cases contains, beside the largely predominating green hornblende, a few sections of the brown mineral, presenting, in many points, a strikingly peculiar aspect, while in andesites two kinds of hornblende never occur together.

f. The propylitic hornblende is often distinctly built up of thin needles or staff-like microlites, and therefore is not regularly cleavable; which has never been found to be the case in andesites.

g. The production of microscopical epidote (mainly by the alteration of hornblende), so very common in propylites, has, with one exception, never been observed in these andesites, and it is also unknown in the European occurrences.

h. Augite often occurs as an accessory constituent in andesites, but it is comparatively very rare in propylites.

i. The andesitic groundmass here and there seems to possess a half-glassy development: a glass-bearing propylitic groundmass has never been found; and herein is another point of resemblance to the old diorite-porphyries.

All these differences between propylitic and andesitic hornblende also extend to both of the quartziferous members, quartz-propylite and dacite.

SECTION IV.

DACITE.

All the rocks described under this title in the following lines are from a few illustrative localities inferred to be younger than propylites and older than trachytes. They stand in close connection with the quartzless member, andesite, being generally of later eruption.

At the West, the first excellent dacites occur in the hills above American City, Washoe [265, 266], where two varieties are presented. One has a brownish-gray and the other a greenish-gray groundmass. Both contain macroscopical feldspars, all, or nearly all, of which are more or less distinctly striated. They also bear quartz grains, which range in size from the dimensions of a pea downward. The first variety [265] is made especially interesting by the fact that its groundmass has a perfectly rhyolitic structure. Its crystalline secretions, plagioclase and hornblende, separate it from the rhyolites, and refer it to the andesitic group, and the quantity of quartz it contains pronounces it a dacite. The groundmass presents for the most part a sphærolitic microstructure of a perfection seldom observed. The balls (of which the average diameter is 0.1^{mm}) are composed of fine, pale yellowish-gray fibres of various lengths, having a splendid radial convergence to a common centre. Beside the more perfect normal sphærolites, rudimentary and malformed ones are seen constituting only a sector, with a diverging structure like an ice-flower. The sphærolitic material either polarizes feebly, with a very indistinct transmission of light, or not at all; and it must therefore be of a microfelsitic nature. The feldspars are no longer fresh in their sections. With a low magnifying power, they show only an indistinct and rudimentary striation; but it is evident that they have once been beautifully lamellated. A high magnifying power ascertains that carbonate of lime already constitutes a considerable part of their mass. This lime, present in the form of calcite, replaces the feldspar in some spots, and forms irregular masses, which have a very distinct rhombohedral cleavage. Whoever is acquainted with the peculiar polarization of finely distributed particles of calcite, which appear like glittering polychromatic scales, will immediately observe that calcite powder is also largely interposed in the plagioclases, a fact with which the obliteration of the twin-striation is connected. The whole feldspar section appears finely stippled and speckled with the most minute calcite points. It may be allowable to account for this by the comparatively basic nature of the plagioclase and the relatively high amount of lime present in it. And C. Doelter has shown that the plagioclase of the typical dacites around Vöröspatak in Transylvania belongs to labradorite and contains 10. to 11.5 per cent. of lime.[1] The feldspars of the Washoe dacite also have small but very distinct fluid-inclusions: this is remarkable, for it is the first time liquid-inclusions have been discovered in the feldspar of a trachytic or andesitic rock. Its quartzes, which are very fine ones, are wanting in fluid and also in proper glass-inclusions; but they contain rounded, oval, and variously-shaped particles of the sphærolitic fibrous groundmass, which exactly agrees with the main body of the mass in substance and structure. Groundmass enters the quartz crystals in the form of rounded bays and inlets, precisely as in the older felsite-porphyries and rhyolites. The hornblende has a feebly black border, and sometimes, under the protection of this zone, has slightly altered, developing these substances: a, a pale greenish-yellow or yellowish-green substance (viridite), which seems to be homogeneous, but polarizes, often found in abundance, traversing in veins; b, excellently rhombohedral, fissile calcite; c, red and brownish-red grains of oxyd of iron; d, dark yellowish-green, rounded grains, often arranged in lines or heaps, which is probably epidote. Aggregations of these four substances often entirely fill the space formerly occupied by the hornblende, and splendid polysynthetic pseudomorphs are exhibited. There is no augite present. Prisms of apatite are occasionally found. The other variety [266], having a greenish-gray groundmass, for the most part repeats the peculiarities of its above-described neighbor: there is the interposition of lime in the plagioclases, the remarkable phenomenon of hornblende alteration, etc. Its groundmass, however, is not at all sphærolitic, but instead

[1] Mineralogische Mittheilungen, gesammelt von Tschermak, 1874, page 13; for instance, the plagioclase of the dacite from the Suligata has 9.95 per cent. of lime, and the plagioclase of the dacite from the Zuckerhut near Nagyag has 10.10 per cent. of lime; and, again, the plagioclase of the dacite from the Haitó, 11.42 per cent. of lime.

microfelsitic, possessing fine, indistinctly polarizing grains, of which egg-shaped inclusions (some even with a bubble) are interposed in the quartzes. A quantitative analysis of this dacite from the hills above American City, Washoe, was made by Mr. C. Councler, of Leipsic, with the following result:

Silica	69. 3
Alumina	17. 9
Protoxyd of iron	4. 1
Lime	1. 6
Magnesia	1. 3
Potassa	3. 6
Soda	2. 0
Loss by ignition	2. 1
	101. 9

It will be seen by this analysis that the amount of silica present is much higher than in andesite (see page 124), and approaches in quantity that in rhyolite, and that the general composition of the rock resembles that of quartz-propylite. A parallel to the striking fact that, in this rock (the larger feldspars of which are triclinic) potash slightly predominates over soda, is seen in the analysis of Transylvania dacites. With reference to this, we shall not quote the analyses made by Sommaruga, who found, in some of these dacites, ten or fifteen times more potash than soda; for it has been asserted[1] that all his conclusions concerning the alkalies are incorrect. Careful chemists like K. v. Hauer, however, have sometimes noted an amount of potash more or less in excess of the soda, or nearly equal to it; for instance, potash : soda $= 4.91 : 3.12$; $5.40 : 3.86$; $3.58 : 3.64$ (Streit Tschermak); $3.33 : 3.59$ (v. Andrian). This seems to prove that sanidin is often present in the groundmass of dacites in a not inconsiderable quantity. J. Roth is even inclined to believe that dacite and rhyolite are to be distinguished by the circumstance that the former contains plagioclase and quartz in a groundmass relatively rich in potash; the latter, sanidin and quartz in a groundmass relatively rich in soda.[2] For the sake

[1] C. Doelter, Mineralog. Mittheilungen, gesammelt von Tschermak, 1873, 92.
[2] Beiträge zur Petrographie der plutonischen Gesteine, Berlin, 1869, 187.

of illustration and comparison, we quote some newly-made analyses of European dacites.

No. 1 is from Illova Valley near Rodna, Transylvania;[1] No. 2, from between Szekelyo and Rogosel, Transylvania ;[2] No. 3, from Sebesvár, Transylvania ;[3] No. 4, from Nagy-Sebes, Transylvania ;[4] No. 5, from Kis Sebes, right bank of Körös, Transylvania;[5] No. 6, from Monte Alto, Euganean Hills, Italy ;[6] No. 7, from New Prevali, Karinthia.[7]

	1	2	3	4	5	6	7
Silica	66.41	66.30	66.91	67.17	66.32	68.18	63.44
Alumina	17.41	15.63	14.13	16.96	14.33	13.65	19.31
Sesquioxyd of iron	4.12	4.59	5.00	3.45	5.53	....	1.61
Protoxyd of iron	....	....	....	1.20	0.25	6.69	1.08
Lime	3.96	2.76	2.35	4.46	4.64	2.23	3.97
Magnesia	1.82	1.33	0.95	1.50	2.45	0.42	1.94
Potassa	1.65	4.91	5.40	1.55	1.61	1.73	3.58
Soda	3.83	3.12	3.86	3.70	3.90	6.00	3.64
Loss by ignition	0.81	1.76	1.42	0.89	1.13	0.55	2.06
	100.01	100.40	100.02	100.88	100.16	99.45	100.63

Washoe dacites have a comparatively high amount of silica, but are not the richest in it; Marx having analyzed a dacite from Leon de Nicaragua el Cerrito, Central America, with even 71.27 per cent. of silica, and 18.46 of alumina.[8] The low percentage of lime in our rocks is probably due to alteration, which is to be counted in with the high loss by ignition; a quantity of this substance having been carried off as a soluble carbonate.

Dacites from the hills west of Devil's Gate, Washoe [267, 268, 269], generally bear a more or less close external resemblance to those above described; the behavior of the feldspar and hornblende being the same. The groundmass is a pale yellowish-gray, microfelsitic substance, in which a

[1] Tschermak (Slechta), Wiener Akad., Ber.,1867, 295.
[2] K. v. Hauer, Verhandl. d. geol. Reichsanst., 1867, 119.
[3] K. v. Hauer, ibid., 1867, 118.
[4] C. Doelter, Mineralog. Mittheil.,von Tschermak, 1873, 92.
[5] C. Doelter, ibid., 1873, 93.
[6] G. von Rath, Zeitschr. d. d. geolog. Gesellsch., 1864, 500.
[7] Tschermak (Streit), Wiener Akad., Ber.,1867, 302.
[8] Zeitsch., d. d. geol. Ges., 1868, 524.

feeble individualization has begun to show itself here and there, presenting between crossed nicols a quite dark isotrope base, out of which small points occasionally shine out indistinctly. Along undulating lines, a somewhat more decided individualization has happened, producing waved bands, which polarize better, and which present in ordinary light a somewhat micro-crystalline composition made up of colorless grains. By the curvature of these granular bands and stripes, which at both extremities soon pass into the microfelsitic base, fluidal wave-phenomena are well shown. In this groundmass also splendid sphærolites in different stages of development have been discerned. Beside entirely round, perfect balls, there are rudimentary tendencies to horseshoe-like forms, and many poor, little bunches, which scarcely constitute the tenth part of a circle. A ring of fine and delicate sphærolitic fibres (the single ones in radial position) is sometimes found wreathing a rounded kernel of a non-fibrous, prevailingly micro-felsitic, mass; and surrounding this is another ring exactly like the first one; the effect being that quite a gradual passage between the fibres and the micro-felsite takes place. The quartzes have rare but perfectly characteristic glass-inclusions but none of fluid.

Another dacite [270] is found in Basalt Cañon, Washoe. It also bears a really rhyolitic base, with excellent fluidal lines, produced by the zonally different, more amorphous, or more indistinctly crystalline-granular behavior of the groundmass. Here and there, black trichites, aggregated fascicularly, are interposed in isolated patches, being more or less dismembered into grains. Quartzes contain the most beautiful hexagonal and rhombic inclusions of brownish glass, and of groundmass pressed into the shape of quartz. The rock bears splendid brown mica instead of hornblende, and is therefore a mica equivalent of the common (hornblende) dacite. Moreover, this dacite, as well as the former one, has a very little sanidin accompanying the prevailing plagioclase. All these rocks are filled with fine pores; and it appears under the microscope that little plagioclase crystals, which in all probability were previously wholly altered into carbonate of lime, had suffered complete removal.

Among the andesites of the Gould and Curry Quarry, Washoe, occur quartz-bearing members, some even rich in quartz [271]. The hornblende is brownish, with a tinge of green. The quartzes contain magnificent glass-inclusions.

Dacitic rocks also appear in Berkshire Cañon [272, 273, 274, 275]. They are yellowish-gray or bluish-gray felsitic masses, rich in dark, macroscopical quartzes, which are for the most part pretty well crystallized. They are poor in larger feldspars. Where the latter are visible, they show distinct traces of striation, notwithstanding the development of carbonate of lime has made considerable progress. This circumstance may make it justifiable to classify these rocks as dacites, although no hornblende can be recognized, and dark plates of biotite can be seen only here and there. The groundmass is in some places more truly crystalline than in the foregoing rocks, and is entirely rhyolitic, sometimes showing a tendency to form sphærolites and those curious, axially fibrous, longitudinal bodies which will be described in the chapter on rhyolites. These rocks are also geologically older than the sanidin-bearing rhyolites from Berkshire Cañon, and are, moreover, no poorer in quartz.

One of the most typical dacites is that from Mullen's Gap, west side of Pyramid Lake [276]. In this grayish rock, it is easy to detect, with the unaided eye, many striated feldspars and beautiful quartzes. Its groundmass, again of rhyolitic nature, is a simply refracting, homogeneous base, in which a great quantity of polarizing particles had begun to be secreted. Almost all the feldspars are triclinic and fresher than in the above-mentioned dacites: they are extremely rich in inclusions of glass and of the groundmass, and also in sometimes irregularly cylindrical, and sometimes flat-pressed, empty pores, in which, however, carbonate of lime is occasionally found parasitically deposited. The hornblende is no longer fresh, but it is very distinctly visible. Where its original condition has been in some measure preserved, it becomes evident that its color was brown.

Another good dacite occurs on the east slope of the hills, south of Rabbit Hole Spring, Kamma Mountains [277]. The structure of its groundmass is the same, but its color is a somewhat darker yellowish-gray. Many quartz grains appear under the microscope, and so also do distinctly predominating, very well striated, but small plagioclases and some hornblende attacked by decomposition. Macroscopically, the felsitic rock does not present any crystals.

The dacite from Shoshone Peak, Shoshone Range [278], is a dark greenish-gray rock, with quartzes nearly the size of a pea, filled with superb, almost colorless, glass-inclusions having a thick, dark bubble. The quartz also contains hornblende-microlites, which is a rare phenomenon in these rocks. In one instance, one of them was seen in the quartz partly surrounded by a bubble-bearing glass-drop, and itself possessing two little glass-inclusions (Plate I, fig. 17). The hornblende is rather distinct. Feldspars have many gas-cavities, and are already in the early stages of decomposition.

That from south of Palisade Cañon, Cortez Range, a light grayish-brown variety, appears generally andesitic, but it contains beautiful quartzes [279]. Pellucid feldspars up to the size of 4^{mm}, nearly all of which are triclinic, may be seen in the section with the unaided eye. The external part is a quite dull, milky layer, forming a plain frame. Under the microscope, one discovers that innumerable bubble-bearing inclusions, or fragments of a fine, porous, light grayish-yellow glass, are imbedded in the feldspar, almost wholly replacing the feldspar substance. The hornblende, under preservation of its outlines, is often altered into a radially fibrous, pale-green substance, and sometimes into a mixture of this and calcite. Less decomposed individuals show that their original color was brown. In strong contrast with this hornblende, the biotite laminæ present have remained entirely fresh. A large part of the groundmass has a microfelsitic base, in which a considerable quantity of delicate, brownish-black, triclitic needles are scattered without order.

A peculiar dacitic rock [280, 281] occurs in Wagon Cañon, Cortez Range. Its prevailing mass is a dark blackish-brown, in which, beside quartzes the thickness of a pepper-corn and some plagioclases, strange angular particles of a dull, milky-looking substance, which are seldom larger than a pea, are richly disseminated. The sections make it instantly apparent that the rock is a miniature breccia; and it is surely an eruptive breccia, not of sedimentary clastic material. Without doubt, the quartzes, and probably the plagioclases, belong to the prevailing dark mass; for its secreted ingredients are not of a foreign, fragmentary nature. Included milky splinters, often densely crowded, have a felsitic microstructure, and contain plagioclases and quartzes. The rock is, in short, a dacite, which envelopes so many strange fragments of another variety of dacite as to form a real breccia.

In conclusion, some comparative observations upon the relation of dacites, as well to quartz-propylites as to andesites, will not be amiss. Of course, these remarks refer only to the rocks examined in the foregoing pages, and a summary generalization as to those of foreign regions is not attempted. It should be understood, nevertheless, that these rocks are thoroughly classic, and represent the best forms of their respective kinds. The difference between dacite and andesite does not consist only in the presence of quartz in one, while it is lacking in the other; the microscopical structure of the groundmass of the two rocks being entirely different: that of the dacites has a rhyolitic structure, presenting a microfelsitic, here and there more or less granular-crystalline, mass, with a frequent tendency to form sphærolites; while the andesitic groundmass is a simple aggregation of microlites. In its original state, the color of hornblende in both rocks is brown. Augite often accompanies the prevailing hornblende, as an accessory element, in andesites; but it is entirely wanting in the dacites. Herein is another point of close likeness between dacites and rhyolites. As to quartz-propylites and dacites, it has been shown (page 133) that all the differences between propylitic and andesitic hornblende also exist between the quartziferous equivalents of the two rocks. The microscopical structure of quartz-propylites being the same as that of quartzless members, it becomes apparent that a considerable difference must exist between it and that of dacites, and it also equally differs from the andesites. But there is another and more remarkable point of contrast: the quartzes of the quartz-propylites abound in fluid-inclusions (as in the older diorite-porphyries), but do not contain any glassy ones; while the quartz of the dacites (as in the rhyolites) do not bear any liquid, but possess excellent glass-particles. Upon this point, it is interesting to know that the only hornblende-plagioclase rock of Transylvania, that from Borsa-bánya, in the quartzes of which inclusions that are doubtless fluid have been observed, does not belong to the dacites (as has been suggested), but is, according to Richt-hofen,[1] a quartziferous propylite.   J. O. Doelter once mentioned liquid-inclusions in real dacites of Transylvania, but subsequently withdrew the statement.[2]   It was formerly thought that the limit between the fluid and glass-bearing quartzes was at the beginning of the Tertiary age; but now, after study of the quartz-propylites, it must be advanced and placed within the Tertiary, between propylites and dacites (andesites).   While the quartz-propylites are rich, the dacites (again like rhyolites) are extremely poor in apatite.   In general, therefore, there is even a stronger contrast between quartz-propylite and dacite than between propylite and andesite : the difference has a stronger expression in the quartziferous members.   The contrast between quartz-propylite and propylite is confined merely to the presence in one of quartz, and its absence in the other; but, between dacite and andesite, the discrepancy is far wider.

---

[1] Zeitschrift d. d. geolog. Gesellsch., XX, 1868, 687.
[2] Mineral. Mittheil., v. Tschermak, 1874, 14.

CHAPTER VII.

TRACHYTE, RHYOLITE.

Section I.—Trachyte.
Section II.—Rhyolite.
Section III.—Hyaline Rhyolites: Glassy
and Half-glassy Rocks.

SECTION I.

TRACHYTE.

About the level of Virginia City, Washoe, and not far to the east of it, a line of trachyte outcrops. The most northerly is on Graveyard Spur, at what is known as The Quarry. Here a comparatively thin sheet of sanidin-trachyte is found capping an abrupt hill; the greater mass being formed of inclined, rudely hexagonal columns, varying in size from a foot to four feet across. A second outcrop occupies a bench just above the Geiger grade, near the Sierra Nevada works. The main ejection of trachytic rocks occupies a broad zone extending from the Washoe foothills to Pyramid Lake, a distance of forty miles. It has flowed out, in a nearly meridional direction, along the heights of the range, and almost all the prominent eroded summits (Sugar Loaf, Mounts Rose, Kate, Emma) and elevated table-lands are formed of it. In the pass north of the Gould and Curry mill, a narrow dike of trachyte, less than one hundred feet wide, breaks through propylite, and up out of this small opening the whole mass of the formation has come. Wherever the country is eroded to any

163

great depth, for instance, at Six Mile Cañon, at the base of Mount Rose, traces of an earlier variety of trachyte may be seen; fragments being imbedded in the breccia, which immediately succeeded it. These breccias form the greater part of the whole outflow, containing masses varying in size from a mere pebble to blocks twenty feet in diameter. Capping the breccias is a broad thick overflow of normal sanidin-trachyte, varying in thickness from one hundred to one thousand feet.[1] In other localities along the Fortieth Parallel, two kinds of trachyte occur, which are distinguished by age. The younger eruptions break through the masses of the older trachyte formation, flow over their rounded forms, and generally occupy the summits and higher parts of mountains. Petrographically, they differ in essential points. The older ones still recall the andesites, which are just antecedent in geological age. They are rich in plagioclase (so that both feldspars often maintain a balance, and the sanidin but slightly predominates), and proportionally rich in hornblende, which is of a brown color, like that in andesites. The younger trachytes are poorer in plagioclase, contain more sanidin, much less hornblende, and in general possess many macroscopical laminæ of biotite. Moreover, they are somewhat rougher and more porous than the older ones.

The older trachyte from Mount Rose and Sugar Loaf [282] also so far microscopically resembles the andesites that proper hornblende does not enter into the composition of the groundmass, which is composed of feldspar microlites, dark brownish or blackish grains of ferrite, and opacite, with here and there some colorless glass. The reddish-gray, younger trachyte from these mountains [283] contains excellent microscopical aggregations of tridymite, precisely resembling those in the trachytes from the Siebengebirge in Hungary, the Euganean Hills in Northern Italy, and Montdore and Puy-de-Dôme in Central France. The tridymite forms little thin and delicate colorless laminæ (which are seldom of more than 0.02^{mm} in diameter), having a six-sided or irregularly rounded outline. These laminæ are arranged, generally in great numbers, one above the other, presenting something the appearance of roofing-slate or shingles (Plate I, fig. 14). The younger trachyte from Cross Spur Quarry, Washoe

---

[1] Clarence King, Geology of the Washoe Mining District, vol. III, 33.

[284], is separated into large columns, and shows in the smaller sanidins beside minute inclusions, real kernels of yellowish-brown glass, which are rectangular in shape, like the crystal section. Their size is sometimes larger than the narrow outer zone of pure feldspar. The hornblende sections have a curious intermediate color between green and brown. Splendid, richly-lamellated biotite is perforated by numerous apatite needles; and again the pores contain dense accumulations of tridymite.

Among the trachytes of the Fortieth Parallel there are some peculiar rocks, which present a combination of prevailing ingredients that has never been observed elsewhere in these Tertiary eruptive rocks, namely, sanidin and augite.

The first of this new group of augite-trachytes forms the low hills between Sheep Corral Cañon and Wadsworth [285]. It is a dark brownish-black, half-glassy-looking rock, and is younger than propylite. All the larger crystals are doubtless sanidin, which places the rock among the trachytes: there is pale-green augite and some plagioclase and brown hornblende; the latter being decidedly inferior to the augite. The very abundant groundmass consists of little colorless crystals and microlites, which are probably for the most part sanidin, and very pale-greenish microlites, belonging by analogy more to augite than to hornblende, imbedded together with magnetite in a nearly colorless glass-base; a micro-structure which in every respect resembles that characteristic of the groundmass of augite-andesites, to be described hereafter. At the time the examination of this and other American augite-trachytes was made, G. von Rath showed that the same peculiar combination also occurs among the older rocks.[1] He described as "augite-syenite" the rock which forms the largest part of the Monzoni Mountain in South Tyrol; the most characteristic variety occurring at the Toal dei Rizzoni. These older rocks contain, besides the principal constituents, orthoclase and augite, some plagioclase, and, rather as accessory ingredients, titanites, hornblende, iron-pyrites, magnetite, and apatite. At the same time, he discovered that some varieties of the famous syenites from the southern coast of Norway,

---

[1] Sitzung der niederrheinischen Gesellschaft f. Natur- und Heilkunde, 8. März 1875.

10 M P

especially the occurrence at Laurvig, belong to the augite-syenite group. These results are the more remarkable because it was formerly considered a petrographical law that augite is, without exception, confined to the basic rocks, and that it never occurs in conjunction with a member of the feldspar group as rich in silica as the sanidin or orthoclase is. A quantitative analysis of this augite-trachyte, made by Dr. Anger in Leipsic, gave the following results:

Silica	68. 81
Alumina	13. 62
Protoxyd of iron	3. 91
Lime	4. 30
Magnesia	2. 74
Potassa	2. 56
Soda	2. 68
Loss by ignition	2. 30
	100. 92

The preponderance of sanidin in this highly silicated rock is indicated by the comparatively large amount of potash, as compared with the soda. Its high amount of silica, which even surpasses the sanidin, in spite of the presence of basic augite, is, as in the augite-andesites, produced by the glass.

A genuine trachyte from the summit at the head of Sheep Corral Cañon, Virginia Range [286], is a peculiar reddish-gray variety, bearing, along fissures, excellent hyalite. Thin sections show an alteration-product of small gray and pale reddish-yellow spots; the first being the freshest portion of the rock. The groundmass consists of water-clear feldspar-microlites, opaque black grains, and a light-gray cementing and imbuing glass-base. In the reddish places, the color of which is doubtless secondary, all the microlites are colored brownish-yellow; and the hornblende, in other parts of the mass a good brown and entirely fresh, is here, wholly or in veins, altered into a dull, dirty yellow substance, inclining one at first sight to mistake it for serpentinized olivine. Beside the prevailing sanidin, there are some plagioclases and biotites present. There is no tridymite, however; probably on account of the abundant acid glass-base.

Other trachytes occur in the Truckee Cañon between Glendale and Clark's Station. One variety presents even macroscopically the two kinds of feldspar.

A characteristic trachyte locality is met with at Truckee Ferry, Truckee Cañon. On the side of the ferry, a beautiful variety appears [287], which is very rich, both in sharp crystals and glass. The included macroscopical and microscopical crystals, among which hornblende and biotite are found in individuals 3^{mm} long, are *a*, sanidin, in some places macroscopical, charged with a remarkable quantity of glass-inclusions; *b*, quite an unimportant amount of plagioclases; *c*, abundant, excellently fissile, deep-brown, fresh hornblende; *d*, biotite, in about the same quantity as hornblende; *e*, much rarer, light greenish-yellow augite, pierced by apatite, which does not occur as an independent constituent; *f*, magnetite. The copious groundmass, of resinous lustre, is very rich in almost colorless glass, and it also contains a large quantity of colorless microlites of the same material, and rectangular crystallites, each of the four corners of which are drawn out into a long acicular spire or thorn. No colored microlites which could belong to hornblende or augite are present. Macroscopical, pumicestone-like protuberances cover hollows in the rock.

Purple Hill, at Truckee Ferry [288], consists of rather dark and more common trachyte, with narrow and unstriated ledges of sanidin, 7^{mm} long, in an unusual degree charged with long microscopical fragments of groundmass. In the groundmass, which chiefly consists of feldspar ledges, among them many that are triclinic, and microlites of feldspar, neither hornblende nor augite can be detected: a quantity of small black magnetites and yellowish-brown or brownish-yellow grains of ferrite accompany the feldspar.

A light-gray rock, which belongs to the augite-trachytes, but represents a different variety from that above described, occurs on the left bank at the Truckee Ferry [289]. It is for the most part a nearly crystalline mixture of feldspar impregnated with augitic dust and pale brownish-yellow augite. Many of the feldspars are striated, but there is no doubt that the predominating quantity is monoclinic. Augite prisms are often found grouped in oval, imperfectly radial accumulations, measuring as high as

0.3^{mm} in diameter. Long tails, composed of black hornblende grains, which appear in the light, thin sections as delicate, short, black lines, were among the phenomena noted. Here and there are feeble spots of a half-glassy, globulitic, brownish-gray substance; but the abundance of imbuing glass, characteristic of the former augite-trachyte, is in this variety totally wanting. There is no olivine, which expresses the absolute separation of the rock from basalts.

A peculiar trachyte forms the foot-hills north of Nevada Station, Truckee Range [290]. It is a brown and somewhat porous rock, appearing almost half-glassy, and contains many macroscopical biotite plates. Under the microscope, all the feldspars, which, although they approach the length of 1^{mm}, are not visible in the hand-specimens, are discovered to belong, with very rare exceptions, to sanidin. In two thin sections, only one very small, dark-bordered hornblende section could be detected; but light yellowish-green augite crystals were rather numerous. The biotite forms, as is often the case, only macroscopical, and no microscopical, individuals, so that the amount seen with the unaided eye is not increased under the microscope. These individuals are partly altered into a striped aggregation of small, dark grains, in which they resemble the rubellans in the lavas around the Laacher See. The groundmass is an accumulation of colorless feldspar-microlites, pale-green microlites, which are most probably not hornblende but augite, black magnetites, and vestiges of glass. There is no apatite.

At the north end of the Kawsoh Mountains, a somewhat rough, brownish-gray trachyte occurs [291, 292]. All the macroscopical feldspars and nearly all the larger microscopical ones are sanidin. Large hornblendes are present, but rare, and also a few augites: biotite is wanting. Larger feldspars are full of roundish, oval, and cylindrical pores, and unexpectedly numerous, dusty-brownish apatite prisms. The groundmass consists of feldspar-microlites and very minute, indefinable, dark needles and grains. It also bears blood-red laminæ of specular iron, which is also settled in fissures of the rock and on the borders of feldspars, and rather numerous aggregations of tridymite.

The summit of the island in Pyramid Lake is formed of trachyte [293].

It has a fine, reddish-gray groundmass, in which are larger sanidins and some plagioclases. The groundmass is a very intimate mixture whose parts can only be resolved microscopically with great difficulty. It seems to be composed mainly of feldspars, together with which are little black grains, black, granulated prisms, and irregular spots, the latter appearing macroscopically in the thin section, and being, without doubt, totally altered brown hornblende.

A gray trachyte appears in the range south of the Kamma Mountains, Nevada [294]. It contains feldspars measuring as high as 3^{mm} in diameter, and hornblende that is entirely decomposed (its border of dark grains being preserved) into a seemingly homogeneous, but aggregately polarizing, mass of an aquamarine or pale-green color, which might, at the first glance, lead one to mistake these sections for serpentinized olivine. This light-green product of alteration bears in its fissures dendritic laminæ of specular iron, which are, therefore, of still more secondary nature. Apatite is present, but augite and biotite are wanting. There are no proper hornblende microlites in the groundmass. The mass contains, beside the feldspar, reddish-brown ferrite and black opacite grains, the latter of which, as in many of the above-described trachytes, after feldspar, are the chief components.

At a point twenty-five miles north of Rabbit Hole Spring, Nevada, is a somewhat rough but quite fine-grained trachyte [295], in which all the feldspars are strikingly pure, and are all, with rare exceptions, sanidins. No macroscopical or microscopical crystallized ingredient is imbedded in the groundmass except the feldspars—neither hornblende, nor mica, nor augite; but it contains numerous reddish-brown and brownish-yellow grains of ferrite, which surely do not belong to either hornblende or augite, but are a kind of substitute for them, in part presenting a chemical equivalent to fill their place. The black opacites here are so excellently quadrangular that they doubtless must be taken for magnetite.

At Chataya Pass, Pah-Ute Range, western Nevada, occur yellowish-gray trachytes, with splendid sanidins, sometimes as large as peas [296, 297, 298], rich in gas-cavities. Quartz is wanting, and there is no proper hornblende present. These rocks somewhat resemble the rhyolites in the microstructure of their groundmass. One variety contains a groundmass which consists of undulating, twisted, and entangled axially fibrous strings and bands, between which is a little felsitic substance that is nearly structureless but rich in heaps of ferrite and opacite. This type of groundmass is as common in rhyolites as it is rare in trachytes. In another specimen, this structure is wanting; the groundmass being here, as in most other trachytes, an aggregation of feldspar, opacite, and ferrite, which are, in the usual manner, accumulated in little heaps with rounded outlines. Hornblende is wanting.

There is one variety among these trachytes which has been altered by solfataric action [296]. In one of its attacked feldspars, the microscope discovered even some grains of calcite with rhombohedral cleavage and twin-striation parallel to $-\frac{1}{2}R$. Hornblende is present, but it is entirely altered. It is remarkable that the brown and black grains whose intimate accumulation borders the former hornblende, and which usually encircle a central, pale-green or aquamarine-colored substance, exactly agree with the ferrite and opacite of the groundmass, and are even plainly seen to pass into them, the external margin gradually dissolving and becoming looser. If we consider that the groundmass is often very fresh and unaltered, and also make note of the regular and equal distribution of the ferrite and opacite grains through it, it can scarcely be believed that the latter had anything to do genetically with decomposed hornblende, of which only alteration products were left. There is some titanite.

Trachytes are found on Coal Creek, Seetoya Range, Nevada [299]. A very fresh, light-gray trachyte possesses, beside sanidin, much plagioclase; but it has no other secretions, except very rare, minute laminæ of biotite. The feldspars are beautifully built up zonally, with excellent zonal inclosure-lines of half-glassy grains. The groundmass is nearly colorless or very light gray, finely microlitic and granular-feldspathic, containing but little ferrite and opacite. Some titanite is also met with. Another variety, from the River Range, near Susan Creek, Nevada [300], is a somewhat earthy, pale-reddish, and domite-like trachyte, and presents macroscopically some feldspar and biotite. This rather remarkable rock possesses a light, globulitic, glassy base, in which numerous feldspar ledges almost wholly devoid of striation, and subtil, half-transparent grains or needles of a brown and brownish-red color, are disseminated. There is no microscopical biotite, hornblende, augite, or apatite. Nevertheless, there occur, appearing even macroscopically in the sections, granular aggregations of pale, rose-red, isotrope garnet, in seemingly broken grains, free from any interposition, and resembling in all respects the garnets in the Saxon granulites, which, as members of the old crystalline schist series, are doubtless of a different geological origin from these Tertiary eruptive trachytes. Only in one other case has garnet been observed as an accessory ingredient of trachytes, namely, in the Castle Rock from the island of Ischia in Italy.[1] Rarely but evenly disseminated through the groundmass, are some sharp grains which in color are an azure or Prussian blue, measure only 0.0025^{mm}, sometimes possess a distinct hexagonal shape, and in all probability belong to haüyne: they perfectly resemble those microscopical blue crystals which are found well preserved in the sanidins and highly altered in the groundmass of the trachyte from the Pferdekopf in the German Rhön Mountains.[2] The rock also bears, besides aggregations of tridymite, water-clear portions of a wholly isotrope substance, rather strongly refracting, traversed by quite irregular cracks, and forming singular spires and denticles: the individuals of this substance seem to be thick, angular particles of glass, and precisely identical with an occurrence which has been observed in the rhyolite from the Hohenburg, near Berkum, Rhenish Prussia.[3]

The Wah-we-ah Range is an interesting trachytic region, and a large number of specimens from there were examined. One variety [301] is a very rough gray rock, with feldspars nearly as large as a pea, biotites, and, in spite of its roughness and richness in biotite, two characteristics common to the younger group of trachytes, very many plagioclases and predominating sanidin. The feldspars have the most distinct and well-developed glass-inclusions, which are not very common in trachytes. The micas are often cleft and broken, as well transversely and longitudinally as parallel to the lamellation, often showing bent stripes. They are no longer in their original condition, but present externally a loose aggregation of dark grains; which extend with a varying width somewhat into the inte-

[1] J. Roth, Der Vesuv u. die Umgebungen von Neapel, 1857, 201.
[2] F. Z., Die mikroskopische Beschaffenh. d. M. u. Gest., 386.
[3] Ibid., 343.

rior. The many biotites present look like mere shadows of the mineral. Hornblende is altered from its original brown color. These two last-named ingredients do not occur in very small microscopical individuals. The groundmass has a microfelsitic base, showing here and there a tendency to form sphærolites, and containing feldspars, ferrite, opacite, and, very rarely, the blue haüyne grains mentioned in a preceding occurrence. These haüyne grains are also included in the feldspars near their borders. There is some apatite.

In other greenish-gray varieties from the same locality [302], with sanidins 2^{mm} long and many excellently lamellated and strongly absorbing biotites: the rare hornblende is altered into an impellucid gray substance, which is seen in reflected light to have an earthy surface. This is a very strange product of decomposition, and it could scarcely be referred to hornblende if the outlines and the directions of cleavage were less distinctly preserved. Rocks from the same region which are in other respects similar to this, do not contain any hornblende and only a little biotite, therein illustrating the freedom of petrographical modification possible to a single rockmass. Sometimes the brown ferrite corpuscles of the groundmass are found to have aggregated into needles and irregularly rectangular forms. Many of the groundmasses seem to contain not a few plagioclases in narrow, striated ledges. A beautiful trachyte [303] bears very fresh feldspars (sanidin predominating), splendid biotite with a black border, but no distinct hornblende, quartz in good hexagonal sections, entirely surrounded by a narrow zone of a fibrous sphærolitic nature, only 0.01^{mm} in width, the limits of the zone both on the side of the groundmass and of the sections being sharply defined. The substance of these zones was, singularly, confined to the peripheries of the quartzes.

The augite-trachytes are also represented in the Wah-we-ah Mountains. A very dark gray rock [304, 305], with a groundmass that seems to be homogeneous, and macroscopically secreted feldspars, for the most part plagioclases, shows, in the sections, to the unaided eye, a large quantity of greenish-yellow grains, excellent augites rich in glass-inclusions, and biotite, but no hornblende. The groundmass is an aggregation of colorless microlites, imbued by considerable recognizable glass. By this structure, and by the predominance of augite and the comparative richness in plagioclase, the rock shows a certain approach to augite-andesites; but geologically these rocks belong to the trachytes. The feldspars contain the most beautiful inclusions of colorless or pale brownish glass. There is some apatite.

The cliffs along Palisade Cañon, Cortez Range, Nevada, are formed of a thoroughly typical trachyte [306]. The feldspars are nearly all sanidin, appearing as dull plates measuring as high as 4^{mm} in the brownish-gray groundmass, which also contains a large quantity of brown biotite laminæ, the individuals of which reach the extreme minuteness of only a few thousandths of a millimetre. There are some pretty thoroughly decomposed remnants of hornblende and some apatite, but no augite. In this somewhat decomposed rock, the magnetite grains have projecting from them very neat dendritical tongues of sesquioxyd of iron.

A remarkable trachyte occurs in Wagon Cañon, Cortez Range [307]. It is a yellowish-gray mass, with quite dim and dull, small feldspars and laminæ of biotite. Between crossed nicols, the feldspars seem to be covered with a glittering dust, partly a product of alteration (probably calcite) and partly an accumulation of strange, minute, greenish particles (probably hornblende). The feldspars have lost their pellucidity, but it is distinctly visible that most of them are simple monoclinic crystals or Carlsbad twins: polysynthetic twin-striation can be detected but rarely. It is sure, however, that the latter structure is now visible wherever it has existed. So in this rock orthoclastic feldspar decidedly predominates, perhaps in a higher degree than in most other trachytic occurrences. Nevertheless, hornblende in small particles enters largely into the composition of the groundmass, which chiefly consists of dull feldspar, and the few tolerably well-preserved crystals show that their original color was green. In nearly all these points, the rock exhibits a considerable measure of similarity to propylite, and it would be so classed if orthoclase did not unquestionably predominate. The biotite has this peculiarity, that quite colorless layers, which are probably muscovite, are intercalated between the brown laminæ of its transverse sections, and that in the darker brown substance of the basal sections, poorly defined, colorless spots appear. Some apatite is found.

A rock from north of Cave Creek, Humboldt Range, should be mentioned among the trachytes, although it differs from them considerably in some points [308]. It is a somewhat rough, gray mass, containing macroscopically very numerous biotite plates; some feldspars, and here and there a grain of quartz: the latter, however, appear almost like strange inclusions. The structure of the groundmass is for the most part unmistakably crystalline-granular. The large, dark mica plates are perforated by an enormous quantity of colorless microlites, part of them showing the most sharp hexagonal transverse sections; and although there may be apatite among them, the needles are present in almost too large numbers (one biotite plate, 0.5^{mm} in diameter, often containing as many as 40) for referring all of them to apatite; and this theory is strengthened by the fact that independent prisms of apatite are abundantly disseminated through the groundmass. The feldspars are tolerably fresh, amongst them much plagioclase; and there is some badly crystallized green hornblende. Fine particles of the hornblende also enter into the composition of the groundmass: this is a peculiarity of propylites, but rare in trachytes. The rock does not contain any quartz except that in macroscopical crystals.

A more distinctly characterized trachyte occurs on the ridge crossing Peoquop Creek, Peoquop Range [309], containing dull feldspars 8^{mm} long. In its prevailing yellowish-gray groundmass, which has a somewhat globulitic, pale, brownish base, are feldspar-microlites and opacite and ferrite grains. There is no trace of biotite; but there is a dirty, yellowish-green product of alteration, the connection of which with hornblende cannot be with certainty determined. Feldspars are largely plagioclases, and the rock is probably a trachyte of the older division. The small hollows of the rock are filled with silicious deposits, which appear macroscopically, in the section, with refracted light, as small, dim, white spots. External layers of these secretions are of a very fine-grained hornstone; next comes a verrucose zone of coarser fibrous quartz, of which the pike-formed ends of the individuals project inwards, and the interior or kernel is composed of very finely fibrous quartz, which presents splendid aggregate polarization between the nicols.

The rock from Emigrant Road, north of Palisade Cañon, Cortez Range [310], has sanidin, which predominates, and a fine microlitic groundmass, probably bearing a considerable quantity of glass base, but neither biotite nor augite. The hornblende is granulated, and has a brown or black color, and is encircled by a dark border, which at its outer margin is disintegrated into single grains. There are quite a good many aggregations of tridymite.

The trachyte from the southern wall of Palisade Cañon [311] resembles that last described. Some of its transverse sections of hornblende are entirely hollow in the middle, being only an empty frame of brown, granulated, altered border-material. In one place, the continuity of this border is broken; and through this gap the groundmass has entered and filled up the whole of the interior (once occupied by hornblende), with its microlitic mass, which is here of the same structure and state as the general surrounding material; a piece of testimony to the strength of the mechanical force which destroyed the hornblende. There are also some sections of quite fresh, pale, greenish-yellow augite. In the groundmass, which contains some coarser elements, there is, beside the ledges and microlites of feldspar, a large quantity of yellowish-brown, indistinctly crystallized, crippled, and somewhat fibrous prisms. They measure as much as 0.05^{mm} in length and 0.015^{mm} in thickness. Although undichroitic, they may very probably belong to hornblende; surely not to biotite or augite, or to any other known mineral. They are chiefly found surrounding in great numbers, and often in tangential position, the hornblende lumps, so that the latter sometimes seem to be dissolving into the encircling periphery. Perhaps they are later hornblende, which crystallized out of the unsolidified rock-mass after the larger individuals of hornblende previously formed had been attacked and destroyed by the molten magma.

On the east base of the Aqui Mountains, Utah, occurs a trachyte [312], which has a fine, porous, grayish-white groundmass containing black biotites and hornblende in quite small prisms. No macroscopical feldspar can be detected. Under the microscope, the rock is enormously rich in biotite, which forms delicate, lighter or darker, brownish laminæ, the most regular hexagons, whose single sides are of different lengths, and even rhombs: sometimes two thin plates of diverse form are found one upon the other. But hornblendes smaller than the macroscopical ones are very rare. Much feldspar is scattered through the groundmass in ledge-formed and broader sections; so also are comparatively many plagioclases. In the groundmass are also some little brownish spots looking like cavities filled with dust, rounded or irregular in shape, and always simply refracting light. They are exceedingly fine, globulitic, glass-stains, but they might very easily be mistaken for noscan, the more because they are usually encircled by a delicate colorless zone, which is indifferent to polarized light. The greatest diameter of these glass spots is 0.06^{mm}. The combination of so widely isolated glass-particles with purely crystalline ingredients (feldspar and mica) is rather uncommon. There is some apatite present.

A very fine trachyte comes from the east end of Traverse Mountains [313]. It bears fresh, beautiful feldspars, built up in regular zones, and filled with splendid glass-inclusions having thick bubbles; abundant dark-brown, entirely unaltered hornblende, having a very distinct cleavage, and lacking the dark border; some biotite plates; not a little pale greenish-yellow augite, between which and the hornblende there is an excellent contrast of color; very much apatite, but no quartz. Most of the feldspars are sanidin, but not a few are plagioclases. The aggregation of feldspar microlites and magnetite grains constituting the groundmass is impregnated throughout with glass base.

The very characteristic and typical trachytes of the Wahsatch Range, which are generally rich in well-developed macroscopical crystals, are similar to the last-mentioned specimen. That from City Creek [314] has a rough, dirty-gray groundmass, in which hornblende and biotite are included. The macroscopical feldspars, among them many plagioclases, are not very distinct. There is an abundance of deep-brown hornblende, with a narrow, black border which is partly well shaped and partly somewhat rounded. One hornblende section was quite pale in the interior, and became colorless by gradual passage; nevertheless, cleavage was evident in it; and in the centre of another a number of gas-cavities were found, also (an exceedingly rare phenomenon in hornblende) some subtil fluid-inclusions, with moving bubble. Intensely brownish-yellow mica, having a fine black border, is present, but it is rarer than hornblende. It often occurs in fragments and shivered pieces. The rock also bears excellent pale-greenish augite with glass grains, and is remarkable for containing tridymite in an abundance and distinctness of aggregation only surpassed by the trachyte from Cerro de San Cristoval near Pachuca, Mexico, where it was first found. It does not properly enter into the composition of the groundmass, being merely attached as an incrustation to the walls of microscopical hollows. There is apatite, but no quartz.

Tridymite also appears in the similar trachyte from East Cañon Creek, Wahsatch [315].

A trachyte from the Upper Provo Cañon, Utah [316], is also very rich in crystals of feldspar and hornblende, but is wanting in biotite, augite and tridymite. The transverse sections of the larger hornblende prisms show that they are beautiful twins; a line parallel to the truncation of the obtuse angle dividing them into two parts, which polarize at the same time with different colors. The apatite contains a yellowish-brown dust. Around the hornblende crystals, the groundmass shows splendid fluidal structure, and contains a large number of sharply hexagonal, blood-red plates of specular iron, some of which are as small as 0.003^{mm} in diameter.

The brownish-gray trachytes from the divide between Provo and Silver Creeks [317, 318] contain sanidin in predominating quantity. A plagioclase crystal, which contained, as do the other feldspars, very distinct glass-inclusions, had, in the interior of one of its glass grains (0.03^{mm} in diameter), an excellent fluid-inclusion with a moving bubble. This remarkable combination of glass and liquid is not unknown in some other rocks; analogous phenomena occurring, for instance, in the leucites of the lava from Capo di Bove and from the Solfatara, Italy. The bubble in the fluid-inclusion was not absorbed when the thin section was heated up to 120° C. Hornblende is mostly blackish and decomposed; but another greenish-gray variety of trachyte from the same locality contained entirely fresh and unaltered crystals. This ingredient here shows the most extraordinary phenomenon of rupture. On the walls of the pores of this rock, numerous lighter or darker, isabel-colored, stalactitic or mammillated, finely stratified, secondary, silicious deposits appear. The tops and warts are usually still covered with extremely delicate fibres. The same kind of material also penetrates through the rock in the form of small veins traversing the groundmass, the feldspars, and even the hornblende. No tridymite exists here, perhaps because the substance just described as filling the hollows and traversing the fissures plays its usual part. The groundmass contains some dark-gray, very fine, globulitic or microfelsitic base.

Trachytes from the mouth of Silver Creek [319] and from near Kimball's in Parley's Park [320] also very well represent this general type of the Wahsatch trachytes, being rich in crystals of sanidin, plagioclase, rather fresh brown hornblende, biotite, often augite, and occasionally tridymite. In the former specimen, the biotites are perforated by numerous apatite prisms, and the feldspar sections are richly set with glass-inclusions.

Another characteristic trachyte of a brownish-gray color occurs on the divide between the North and Middle Parks, Colorado [321]. The beautiful, lucid feldspars, formed in regular zones, are mainly sanidins in simple individuals and Carlsbad twins. Sharp, yellowish-green augite and brown hornblende with a black border, occur together. The augite, rather than the hornblende, predominates. There is some biotite and dusty-brown apatite. The groundmass is an aggregation of microlites, with grains and needles of opacite and ferrite. This rock is in an almost entirely unaltered state, and presents excellent fluctuation phenomena.

A second trachyte from this same region [322] is not unlike that last described. Like the above, it bears predominating sanidin, but also has a great deal of green augite. The hornblende present is in a much smaller quantity, and is generally found in the form of loose aggregations of black grains and dark-brown needles, which show more or less of the original hornblende contours. Small, but thick, yellowish-brown, indistinctly crippled prisms, which are entirely undichroitic, are disseminated through the groundmass in considerable abundance: they may be related to hornblende, but this is uncertain. Biotite is present. The groundmass contains colorless, dazzling, and cracked angular glass-grains, like those found in the trachyte from the Aqui Mountains, Utah (see page 156).

Before concluding this section, the singular quartz-bearing trachytic rocks of the Elkhead Mountains, a part of whose composition is very remarkable, must receive attention.

The rough, gray trachyte from Skellig's Ridge, Elkhead Mountains [323], bears sanidin, hornblende, and biotite, accompanied by some grains which are doubtless quartz, distinctly visible to the naked eye. Nevertheless, the whole habitus of the rock is trachytic, rather than rhyolitic. And all those quartzes which are highly cracked, much fissured, split apart, and burst asunder, possess more of a dull greasy than a bright glassy lustre: they are rounded grains which easily drop out of their places, leaving little hollows. The highest magnifying power does not discover any more quartz than that visible to the unaided eye; and while what is present may not properly be designated as a strange erratic body, it is in every case unimportant and purely accessory, and does not at all influence the aspect of the rock: it is, in short, of no more significance than the presence or absence of tridymite in a trachyte. Under the microscope, this rock is extremely rich in small crystals of hornblende, and even richer in brown mica. It also bears not an inconsiderable quantity of pale, yellowish-green augite. The apparently homogeneous groundmass is composed of feldspar microlites, very small prisms of augite and hornblende, and minute biotite plates, all imbedded in a pale brownish, somewhat globulitic, amorphous base. A remarkable fact is that the quartzes are immediately surrounded by a zone of the most delicate and tender, pale-green spikes or needles, probably augite, gathered in a very intimate but confused aggregation, and appearing in the sections like a green ring of a prickly felt. That the substance of the quartzes is not a secondary infiltration into preëxisting cavities, is proved by their sometimes containing splendid glass-inclusions. The same kind of microlitic ring also encircles the quartzes of the trachytes from the summit of Crescent Peak, Elkhead Mountains [324]. When, in preparing the section, the quartzes fall out, this ring keeps its place as a sort of frame in the cavities, and shows where the quartzes have been.

A rough, reddish-gray trachyte from the summit of Whitehead Peak, Elkhead Mountains [325], is still more remarkable. It presents, beside sanidin, very many cracked quartzes as large as a pea, hornblende and augite, and, what is remarkable, not very numerous but doubtless characteristic half-serpentinized olivines, the sections of which, measuring as high as 0.75^{mm}, are visible even to the naked eye in the slides. The peculiar quartz occurring here is, therefore, accompanied by a mineral which has never before been observed in a sanidin rock. Perhaps the explanation of the formation of this uncommon quartz out of a rock-magma of trachytic constitution may also account for the presence of the olivine in the same mass. It almost seems as if the uncalled-for secretion of free silica had been counterbalanced and neutralized by the contemporaneous production of as basic a mineral as the olivine.

Another highly interesting quartz-bearing trachyte occurs at Steves' Ridge [326]. It bears remarkably good sanidins, measuring more than an inch in length. In other respects than the size of its sanidins, also, this rock strongly resembles the famous trachyte from the Drachenfels, on the Rhine; especially when one observes, with astonishment, a quantity of quartz grains the size of peas, which are riven by multitudinous cracks, and look glassy. The large, imbedded individuals of feldspar are especially remarkable, because, in spite of the proper and natural physical behavior of the sanidin, they possess crystal faces which we have been accustomed to observe only in the old, compact and dull orthoclases of the porphyritic granites, or in those of some felsite-porphyries. The crystals where the trachyte is somewhat decomposed, can easily be loosened and removed from the rock-mass, presenting the faces T (∞ P); z (∞ $\mathcal{P}$ 3); M (∞ $\mathcal{P}$ ∞): P (O P); y (2 $\mathcal{P}$ ∞); even n (2 $\mathcal{P}$ ∞). Sanidins of like richness of crystallization have never been found in trachytes. Beside the sanidin and quartz, macroscopical black biotite is also present in the whitish-gray groundmass. Some plagioclase is dicovered with the microscope. The mica often has a black border. Hornblende is rare, and augite is entirely wanting. As usual, microscopical quartzes could not be detected. The larger quartz grains bear beautiful glass-inclusions. There are some thick titanites, and also apatite prisms. The groundmass is chiefly composed of feldspathic particles. A thin section was made of one of the large sanidins; which thus prepared, showed an almost perfectly water-clear mass which looks at first sight somewhat homogeneous, but the microscope and polarized light prove the contrary. It contains other smaller, differently situated feldspars, simple sanidins and Carlsbad twins, and some (much rarer) striated plagioclases. None of these bodies appear distinctly before polarized light is used. The sanidin also exhibits excellent hexagonal and rhombic sections of pure and homogeneous quartz, measuring as high as 0.5^{mm} in diameter, and polarizing with intensely brilliant colors. Sometimes the quartzes are broken and the pieces separated by the sanidin substance; but the fragments lie so close together that it seems as if they might easily be put together again, and each individual made complete. Lastly, the sanidin contains some groups of pale-green, sometimes dismembered microlites, and a quantity of empty cavities, but neither glass, nor fluid-inclusions.

The trachytic rock from Camel Peak, Elkhead Mountains [327], also bears quartz with a green ring around it and olivine; but it has no large sanidins. Seen under the microscope, augite predominates; but there is only a little hornblende, some biotite and much magnetite. This rock, surely of a more basic composition than the others, therefore resembles the basalts. Perhaps it is pretty closely related to the quartziferous basic rock [328] from the benches along the Upper Little Snake River (see Basalts).

A trachyte from the Little Snake River, Colorado [329], has a dark, bluish-gray, seemingly homogeneous groundmass, in which are a great number of cracked quartzes of the unusual size of a hazel-nut, very glassy sanidins, and large, light brownish biotite plates. Under the microscope, considerable augite appears; but there is no distinct hornblende, and olivine is wanting. To this rather poorly characteristic group belong the rocks from the South Shoulder of Crescent Peak [330], and from Hantz Peak, Elkhead Mountains [331]. The latter, of a brownish-gray color, is somewhat decomposed. One of these eastern trachytic rocks, which forms the mouth of Slater's Fork, Elkhead Mountains [332], contains what is most probably nepheline. It is a yellowish-gray mass, of which the only macroscopical ingredient is long stripes and rays of yellowish-brown mica similar to that in the interesting leucite rocks to be described hereafter. Under the microscope, very little striated feldspar can be detected, but considerable monochromatically polarizing sanidin is discovered; and the instrument also reveals a colorless mineral having short, sharply rectangular sections, which have sometimes become somewhat fibrous on the borders; a

11 M P

phenomenon strongly characteristic of decomposing nepheline. But hexagons of this mineral could not be found in sufficient distinctness to make the identification of it sure. When powdered and treated with hydrochloric acid, the rock very soon secretes flocculent silica; and the inference of the presence of nepheline based upon the microscopical examination is thus corroborated. Neither hornblende nor quartz enters into the composition of the rock; but comparatively numerous, beautiful augites, and occasional olivines, are found. It is a remarkable fact that this sanidin rock, in all probability containing nepheline, and the nepheline-bearing basalts from Fortification Peak, Upper Little Snake River, Yampah River, etc., occur in general not far from leucite rocks.

SECTION II.

RHYOLITE.

The scope of this section will be confined to a description of the proper felsitic or porphyritic rhyolites; for the almost granitic rhyolites (nevadites) are wanting in the examined territories, and the chemically and geologically identical glassy rocks (hyaline-rhyolites), like pearlite and obsidian, will be treated in a section devoted especially to themselves. Of all rocks, these rhyolites most excel in variety and diversity of microscopical structure; and since better facilities for investigation than had ever before been enjoyed, were furnished in this case by the extraordinary number of occurrences at hand, it is highly probable that the following pages will be found to explain all, or nearly all, the most characteristic types of which the rhyolitic structure is capable. Particular attention has been paid to these interesting varieties, examples of which will doubtless be found in studying the comparatively unknown rhyolites of other countries.

Proceeding from west to east, the first occurrence is found on the west side of American Flat Cañon, Washoe [333]. It is an excellent specimen, and represents one of the most widely spread and characteristic types. Its color is a pale yellowish-gray, and it is apparently an almost perfectly homogeneous, felsitic mass. Beside its microscopical crystals, the rock under the microscope is found to be composed, first, of a light sphærolitic material, and, secondly, of lines and strings of dark grains. These latter appear in the slides as short, fathom-like, bent, and undulating stripes, made up of fine, dark-brown, closely aggregated grains. As usual, the undulations of these lines here produce a very distinct microfluidal texture, and wind around larger and smaller microscopical crystals, imparting to them the appearance of eyes. Generally, these stripes have, along their length, short, ciliated, or prickle-like hairs, which, for the sake of illustration, may be compared to thorns upon a stem, consisting of very minute, lineally grouped grains, growing finer towards the projecting end, so that they taper to a point. The spaces between these curved grain-stripes are now occupied by the sphærolitic substance (see Plate VIII, fig. 1, which refers to another rock of precisely the same structural type). The sphærolites are colorless and more or less distinctly fibrous. Often a granular composition of the single, radiated fibres may be observed, particularly in the larger ones. The sphærolites are but feebly affected by polarized light, giving between crossed nicols merely an indistinct shimmer, which seems to be somewhat more intense in the granulated fibrous members. But this is certainly not such chromatic polarization as is proper to really crystalline bodies, even of the most extreme minuteness; so we surely have here to do with an indistinctly crystallitic and imperfectly individualized substance. The dark strings do not pass through the sphærolites, but run between them, marking the outlines of the individuals: because of their fluidal structure, the brown grain-lines have in general, excepting their undulations and curvatures, a parallel direction. The sphærolites do not have the usual rounded shape, but are also for the most part drawn out lengthwise; and very many, if not by far the greater part, of the sections must be derived more largely from longitudinal, cylindrical clubs, fibrated axially or concentrically, than from globular balls. Viewing the whole mass, the conclusion is that the sphærolites do not generally appear isolated, and several of them, or some of the rudimentary stages thereof, are often found developed in close connection between the dark strings; so that the section of one sphærolitic spot sometimes presents a number of centra, or axes of attraction, towards which the fibres tend. Fine hair-like or prickle-like appendages, attached to the surface of the grain-lines, protrude into adjacent sphærolites; and the appearance of the whole mass gives an impression that the intricate system of line-strings was formed first, and that subsequently included sphærolites were developed. As in individualized elements, so in this rock occur colorless, fresh feldspars not exceeding 0.6^{mm} in length, most of which belong to sanidin; and, in one of them, unmistakable fluid-inclusions, with moving bubbles, was detected. In the light of all previously known upon the subject, this phenomenon of a liquid-inclusion in a rhyolitic feldspar at first seemed to us very strange, but it was frequently observed in other feldspars of these American rhyolites; and it was doubtless merely chance that liquid-inclusions were never before found in rhyolitic feldspars, for they have long been known to occur in the plagioclases of nearly contemporraeous basalts. The rock contains but very little quartz, and biotite is present only in the form of microscopical laminæ. Some indistinct sections which were noticed appeared to be decomposed hornblende. There were a very few opaque, black magnetite grains, but no augite. A characteristic feature of the rhyolites observed in this variety is the total absence of microlites. The crystalline ingredients do not appear in very great microscopical minuteness, an enlargement of 60 showing all that are present.

West of Spanish Spring Valley, a rhyolite is found, forming a dike in granite-porphyry [334], externally resembling the former, but having an entirely different microscopical structure. The strings of dark grains so abundant in the other, are wholly wanting here, and the main body of the mass is a true microfelsite (see page 3); an unindividualized substance which is neither homogeneous glass, nor an aggregation of single crystalline particles discernible in ordinary or polarized light. It becomes quite characteristically dark between crossed nicols; indistinct shimmers, as from pin-points, rarely appearing. Very minute, dark grains which are probably opacite, are sparingly disseminated through this feebly gray, almost colorless, typical microfelsite. Here and there a tendency to form fibres is seen; the rudiments observed being always rough, and more frequently arranged along longitudinal axes than around a centre. There are no crystalline secretions at all, except a very few small feldspars: this is a general rule with microfelsitic masses. Microlites also are wanting.

The region of Truckee Cañon, Virginia Range, is very rich in rhyolites, which differ somewhat in macroscopical but still more in microscopical structure. On the foot-hills at Sheep Corral Cañon is a reddish-brown rock [335], in which dull, milky feldspars and small quartzes can be detected with the unaided eye. The thin section appears, under the lens, like finely mottled marble, having reddish and colorless spots. In general, this variety is the same as the Washoe rhyolite first described; but, between the more pronounced and axially fibrous groupings, those thin, line-like strings common to the other are wanting, their place being taken by broader, brownish-red stripes and bands, which also consist of little grains. The aggregation forming these stripes is probably imbued with some glass. These stripes are sometimes shorter than the strings of the other, and are often extraordinarily bent, winding like manifoldly twisted veins through the surrounding mass, or woven together in the form of a net. The nearly colorless fibres are sometimes distinctly seen to be composed of granular particles, more particularly on their thicker, outer ends. The number of quartzes visible macroscopically is not at all increased under the microscope. They are well shaped; and contain even macroscopically the most excellent sphærolitic particles, having a divergent fibration like the fibres of a quill: the quartzes also bear, beside these, splendid glassy but no liquid-inclusions. All the feldspars are sanidins (which fact pronounces the rock not a dacite), and they present a very remarkable microstructure. While naturally inclining to think that their dull aspect is produced by molecular alteration, one observes with astonishment that their quite fresh and clear mass is thickly filled with empty, round and cylindrical cavities, and, surprisingly, with countless small, but for the most part rather distinctly recognizable, fluid-inclusions, containing moving bubbles. These interpositions give the rock its milky, opaque appearance. It is certainly very curious that the feldspars of this volcanic rhyolite should be as rich in liquid-inclusions as the orthoclases in granites or crystalline schists; and that, in striking contrast, its quartz bears only glassy and its feldspars only fluid-inclusions. Biotite, hornblende, and microlites are wanting in this rock.

A collection of rhyolites obtained from the railroad-cut, Truckee Cañon [336], well exhibits the great diversity of characteristics often found in different rhyolitic groundmasses. There are some in which the above-described brown grain-strings appear; the included roundish or angular portions being very well fibrated. The individual members of these roundish or angular portions consist of several systems of fibres arranged close against one another. Where the dark, granular lines run approximatively parallel for some distance, there the intervening mass becomes, not concentrically and radially, but longitudinally and axially, fibrous; and the effect is very beautiful where the parallel fibres, extending from the strings, meet in the middle and form a real linear suture. Aggregations of fibres evenly arranged along a linear axis like the calcareous fibres in a belemnite or in a stalactite, and which are more or less cylindrical in form, in general fill an important place in the rhyolites; and it is the more necessary to lay stress upon this phenomenon, because it has never before been described, and because it is coördinate with the long-known fact of sphærolites possessing a concentric radial structure. In the latter, the attraction acted from a centre, apparently with equal force, in all directions; while, in the longitudinal or axial bodies, it acted along a line; the substance, however, being the same as in the first instance was employed in the formation of sphærolites. This newly discovered manner of arrangement (see, for example, Plate VII, figs. 1, 4) might be named axiolite. It is remarkable that in the older felsite-porphyries, in which thoroughly typical sphærolites are often found, axiolitic formations do not seem to play the same part as in rhyolites.

Other rhyolites from the same railroad-cut present only indistinctly visible grain-strings; these strings or lines being often replaced by irregularly disseminated grains of opacite and ferrite. In these cases, the fibrous material, which develops from a microfelsitic substance, is distributed without any order, or else the groundmass is an indistinctly granular material, which becomes feebly fibrous in some places. But this groundmass is not at all crystalline-granular. It does not show any such state of development, as, for instance, the groundmass of most felsite-porphyries, which is in fact granitic and of the opposite type. There are no distinctly outlined grains here, all blending together in ordinary and polarized light, with the exception of some better-individualized particles which shine forth from the mass between crossed nicols. Rocks of this description contain only a very few of the larger crystalline secretions. In one variety, manifoldly undulating and curving bands of the undeveloped granular material, varying in width, alternate with others which are rather distinctly crystalline-grained, the particles being very fine. The course of the latter, and the contrast of the two, however, are not easily visible without the use of polarized light. Between crossed nicols, the last-described mass is found to be an aggregation of vividly polarizing grains. All the feldspars in this specimen [337], measuring as high as 3^{mm} in length, are sanidins, and contain inclusions which (although one could not positively pronounce as to the mobility of the bubble), judging from their whole aspect, are of a fluid nature. The quartzes are rare, and they contain the most beautiful hexagonal inclusions of glass but none of liquid. There are a few thick grains of magnetite, but no biotite.

In the ravine north of Truckee Road, between Glendale and Clark's Station, a light-gray rhyolite occurs [338]. Viewed macroscopically, it is a quite homogeneous rock, devoid of crystalline ingredients. The proper base is a microfelsitic substance, in which, nevertheless, numerous polarizing grains are disseminated, in some spots so abundantly that they produce a nearly angular aggregation. The rock contains many accumulations of tridymite, which are mostly oval in shape, together with isolated, splendidly fibrous and well-rounded sphærolites that have a strong action in polarized light.

Tridymites and sphærolites were also found in another specimen from the same locality [339], of which the groundmass has the same structure as the other. The mass consists of a striped and spotted mixture of a pale brownish and a colorless substance in which very short, light and dark, prickle-like microlites are imbedded. In polarized light, between crossed nicols, the brownish mass appears dark over nearly its whole extent, being a real microfelsite; while the colorless material, appearing in ordinary light to be homogeneous, is found to be an aggregation of polarizing granular particles.

An entirely different type of structure is found in a rhyolite from above Clark's, Truckee Cañon [340]. It is a light brown rock with a somewhat resinous lustre, and contains sanidins. Under the microscope, it is seen to be a glass-bearing mass, rich in crystals. The feldspars and microscopical quartzes are extremely rich in light brownish-yellow glass-inclusions, which have often become confusedly fibrous, but nevertheless contain a dark bubble. The groundmass is a felt-like aggregation of indistinct microlites, charged through and through with brownish-yellow glass.

The rhyolite from Purple Hills, Truckee Ferry, possesses the microstructure which is rather common in that region [341]. In color, it varies from a brownish-red to a brick-red. Its groundmass is a typical light-gray microfelsite, containing some indistinctly polarizing spots, and it has a very great quantity of fine grains of reddish or brownish-black ferrite and opacite disseminated through it, which are often crowded so close together as to produce rather distinct, curving, fluidal lines. Feldspars 1 ▀▀ in length show plainly, under the microscope, a partial alteration into carbonate of lime; the newly-formed calcite within the feldspar presenting not only the rhombohedral cleavage of the latter, but even the twin-lamellation after — ½ R Similar phenomena were to be observed in the feldspar crystals. There is some rather milky and dull biotite, but no quartz.

Berkshire Cañon, Virginia Range, is a most excellent region for rhyolites. The varieties [342, 343, 344, 345, 346, 347, 348, 349] are chiefly gray, but in part somewhat reddish, and are usually very rich in quartz, and often extremely porous, resembling the so-called millstone-trachytes from the environs of Schemnitz, Hungary. They abound, like the latter, in little veins of a brown, jasper-like substance, and in other silicious concretions. All the rhyolites from this vicinity agree pretty well with each other, but they differ somewhat from those heretofore described. In ordinary light, their groundmass is apparently composed, for the most part, of little colorless grains, and polarized light proves that it is indeed chiefly constituted of angular, feebly double-refracting particles; a structure which is not very common in rhyolites. When arranged in single bands, as they sometimes are, the grains become a little larger; and these coarser crystalline stripes present here and there signs of fluidal structure. Nevertheless, there run through the groundmass linear arcs, half rings, and perfect circles, composed of the very finest black grains densely strung together, comparable in their direction with the roundish cracks which the pearlite sections offer, by reason of their shaly, globular composition. Faint little fissures were sometimes observed running in the middle of these curved, granular lines. Usually, the dark grains are confined to the lines, and are not generally scattered through the rock. These bent lines are often accompanied on either side by a narrower or broader zone, which has a peculiar modification of the prevailing groundmass, a variation of grain-dimension (for instance, a somewhat coarser-grained substance), or a development of fibres the most of which are arranged axially along the lines. Small sphærolites are occasionally found in these rhyolites. Rings of sphærolitic fibres are often seen partly or wholly surrounding smaller quartzes and feldspars, giving them the appearance of being set in frames. It is possible that some glassy or microfelsitic base is present in the granular aggregation of the groundmass; but this cannot be decided with anything like certainty, on account of the fineness of the composition of the mass. Arms of the ground-mass intrude into the quartzes, which are pretty well formed, and their outlines sharply defined; and they contain a few excellent glass-inclusions. The feldspar is partly plagioclase. The macroscopical sanidins are for the most part dull; which, as the microscope shows, is produced by a great quantity of interpositions so extremely minute that their nature cannot be discovered even with Hartnack's immersion No. 10. They would seem to be fluid-inclusions and gas-cavities. Comparatively large fluid-inclusions were observed in the feldspars of one of these Berkshire Cañon rhyolites. Here they measure 0.006^{mm}, but they are decidedly rare. The plagioclase has given rise to the formation of carbonate of lime, which in some cases has been transported from its native place, and deposited in cracks of the ground-mass. It may not be a mistake to suppose that the porosity of these rocks is produced by the far-advanced decomposition of a part of the feldspars. Altered hornblende is present, but very rare. Tridymite and biotite are wanting.

Southeast from Wadsworth, three brownish rhyolites, appearing to be half-glassy, were collected. They possess interesting individual peculiarities, but there is an unquestionable likeness between the three. All contain pearlite flaws, or narrow, dark, granular lines, which are at times rounded, semicircular, oval, and irregularly formed, traversing a glassy mass, giving the appearance of a net-work. In one variety [350] (Plate VI, fig. 1), the glass-mass is nearly colorless, and the cracks are bordered on either side by a narrow zone of true microfelsitic substance, varying from light to dark brown. Thus a manifoldly entangled vein traverses the colorless glass, and gives it the appearance of running hurdle-work. The cracks and their micro-felsitic walls are often cut in obliquely, and so the substance of the latter seems to be broader than it really is; the thickness of one lateral zone not exceeding 0.008^{mm}. The microfelsite is quite isotrope, like the glass into which it gradually passes. By the use of the right focal distance, the chasms of the cracks may be observed on the surface of the thin sections. Often, however, the cracks seemed to be cicatrized. There are no crystalline ingredients except the feldspars, which are clear and pure, and have many cleavage-fissures. So, in its microstructure, this rock in general resembles the well-known pitchstones from Meissen, Saxony; in the latter, however, the substance of the zones bounding the cracks on either side has a better crystalline development. It seems that the formation of the microfelsitic mass happened during the solidification of the rock along the previously opened cracks, instead of being produced in the lapse of time by a molecular alteration of the glass. In another of these three varieties [351] (Plate VI, fig. 3), the same figures are produced by faint, dark, granular lines, which, by their fluidal running, form a net with a multitude of meshes of a long-oval shape. It is impossible to determine with accuracy whether or not, in the midst of these lines, an extremely narrow crack is present. Sometimes it would seem that there is such an one. The lines surround pure glass spots, forming manifold undulations and curves; the interior being brownish-yellow, gradually growing paler and paler towards the outlines, where they come in contact with the dark lines. Here, also, there are no crystalline secretions but feldspars, which latter are often broken into pieces; the single fragments lying close together. The third rock from the same locality [352] (Plate VI, fig. 2) has the same net of dark, granular, fluidal lines. But the included glass, pale yellowish-brown portions of which represent the meshes of the net, is not a homogeneous substance, but distinctly fibrous. The fibres of the single oval or roundish portions are at times concentrically and again axially grouped. Although the fibration is quite distinct, polarized light has but a very feeble effect. Here also the brown color becomes decidedly pale towards the dark lines. Some of the parts, and among them the smallest ones, have not become fibrous, but remain pure, homogeneous glass. There are very few crystalline secretions: sanidins, rare quartzes, and in one slide two unmistakable augite sections were observed.

The specimen from Haws' Station on the Carson River and the outcrop in the valley southeast of the Station [353, 354], are two very similar gray rhyolites, rarely containing feldspars. The groundmass is a mixture of fine, polarizing particles, and colorless glass, the latter appearing, under a high magnifying power, in considerable abundance and much distinctness between the particles. Somewhat coarser-grained aggregations appear in some spots, where the individual, doubly refracting grains have a diameter of about 0.008^{mm}. Brown hornblende prisms occur rarely, and so also do richly lamellated microscopical biotite plates. Almost all the macroscopical feldspars are sanidins in excellent Carlsbad twins.

A fine series of rhyolites outcrop in the vicinity of Pyramid Lake. The most remarkable occur in Astor Pass, between Honey and Pyramid Lakes [355]. This beautiful rock resembles the rhyolite from the Esterel Mountains in the south of France. It is unusually rich in large crystals; bearing quartzes the size of a pea, feldspars half an inch long, small biotite plates and hornblende prisms not as large, with a small proportion of a light-gray groundmass. Under the microscope, the latter is almost wholly crystalline-granular; and it is comparatively so coarse-grained that feldspar and quartz particles seem to be distinguishable. This entirely crystalline microstructure of the groundmass, which bears some relation to the macroscopical one of nevadite, is very rare in rhyolites. The microscope adds another to the crystalline rock-constituents, namely, apatite.

The yellowish-gray, somewhat rough, and porous rhyolite, from the west shore of Pyramid Lake, Virginia Range [356], is a totally different variety from that last described. It looks like a quite homogeneous rock, containing macroscopically only extraordinarily small feldspars; and it has no microscopical quartz, biotite, or hornblende. The groundmass is a microfelsite, with imbedded, feebly polarizing grains and very unevenly outlined feldspar ledges; the latter chiefly Carlsbad twins, but partly triclinic. The microfelsite has become indistinctly fibrous in stripes, which undulate through the groundmass, and produce fluidal phenomena visible to the naked eye in the hand-specimens.

A brownish-gray rhyolite from the ridge at the head of Louis Valley, Nevada [357], is similar to the last-described rock, except in color. Its microfelsitic base contains colorless, feebly polarizing grains, together with dark granules of opacite and ferrite. In the groundmass, and doubtless developed out of it, narrow, longitudinal, brownish-yellow bodies appear, most of them curving like a paragraph-mark, and having a more or less distinct axial fibration. Sometimes a series of thicker ferrite grains runs in the midst of these tails, more distinctly marking their axially fibrous structure. The microscopical aspect of the rock very much resembles that of one to be described hereafter, (represented in Plate VII, fig. 4). Neither quartz nor hornblende is present, but there are many microscopical, splendidly lamellated, brownish biotite plates, which are split and shivered into single leaves in the most extraordinary manner, the folia being often bent (Plate VI, fig. 4).

In strong contrast with this, the brownish rhyolite from Mullen's Gap, Pyramid Lake [358], contains nearly as large a quantity of macroscopical quartzes as of the splintery groundmass. The quartzes bear a few unusually beautiful, light-brown, dihexahedral glass-inclusions, in some of which a little green microlite is present. In some cases, the microlite passes entirely through the inclosure, as if it were the axis of the little body. The ground-mass is principally a microfelsitic base, within which a large quantity of brown ferrite and dark opacite grains have been grouped into rounded lumps, and the base has become, at intervals, somewhat fibrous. Inclusions of brown glass in the quartzes probably date from the time when the separation of the groundmass into light microfelsitic and dark granular matter had not taken place, and when the rock-magma, solidifying homogeneously, still produced a light-brown glass.

Well-developed axiolites (linear aggregations of axially grouped fibres), in color nearly a reddish-yellow, are found in a brownish-red rhyolite from the immediate neighborhood of that last mentioned [359]. Here they are generally much curved and bent, presenting S-formed, semi-circular, and even horseshoe-like figures.

In the hills east of Winnemucca Lake, Truckee Range, is a beautiful yellowish-gray rhyolite [360], containing quartz and feldspar which are almost devoid of foreign interpositions. Here also the groundmass is a microfelsite, having little polarizing grains imbedded in it. An alteration of lighter and darker, or of more homogeneous and more confusedly fibrous bands, has produced macroscopical fluidal drawings.

The brownish rhyolite from the southern end of the Forman Mount-ains, Nevada [361], is more crystalline, and contains many grains and little, short clubs of ferrite, some black-bordered biotite, and what seems to be altered hornblende.

Rhyolites occur in the Forman Mountains, west of Cold Springs [362, 363], with secreted feldspars and quartzes, in a single thin section, of which the groundmass is in one place of a finer crystalline-granular structure, and in others rich in quite light-brownish glassy particles.

The light-colored rhyolites from the Black Rock Mountains are in strong contrast with (for instance) those of Berkshire Cañon, Virginia Range, very poor in macroscopical and microscopical secretions, few of them containing any proper crystalline element at all. This is the composition, too, of the rhyolites from Utah Hill [364], Ruby Cañon[365], Hardin Mountain [366], and Star Cañon [367]. The groundmass (Plate VII, fig. 1) is of a medium character, between that which is so extremely fine-grained as to be indistinct, and the microfelsitic; and it contains straight, curved, and almost circular stripes, composed of thicker, colorless, cuneiform grains placed axially along a central line, a section of which therefore shows two series of roughly wedge-formed grains, with a distinct suture running between them. Bodies of these granular axiolites, which are closely related to the fibrous ones, are very common in the groundmasses of rhyolites. They are more strongly affected by polarized light than fibrous axiolites or fibrous sphærolites.

A rhyolite from Snow Storm Cañon, Black Rock Mountains, contains many spots of colorless glass in a net-work of entwined strings, composed of axial fibres or cuneiform grains [368]. Some quartz crystals, which are partly broken, are each traversed by one of the little strings. Where the strings, or stripes, or cylindrical forms of axial structure, are cut transversely, there the section, of course, looks like that of a little, concentrically radial sphærolite.

Another rhyolite from Snow Storm Ledge [369] possesses the same general microstructure as its neighbor, but it includes very small fragments of strange rhyolitic particles. The latter, with their sharp outlines, very distinctly contrast with the main mass, and are of a very fine-granular or microfelsitic structure; and they, together with angular, broken pieces of quartz, sanidin and plagioclase, and numerous black grains, seem more like foreign inclusions than original crystalline secretions of the rock. The dirty, light-gray specimens do not show macroscopically anything of this partially microplastic composition. It is evident, however, that the rock is not a real tufa, but a massive rhyolite, which has taken up vagrant splinters, grains, and scraps of other varieties with which it has come in contact. These strange fragments are also wanting in other specimens of the same locality [370, 371].

The Pah-tson and Kamma Mountains are rich in rhyolites, characterized by a greater quantity of dark biotite than any described in the foregoing pages. The hills north of Rabbit Hole Spring consist of a very distinctly lamellated rhyolite [372]. The mass contains hardly any secretions, and is neither microfelsitic nor properly crystalline, even differing from that of most felsite-porphyries. It is constituted for the most part of very small and indistinct, uncertain grains and confused, short fibres, which have a rather feeble optical action. In this almost colorless mass, larger and better-polarizing grains (about 0.02^{mm} in diameter) are gathered in little heaps, contrasting with the rest in ordinary light by their yellowish-gray color, and between crossed nicols they appear very distinctly. The faint fluidal lines which give the rock the appearance of being lamellated, are bands, stripes, and layers of these densely crowded heaps, with their better crystalline development.

A rock from the north end of the Kamma Mountains is very similar, possessing the crystalline grains in better development, polarizing so distinctly that they must be considered as true crystalline individuals of feldspar and quartz [373].

The rhyolite from the saddle in the main ridge north of Aloha Peak, Pah-tson Mountains, Nevada, bears macroscopical biotite [374]; but the microscope does not reveal any more than the naked eye can detect. It has no other secretions.

Rhyolite forms the ridge southwest of Pahkeah Peak, Pah-tson Mountains [375], being very rich in crystals and bearing much glass. It has a colorless glass-ground, with imbedded microlites and larger crystals. The latter are microscopical feldspars (some plagioclases), quartzes, and biotites. Feldspars have an enormous number of glass-inclusions; the inner portions of the crystals being in some cases a close aggregation of angular, bubble-bearing glass-grains, in such immediate contact with one another that no feldspar appears between them. The thicker, horizontally lying mica-plates remain almost wholly dark in thin section: the transverse sections, however, become greenish-brown. The rock includes an extraordinary quantity of microscopical biotites in the form of sharply outlined hexagonal laminæ, the diameter of which is only 0.008^{mm}. They vary from dark to light brown, according to their thickness; but their color does not depend entirely upon that alone, for pretty plates were observed, consisting of three or four concentric zones, of different shades of brown, arranged one around another, like frames. In the glass-base, many feldspar-microlites are scattered, and are accompanied by some quite pale-greenish needles, which appear to be related to thicker, indistinctly formed, green individuals probably belonging to augite rather than to hornblende. The base contains numerous oval and rounded, dark-bordered gas-cavities in the glass, whose pellucidity is chemically supplemented by black magnetites.

The peak north of Pahkeah Peak, Pah-tson Mountains, is formed of a beautiful and interesting yellowish-gray rhyolite [376], containing small macroscopical feldspars, quartzes, and biotites (Plate VII, fig. 2). The groundmass is a ramifying net-work of pale-yellowish strings, having an axially arranged composition, of roughly cuneiform grains, or short, thick fibres, with a distinct suture running down the middle. In the most conspicuous contrast, the intervals or meshes of this net-work have become concentrically and radially fibrous, like sphærolites, with a well-expressed centre. These fibrous aggregations of a grayish-yellow color sometimes show, in the sections, alternating lighter and darker concentric rings. Quartzes and feldspars containing glass-inclusions are present. Some large, irregular masses of groundmass, with all its structural characteristics, imbedded in the larger quartzes, prove that this structure is primary. The biotite plates are often shivered and broken into pieces.

A very similar type of rhyolite occurs on the rock from the east side of the Pah-tson Mountains [377]. The rhyolite from the second summit north of Pahkeah Peak possesses a different structure [378]. This rock is rather rich in crystals of quartz, feldspar, and biotite, and does not show any trace

of axial fibration; its groundmass being composed of, long, rough, rudimentary, and perfect sphærolites with more or less distinct centres. The rhyolite
from the south of Pahkeah Peak [379] does not show any fibration at all,
but has an undeveloped, granular groundmass. Biotite is about the only
secretion.

A rock from hills north of Indian Spring [380] is in some places
even devoid of biotite; other specimens [381] showing many macroscopical
feldspars and microscopical quartzes.

The rhyolite from Aloha Peak, Pah-tson Mountains, contains Carlsbad
twins of sanidin, very little plagioclase, and considerable quartz and biotite
[382]. All but the biotite contain good glass-inclusions. The mica is.
partly pretty fresh and partly altered into a dirty brown, granular substance.
The groundmass is microfelsitic, and contains many brownish, partly
pellucid, ill-shaped microlites of an uncertain nature.

Rhyolites of Grass Cañon, Pah-tson Mountains [383, 384, 385], are
related to very characteristic glass-rocks or hyaline-rhyolites, and have
the most varied behavior; in one place containing good sphærolites; in
another, almost free from crystalline secretions; again, devoid of sphærolites,
but bearing fine quartzes (with glass-inclusions), feldspars, and biotites.
The largest part of the groundmass is very finely and indistinctly crystalline, and is traversed by microfelsitic zones, which contain clumsy ferrite
needles produced by aggregations of single grains.

At Karnak Ridge, Montezuma Range, columnar rhyolites occur; single
columns attaining the thickness of a man's body. In light-gray rocks of
this locality [386], large macroscopical biotite plates are secreted. The
groundmass contains many fine crystalline particles, quite pale-green, ill-
shaped grains, and dark grains of opacite. In many places, it has, by
perceptible passage, become radially central-sphærolitic. Axial fibration is
wanting here. The sphærolites, well formed and measuring 0.1^{mm} in diameter, consist of fine fibres, which are nearly colorless about the centre; but,
near the periphery, they have something of an isabel color, so that in low
magnifying power many pale-yellowish rings are seen surrounding colorless
centres. There is also much microscopical, dark-bordered biotite, of which
the granular, outer zone often protrudes far into the interior. The rock also

contains microscopical hornblende in splendid brown sections, clear feldspars, bearing good, thick glass-inclusions, apatite in prisms that are transversely cracked, and pale-green microlites (perhaps augite); the latter being very rare in rhyolitic groundmasses. Quartz is not present. It is a noteworthy fact that apatite only occurs in those rhyolites which are rich in crystals, or else possess a rather crystalline groundmass; and it is wanting in the microfelsitic or indistinctly crystalline rhyolites, although the circumstances necessary to its thorough individualization are as complete here as in other varieties. Thin sections of the outer and inner parts of a little rhyolite column which were examined under the microscope did not at all differ, either in relation to general structure, or to the nature, quantity, and behavior of the included crystalline ingredients.

The rhyolites from Lovelock's Knob, Montezuma Range [387, 388], are made interesting by their microstructure. They consist of, a, very fine, brownish-yellow, granular stripes; b, light-yellow or reddish-yellow axially fibrated strings (both being very much bent and curved, and often presenting section-forms like the letter C); and of roundish, longitudinal bodies, composed either of, c, a distinctly polarizing aggregation of small colorless grains, or of, d, concentric sphærolitic bodies. The strings b, often show in the middle a darker axis, or suture, and a high magnifying power discovers that this is produced by extremely minute black grains, arranged lineally between the ends of the short fibres or wedge-formed particles. There is no well-individualized, microscopical secretion.

Back of Oreana, in the Montezuma Range, a reddish-gray rhyolite, with faint, finely undulating, bluish-gray stripes, occurs [389]. In the sections, short, dark reddish-brown lines are visible, which, under the microscope, prove to be highly altered biotite; the lenses showing them to be an aggregation of dirty reddish-brown grains, in the distribution of which the former lamellation can sometimes be recognized. The prevailing reddish-gray parts of the rock are rich in microscopical biotite plates of the same nature. They are, however, inseparable from accompanying needles, evidently composed of brown ferrite grains; so that there exists here a curious relation between ferrite and decomposed biotite. Both contribute to form the somewhat darker color of these parts of the rock. The bluish-gray stripes show the indistinctly crystalline groundmass to be free from both these elements. There are no secretions beside some very rare, small feldspars.

Rhyolites, northwest from Black Cañon, Montezuma Range, are lithoidal and quite like hornstone, resembling isabel-colored or pale-reddish porcelain, with excellent, fine, undulating fluidal stripes [390, 391, 392]. The groundmass has a very interesting microstructure (Plate VII, fig. 3). It has become very largely fibrous, but the fibres are not grouped into sphærolites or axial, longitudinal bodies, but are arranged in bunches, with parallel aggregation and a slight divergence at the ends, so that they suggest tiny sheaves of grain. These fibrous bunches measure about 0.02^{mm} in length, are heaped together confusedly, and but very slightly affect polarized light. This is a really microscopical structure which strongly reminds the observer of that of artificial porcelain as described by H. Behrens.[1] Stripes about 0.05^{mm} broad, the borders of which are not sharply defined, composed of colorless angular (polarizing) grains, traverse the groundmass, which also contains minute grains and needles of ferrite. There are a few quartzes and feldspars, but no biotite.

The groundmass of the highly lamellated grayish rhyolite from the ridge near White Plains, Montezuma Range, also possesses an interesting structure [393, 394]. With a strong lens there can be seen in the thin sections, a large number of alternating, nearly colorless and duller isabel-colored, narrow, finely undulating stripes. The clearer ones consist chiefly of a water-clear substance, which might, in ordinary light, be taken for a homogeneous glassy base, but between the nicols are discovered to be an aggregation of more or less polarizing grains. A large number of nearly colorless, thin microlites and dark grains and knotted needles of ferrite are imbedded in the clearer stripes, the general direction of the two linear elements agreeing with that of the stripes. The isabel-colored bands appear under the microscope as an aggregation of excellent, parallel-fibrous bunches, almost devoid of polarizing particles, and poor in those microlitic constituents which abound in the lighter-colored stripes. The outlines of the two kinds of stripes are not sharply defined, the passage between them being gradual. This ground-

[1] Poggendorff's Annalen, CL. 386.

mass contains feldspar, large biotite plates, and some hornblende individuals. The stripes wind among and around these crystals.

The gray rhyolite from the Karnak, Montezuma Range [395], has a somewhat trachytic behavior, containing in its groundmass, which is also rather rhyolitic, numerous feldspar microlites (an unusual thing in rhyolites), macroscopical individuals of hornblende and biotite, apatite, and more plagioclase than is common in other rhyolites. There is no quartz. The presence of such a quantity of microlites, however, seems to be merely accidental; for specimens occur at the east base of the Karnak, some of which are rich in microlites, while others are entirely free from them. There is no evidence of a tendency to fibrous structure.

Quartzes nearly as large as a pea are imbedded in the reddish rhyolites from Bayless Cañon, Montezuma Range [396, 397]. They are strikingly free from all microscopical interpositions. Excellent longitudinal, axial fibre systems run through the groundmass, being pale-yellowish along the axis and reddish-yellow along the borders.

The greater part of the rhyolites from the Mopung Hills, at the southern end of the West Humboldt Range, are very poor in crystalline secretions. The rock is usually somewhat porous. Dark and light reddish-gray varieties predominate. They take their peculiar color mostly from grains and short needles of dirty-brown ferrite or from hydrous oxyd of iron, evidently infiltrated into microscopical fissures after the formation of the crystalline ingredients. Often the rocks are highly lamellated, presenting the most characteristic string-structure. In some of the varieties [398, 399], the lamellation is surprisingly complete (see Plate VIII, fig. 2, the representation of another very similar rock). Under the microscope, the rock is seen to consist of alternating colorless and brownish-yellow layers, the line of separation between each being sharply defined, without any passage. The colorless layers are indistinctly granular, or else somewhat fibrous in constitution, acting very feebly upon polarized light, and often containing many short, dark microlites. The brownish-yellow layers of this color are of a globulitic, glassy nature, and do not polarize at all. The delicate, hair-like microlites sometimes consist of a linear grouping of extremely fine, dark-brown grains; and, being generally attached to the surface of the brownish, glassy layers while stretching into the colorless zones, they seem to spring from the globulitic glass; but they are also found isolated in the clearer layers. These are often so extremely thin that a dozen of them together measure only 0.03^{mm}; and, under the microscope, the most delicate drawings appear on them, resembling the finest agate. These systems of layers also curve and undulate very nicely, swelling into beautiful contours around cavities. The single layers are often interrupted, only to be continued at a greater or less distance beyond. The globulitic, brownish-yellow members are generally somewhat narrower than those which are colorless. In such varieties, there are hardly any secretions. Others of the Mopung Hills rhyolites present types of structure already described. Rocks occur [such as 400] which show, in unusual distinctness, the yellowish-brown, axially fibrated, longer or shorter, tail-formed strings, running through a light-gray, ferrite-bearing groundmass, which is principally in an undeveloped crystalline state. The strings are alternately thicker and thinner, show short, wedge-formed ramifications, and are often darker along the suture, and invariably so on the borders (Plate VII, fig. 4). Brownish-green biotite is sometimes met with in such varieties. In other rocks [such as 401], a net-work of brownish-yellow lines, composed of ferrite grains, includes roundish or oval bodies which are observed, in varying distinctness, to be concentrically and radially fibrous. Other varieties possess only rough sphærolitic groupings of fibres in a mainly microfelsitic base.

Other types from the Mopung Hills [402, 403] are also poor in crystalline ingredients, having no quartz, only a little feldspar, and here and there some very much altered biotite; and they are generally made up of a combination of sphærolitic and axially fibrated masses.

In conspicuous contrast with all the more recently described rhyolites, those of the Pah-Ute Range, Nevada, are, for the most part, comparatively very rich, even in macroscopical crystals. The brownish-gray specimen from McKinney's Pass [404] contains quartzes measuring 3^{mm}, and even larger sanidins. The first have very accurately dihexahedral forms, and contain some macroscopical inclusions of groundmass, besides numerous smaller glass grains. The sanidin is entirely fresh, and bears many layers of cylindrical or oval, empty gas-cavities. The groundmass, for the most part, is divergingly fibrous, being composed of long bunches, like ice-flowers. In these bunches, an enormous quantity of dark-brown, bristly, ferritic needles is imbedded, which in their position, curiously enough, follow uniform lines of direction, regardless of the trend of the including fibrous mass. They form strings and bands of parallel needles, and also diverging bunches, which pass transversely through the rough sphærolites. The perfect independence of direction, each from the other, in these chemically different elements, is indeed striking. There is no hornblende: biotite cannot be detected with certainty.

Quartzes in the similar rhyolite from the hills southwest of Granite Mountain, Pah-Ute Range [405], are filled with the most excellent glass-inclusions, measuring as high as 1^{mm}, and are formed in faultless dihexahedrons. The rock contains some long hornblende prisms. There is no sign of axial fibration in either of the two rocks.

The yellowish-gray and brown rhyolites from the Hot Spring Hills, Pah-Ute Range, are, on the contrary, partly very poor and partly inclined to be rich in crystalline secretions. In one place will be found a base belonging between the poorly developed crystalline and the microfelsitic state; in another, axially fibrous strings; in another, more or less distinct sphærolitic aggregations predominating in the groundmass. After careful comparative examinations, no general relation between the microscopical structure of the groundmass and its individualized crystals could be detected. There is one variety [406] which contains large quartzes, measuring 4^{mm}, some sanidius, and small biotite plates, and is composed mainly of very excellent concentric-radial sphærolites in an unusually good stage of development, and they act more vividly upon polarized light here, therefore, than elsewhere. The sphærolites are pretty regularly rounded; and where several of the larger ones, say three, touch each other, the immediate mass around the point of contact has become fibrous; sometimes radially, but always axially where the interval between them had a longitudinal direction. Sesquioxyd of iron has penetrated as a secondary infiltration into the rock, being attached in the form of dendritic lobes to the walls of the cracks in the quartz; and in planes where there has been stronger absorption, they color the sphærolites, in part or wholly, reddish-brown. There also occur here light-brown varieties [for instance, 407], which perfectly agree in microstructure with those from the west side of American Flat Cañon, Washoe (see page 163:—Plate VIII, fig. 1).

The pass below Chataya Peak, Pah-Ute Mountains, is another place where typical varieties of rhyolite are met. Their structure, however, is such as has been already fully described. Most of them are comparatively very rich in moderately large crystals of quartz, sanidin, and biotite. In some of these rocks, the groundmass has this extraordinary composition: alternations of brown, wavy, glassy layers, often containing short dark hairs and lighter microfelsitic or half-crystalline layers (Plate VIII, fig. 2). In others, rough sphærolitic globules are traversed by axially fibrous strings, or by brownish-yellow, microfelsitic bands. The axial strings generally show a darker color along the borders, and are lighter near the axis. Still other ground-masses are chiefly made up of an indistinctly developed, crystalline-granular substance. Through these several varieties of groundmass, ferritic grains or needles are disseminated in more or less profusion. Rhyolites occur here, also, in which crystals constitute fully one-third of the whole mass. The quartzes generally bear good glass-inclusions, and the sanidin often forms distinct Carlsbad twins, and has a beautiful zonal structure. In some varieties of these rocks [such as 408], the sanidins are remarkable for exhibiting the most superb blue color in refracted light, and reach a size of 3^{mm}. This splendid color-phenomenon appears as well in the hand-specimens as in the thin sections. In transmitted light, the thin sections are quite colorless. The blue color is much more intense even than that of the famous "labradorizing" feldspar from Frederiksviirn in South Norway. But, while the luminous shimmer of the latter is connected with the numerous brown and violet-black laminæ and needles which are microscopically interposed in its mass, the same strange bodies being also present in the proper labradorite from the coast of Labrador and from Kiow, Russia, in the feldspars of these rhyolites, no strange particles can be detected, neither needles, nor plates, nor grains, nor a dust-like powder, nor glass or fluid-inclusions. Moreover, these extremely fresh and unaltered feldspars have a strikingly compact mass, being sometimes in transmitted light, there-

fore, not easily distinguishable from the quartz. The latter, however, is
always characterized by excellent dihexahedral glass-inclusions. The cause
of this strange blue color must, for the present, therefore, remain uncertain.
It reappears in the sanidins of some more eastern rhyolites. If the element which shows the color were plagioclase instead of sanidin, the phenomenon could easily be explained as a freak of polarization, produced
by the passage of broken rays from one lamel into another, whose planes of
vibration do not correspond.[1] The rhyolites of this locality which are rich
in biotite, generally possess a peculiar fine porosity. There are varieties
which only exhibit biotite macroscopically, quartz and sanidin being
secreted in the form of very small individuals in the groundmass. Apatite
is comparatively plentiful in these rhyolites, which have many crystals

The greenish-gray rhyolite from north of Shoshone Spring, Augusta
Mountains, Nevada, appears macroscopically to be decomposed; but the
microscope shows it is unaltered [409, 410]. It is rather rich in small feldspars, and occasionally contains quartz. In some places, the groundmass is
radially fibrous, and traversed by fine, undulating axial strings.

An interesting half-glassy rhyolite occurs at Shoshone Springs, Augusta
Mountains [411], consisting of an intimate running-hurdle-work of colorless glass, and somewhat less pellucid bands and stripes of typical light
yellowish-gray microfelsite. The contrast of the two ingredients here is
very instructive as to the nature of the latter. It is evident that the
microfelsite is neither proper glass nor a granular-crystalline aggregation,
and it is not at all affected by polarized light. The glass, often finely
porous, seems to be a little in excess of the microfelsite. Some feldspars
and broken quartzes are imbedded in the rock; and here also bluish, opal-
izing feldspars occur, as in those of the rock from the pass near Chataya
Peak; and here, too, they all present perfectly pure substances.

Excellent rhyolite forms the head of Antimony Cañon, Augusta
Mountains [412]. Its grayish-yellow groundmass consists almost wholly
of longitudinal strings, with good axial fibration, 0.05^{mm} broad. Near the
borders and axis, the strings are darker-colored. Feldspars are rarely met.

<hr/>

[1] Vogelsang, Sur la labradorite coloré. Archives Néerlandaises, 1868, tome III.

At the forks of Granite Point Cañon, Augusta Mountains, a greenish-gray rhyolite occurs [413], which is rather rich in quartz.

In the rhyolite from the mouth of Granite Point Cañon [414], the feldspars seem to bear inclusions of a liquid nature along their borders, but the mobility of the bubbles is uncertain. In the interior of the feldspars, unmistakable glass-inclusions are imbedded. The rock does not contain quartz.

Other rhyolites from the Augusta Mountains are much richer in crystals. From the variety found north of Shoshone Springs [415], which contains sanidin, quartz (bearing many glass-inclusions), and biotite, the imperfectly crystalline groundmass develops in some places the most beautiful radially fibrated globules, their centres being very distinct. The single fibres constituting these sphærolites are of varying lengths, and their surfaces, therefore, have the appearance of being finely fringed. In other places, long axial fibrations traverse the groundmass.

The bluish-green rhyolite, somewhat like hornstone, from the head of the ravine south of Shoshone Pass, Augusta Mountains [416], has the same porphyritical crystals, and strongly resembles the last-described rock in structure. But the sphærolites are more nicely fibrous; and these, as well as the axially fibrous strings present, are immediately surrounded by a zone of groundmass having a better crystalline development than the other; and between the nicols it has a spotted appearance something like a mosaic.

A grayish-black rhyolite occurs in the ravine south of Shoshone Pass [417], which has the porphyritical characteristics, together with brown glass, in considerable abundance, and sanidin. The groundmass is like that represented in Plate VI, fig. 3. The most of these rocks have very small angular fragments of strange varieties of rhyolite imbedded in their mass, of which the prevailing groundmass differs from that of the others in color and in microscopical structure.

In the rhyolite from the ravine north of Shoshone Pass [418], the bluish, labradorizing sanidins again appear.

Reddish-yellow varieties from this same locality [for instance, 419] bear, besides sanidin and quartz, an abundance of biotite, which is penetrated by numerous dazzling prisms of apatite. Light-brownish axial strings of great beauty traverse the groundmass.

Profuse secretions of quartz, sanidin, and biotite are also found in the rhyolites from Clan Alpine Cañon, Augusta Mountains. That from Clan Alpine Mine [420] also contains plagioclase, and its sanidin is very rich in cylindrical and rounded, empty cavities. Long arms of the groundmass are often found protruding into the quartz, and, in its hexagonal sections, hexagonal zones of the groundmass are imbedded; and the quartz is full of isolated rounded inclusions of pure glass, with bubbles, and of the half-fibrous groundmass.

The variety from the head of Clan Alpine Cañon [421] is rich in the same crystals. The brownish-yellow groundmass has become finely but more confusedly fibrous; in some places, the fibres being arranged in parallel, bunch-like systems. It does not act upon polarized light. Faint, black hairs are scattered without order through this mass; but they are more numerous in the immediate vicinity of the quartz crystals. There is no sign of axial fibration.

A rock from the mouth of Clan Alpine Cañon [422] bears, beside large quartzes and sanidins, colorless bodies which seem to be perfectly homogeneous in ordinary light, but prove, in polarized light, to be aggregations of powerfully double-refracting grains, reaching a size of 0.05^{mm} (probably quartz and feldspar), and excellent sphærolitic bodies having a comparatively strong action in polarized light, sometimes almost producing the black cross. In some cases, the better-developed sphærolites of three concentric zones vary in color from dark to light. The colorless portions of the groundmass contain an unknown mineral of a vivid yellow color, in the form of sharp, irregularly shaped, compact grains, and also sharp, rhombic, colorless, little plates 0.02^{mm} long, lying one above another, like tridymites, which are also indeterminable.

The quartz in the rhyolite from the cañon south of Clan Alpine Cañon [423] bears as beautiful glass-inclusions as may be seen anywhere.

Rhyolites from the Desatoya Mountains are also very rich in crystals. On the east side, a black variety, appearing to be very glassy, occurs [424], containing microscopically a deep, dark-brown glass, which even in very thin sections is but slightly transparent, and, remarkably, is almost wholly free from microscopical products of devitrification. The larger quartzes, sanidins, and plagioclases of the rock are filled with inclusions of the dark glass, whose shapes are more like long stripes and rays than roundish grains.

A rhyolite from the mouth of New Pass, near the stage-road [425], is enormously rich in quartz, which constitutes perhaps one-third of the whole mass. Its groundmass is in a peculiar state. The pale-yellowish substance composing it does not polarize at all, except in the case of very rare and very minute, indistinctly individualized particles; yet it is neither a real glass nor the common microfelsite. When carefully examined with the higher magnifying power, it is evident that the groundmass is composed of extremely small globules, heaped together like clusters of grapes or bunches of blackberries; their forms being such as have been named by Vogelsang cumulites.' The single globules are distinctly concentric, at least, not evidently fibrous. Toward the centre, they are a little darker, and merge into one another at the borders. Short, axially fibrous strings traverse this aggregation of isotrope cumulites. Vogelsang has observed similar cumulitic groundmasses in Hungarian rhyolites. In the rhyolites of the Fortieth Parallel, this development seems to be very rare.

Labradorizing sanidin is again found in another rhyolite from the New Pass, Desatoya Mountains [426], and, as usual, it is free from interpositions. The rock contains quartzes, with fine glass-inclusions.

A brownish rhyolite from Gilbert Creek [427] bears many, but very small, quartzes and feldspars, and microscopical biotites, and is traversed by fine axially fibrous strings.

The reddish-brown rock from the head of South Cañon, Desatoya Mountains [428], is very rich in larger crystals, and bears comparatively very thick, dark, grayish-yellow to reddish-yellow sphærolites, polarizing in flame-like stripes. The sections also show concentric, differently-shaded rings, often suggesting the appearance of an old tree-trunk.

Large sphærolites, with distinct centres, are also developed in the rhy-

_____

'Die Krystalliten, 1875, 134.

. I

olites from the New Pass Mines [429]. In some places, axially fibrous and often dichotome bands run through the sphærolitic aggregations; in others, the substance of the latter, gradually becoming indistinctly fibrous, passes into a cumulitic matter, the shaly globules of which are unaffected by polarized light. The yellowish-gray groundmass of this variety, resembling hornstone, contains numerous crystals, among which are many biotites and microscopical apatites.

Quartzes of the rhyolite from the Eastern foothills, New Pass Mountains [430], bear unusually large and clear glass-inclusions, measuring 0.045^{mm} in diameter, the bubbles of which are often remarkably sac-like, curved and twisted (Plate I, fig. 16). Included particles of the groundmass, also bearing bubbles, which have been pressed into sharply hexagonal forms, accompany the dihexahedrons of pure glass in the same crystals.

The saddle northeast of the New Pass Mines also consists of rhyolite.

Rhyolites from Mount Airy, Shoshone Range [431, 432], show an excellent fluidal structure, in the form of groundmass-stripes differing somewhat in color, several of them being axially fibrous. There is no sign of a tendency to form sphærolites. The numerous quartzes and sanidins are entirely free from interpositions, excepting a few gas-cavities.

The rhyolite from Jacob's Promontory, Shoshone Range [423], is of a quite different type, being largely a half-glassy rock. The groundmass becomes dark gray in the section, and is a felty aggregation of small microlites, charged through and through with glass, so that it very much resembles the characteristic groundmass of augite-andesites. Nevertheless, the secreted crystalline ingredients are those of a genuine rhyolite. The rock contains quartz, largely predominating sanidin, accompanied by a little plagioclase, an abundance of excellent brown hornblende with a dark border, biotite, and some lighter augite crystals, with exceedingly abundant glass-inclusions.

A rhyolite from the Hot Springs, Reese River Valley [434], is not glassy, but is rather rich in crystals, resembling those from the Desatoya Mountains.

Rhyolites from the south of Ravenswood Peak, Shoshone Range [435], are much poorer in secreted crystals than the latter, and possess a brownish groundmass, which is a fine combination of very distinctly fibrous, sphærolitic and axiolitic bodies. The latter often have a lighter-colored middle suture, because the axially arranged fibres do not here join each other closely. Delicate, brownish stripes and lines of ferrite-grains wind among the individuals, marking their limits distinctly.

Rocks of Reese River Cañon, Shoshone Range [436], are perhaps rhyolitic tufas. They consist of roundish, dirty-gray bodies of groundmass, rich in ferrite, especially so along the borders. Between these isolated rhyolitic particles, run bands and veins of a colorless substance. In ordinary light, they seem to be homogeneous; but, in polarized light, they are proved to be composed of single, wedge-formed grains, exhibiting a very vivid chromatic polarization. There is no doubt that they belong to a fibrous, granulated hornstone; and it is highly probable that this quartzy material filled up the intervals between the rhyolitic fragments secondarily.

At the north spur of Ravenswood Peak, Shoshone Range, a rhyolite occurs [437], which has been colored a brick-red by dusty ferrite grains, aggregated in lumps, heaps, and long stripes. Those parts of the ground-mass which are poor in ferrite, or free from it, have a delicate, sphærolitic fibration. In this mass, also, are fragments of other rhyolites, as large as 1.5^{mm}, and macroscopically visible in thin sections, being more distinct here than in the hand-specimens. The groundmass is opaque, and of a dark, dirty greenish-gray color.

The rhyolites of the Fish Creek Mountains are for the most part extremely rich in crystals. The quartzes are often evidently broken, and sometimes have a very dark color, like that of the so-called smoky topaz or cairngorm-stone. This color is produced in the quartzes by deposits of hydrous oxyd of iron, or of oxyd of iron, in the numerous fissures of the crystals. These rhyolites also occur on the summit of Mount Moses, Fish Creek Mountains [438]. Their sanidins are often accompanied by a little plagioclase, and both are rendered remarkable by containing an enormous quantity of glass-inclusions and empty cavities; which latter are rare in quartz. In one place, the groundmass is microfelsitic, with small and rare polarizing points; in another, it is in an imperfectly-developed, and in still another a better-developed, crystalline-granular state, and ferritic powder is scattered at intervals through it. Sphærolitic or axial fibration is generally wanting. In one of the examined specimens, however [439], axially fibrated strings of a rather yellowish color were visible. These strings do not, as usual, run singly; but two or three are generally found intimately associated.

A gray rhyolite of Storm Cañon, Fish Creek Mountains [440], has sanidins which are extremely rich in pores, and its groundmass shows a pretty good crystalline development. Occasionally, feeble rudiments of axial bands are seen. The thick magnetite grains of this rock, which are doubtless quadrangular, are covered with a thin, whitish crust, like that which is sometimes seen to veil titanic iron.

The isolated ridge between Winnemucca and Fairbank Point [441] consists of a curious rock, seeming, in the hand-specimens, to be slightly rough, like a trachyte; but it contains quartzes as thick as a pea, and very large sanidins, together with microscopical biotite and apatite. The ground-mass does not contain any trace of either sphærolitic or axiolitic fibration, but is entirely crystalline, polarized light showing it to be constituted of double-refracting particles, which are most probably quartz and feldspar. Nevertheless, this aggregation of colorless grains contains a great abundance of rounded, microscopical pores, a phenomenon extremely rare in crystalline groundmasses.

At the west end of the Havallah Range, Nevada, is a brownish rhyolite [442], which is very rich in quartz, and bears highly porous sanidins. The larger part of the groundmass is remarkably sphærolitic, and this is the more plain because the centre and periphery of the fibrous globes are generally of a somewhat duller and darker gray color.

Golconda Pass, Havallah Range, yields a brownish-red rhyolite [443], which bears fewer crystals. There is some biotite, and here and there pretty, axially fibrous strings. Sphærolites are wanting. The color of the rock seems in part to be of secondary origin, resulting from infiltrated combinations of iron, but it also contains ferrite grains as a primary ingredient.

The rhyolites from the base of the cliffs of Shoshone Mesa, Nevada [444, 445], do not have any signs of fibration, either radial or axial, except around the larger crystals of the rocks, which are encircled by feeble and confused fibres. Almost the whole of the groundmass has a pretty good microcrystalline development, being chiefly composed of colorless particles, with grains of black opacite and brownish ferrite, beside needles of the latter. No microfelsitic matter is visible. Of the larger colorless ingredients, many have a strikingly accurate rectangular outline; but, although some forms occur which might be taken for irregular hexagons, it would not be warrantable to ascribe them to nepheline.

One variety from this locality contains quartz, bearing especially good glass-inclusions, very little plagioclase, many sanidins, and proportionally considerable apatite. Another variety is devoid of quartz, both as an ingredient of the groundmass and in the form of larger crystals; but it contains much plagioclase.

Rhyolites from the top of Shoshone Mesa, east side [446, 447], are less distinctly crystalline than the last described, and they are remarkable for containing tridymite. Long, prismatic bodies are seen in the sections of both specimens: in transmitted light, they appear black, opaque, and somewhat granular; but, in reflected light, they have a dirty, brownish-red color. These bodies are most probably altered biotite.

A light-gray rhyolite from the spurs of the River Range, in the region of Susan Creek [448], is free from macroscopical crystalline secretions, with the exception of a very few, little quartzes; and it is so homogeneous that a likeness between it and porcelain is suggested. Under the microscope, the groundmass is seen to be chiefly an aggregation of small, polarizing grains, no thicker than 0.05^{mm}, which are probably quartz and feldspar. The mass is intricately striped with lines of a rough, axial structure in arabesque drawings, and is almost devoid of any optical action. These stripes sometimes form complete rings around small particles of the crystalline mass.

The rhyolite from Sunset Gap, Rock Creek [449], Nevada, is extremely rich in biotite, with which is mingled sanidin and quartz; and the groundmass bears excellent axially fibrous stripes.

Another variety from Rock Creek [450] is a glassy, brown rock, having a groundmass like that represented in Plate VI, fig. 3; but it bears only sanidin, with a very little plagioclase, and here and there some vividly green augite. Quartz, hornblende, and biotite are not present.

A most remarkable rhyolite is taken from the walls of Upper Cañon, Rock Creek [451]. In the hand-specimens, reddish and grayish stripes, which are more or less indistinct throughout their whole length, may be observed, the first-named of these showing macroscopically a sphærolitic structure. The microscope shows the groundmass (Plate VIII, fig. 3) to be constituted almost wholly of an aggregation of more or less perfectly-formed sphærolites, with a very fine and delicate but moderately distinct radial fibration, and quite an obvious centre. The usual, light-isabel-colored sphærolitic balls contain transparent, prismatic, ferrite needles of a dark-yellow, reddish-yellow, or brownish-red color, their maximum length being 0.045^{mm}, arranged loosely but regularly around given centres. This appearance of ferritic stars in the section is very pretty; the needles composing them often varying in length and thickness. Reddish stripes of the hand-specimens are composed of sphærolites richer than usual in these ferritic microlites, grayish stripes being produced by the small number of them here interposed in the sphærolites. Quartz bearing the most perfect glass-inclusions is present.

Rhyolites from Independence Valley, north of Tuscarora [452, 453], appear somewhat trachytic. The groundmass is not very distinctly granular, and lacks all signs of any tendency to fibration or to waving fluidal structure. Quartz is comparatively abundant. Partly decomposed feldspar, altered hornblende, and much biotite are also present.

Specimens from the west slope of Nannie's Peak [454, 455], Sectoya Range, are poor in crystals, containing only quartz with beautiful dihexahedrons of glass, sanidin, and biotite. The groundmass is in some places indistinctly sphærolitic; but there is no sign of axial fibration.

The brown variety from the east of North Fork, Humboldt [456], is somewhat decomposed, containing an enormous quantity of roundish, brownish-yellow ferrite grains; and there are no larger crystalline inclusions.

A more typical rhyolite is found in the yellowish-gray specimen from Station 39, Toyabe Mountains [457, 458]. Quartz, sanidin, and biotite are present. The imperfectly granular groundmass, inclining to the micro-felsitic state, presents pretty good sphærolitic fibrations and axially fibrous strings.

In a variety of hand-specimens from different localities, very small angular fragments of a blackish-gray, largely half glassy rhyolite occur, containing, under the microscope, colorless feldspar-microlites. The larger of these sharply-limited fragments, which strongly contrast with the including rock, appear macroscopically in the thin sections as dark points or dots. It is strange that these imbedded particles should be so small in size, several having been found which were only 0.3^{mm} in diameter.

The dark-gray rhyolite from the divide between Susan Creek and the North Fork [459] is rather rich in crystals, with which is mingled some biotite and hornblende, the latter of a rust-red color. The whole of the groundmass is confusedly fibrous, the fibres being short. Brownish and reddish-yellow ferrite needles are scattered without order through the mass. In short, this groundmass has the same composition as that of the rock from the summit of Upper Cañon, Rock Creek. There has been, however, no tendency to central attraction here: if there had been, sphæro-lites and radial groupings of ferrite needles would have been developed.

At the top of the hill above Camp Cañon is a confusedly fibrous rhyolite [460], lacking larger secretions, but bearing a great abundance of biotite.

In Reese River Cañon, Shoshone Range, occurs a good rhyolite [461], which has but few secretions of quartz and sanidin, and in rare instances biotite. The pale brownish-yellow groundmass is a good combination of fibrous heaps, having a central radial structure and axially fibrous strings. The thick fibres show proportionally strong optical action.

West of Carico Lake, in the foot-hills of the Shoshone Range, a grayish-white, very quartzose rhyolite occurs [462]. Its feldspars are rather porous, and are decomposed along the outlines, producing a dull, milky border around the clear, transparent kernel; a phenomenon common to the old felsite-porphyries. The rock also bears many beautiful fresh biotites of a comparatively light color; but hornblende is wanting. The groundmass is confusedly fibrous, its individuals being short.

From a neighboring locality in the Shoshone Range, a splendid rhyolite was collected [463], bearing numerous quartzes as large as a pea, in which are excellent, pale-brownish, hexagonal glass-inclusions. These are often covered with a star of six rays, the rays apparently protruding over the borders (Plate I, fig. 15). The rock also contains biotite, but no hornblende

In the southern end of the Wah-we-ah Mountains are some rhyolites [464, 465], which are very rich in quartz, feldspar, and large, fresh plates of biotite measuring 4^{mm} in diameter. Of the quartzes, many have the dark-brown color of smoky topaz; but they do not possess any microscopical peculiarity of structure. Of the feldspars, a comparatively large number are plagioclases. The biotites have a narrow black border, and include a great quantity of black grains and long colorless prisms, a part of which are doubtless apatite. The groundmass of this rock is better crystalline-granular than are those of most rhyolites of this type. It consists of colorless particles which are probably quartz, somewhat duller bodies which have been taken for feldspar, and microscopical brown mica plates, all mingled into an intimate aggregation. In spite of its granular composition, a great number of dark-bordered pores are disseminated among its elements.

The Roberts' Peak group offers a rhyolite [466], which has but a very little quartz; its felsitic groundmass looking homogeneous, and being of a violet color. This mass is imperfectly crystalline, wanting in fibration, and bears blackish-brown and reddish-brown prickly and crippled ferrite needles, scattered without order, together with small, microlitic, colorless feldspar ledges, which are, for the most part, striated. This latter phenomenon is very rare in rhyolites. The larger feldspars contain many black opacite grains, and are devoid of proper glass-inclusions; but devitrified, slaggy inclusions of feeble pellucidity are present in them. There is some biotite and apatite in the groundmass. This variety, therefore, resembles trachyte.

Rhyolites of Wagon Cañon and Rhyolite Cañon, Cortez Range [467, 468], are distinguished from most other rhyolites in these respects: a, their feldspars are, for the most part, altered into a dull, half-kaolinic substance; b, they lack evidence of any tendency to develop fibrous, sphærolitic or axiolitic aggregations; c, their groundmasses, which are in a very imperfectly crystalline state, and are rich in ferrite, contain colorless feldspar-microlites; and, d, they are absolutely free from biotite. Most of the rocks from this locality are rich in quartz, which is very pure, including only narrow lines of empty pores and beautiful, isolated glass-inclusions. The rhyolite from the Roberts' Peak group belongs, in certain respects, to this type.

A specimen from north of Piñon Pass, Piñon Range [469], is a normal rock, exceedingly rich in crystals, particularly quartz and biotite, the latter very much shivered. The groundmass is in an undeveloped crystalline condition, and is rich in ferrite, with here and there the rudiments of a confusedly fibrous state.

At Pleasant Valley, south of Pine Nut Pass, Piñon Range, a remarkable rhyolite occurs [470], composed of large quartzes and sanidins, which are full of dark pores, but wanting in proper glass-inclusions. Under the microscope, the groundmass, which is not very compact, shows a remarkably well-developed crystalline-granular structure, so perfect, indeed, as to surpass that of any rhyolite ever before seen, and to strongly resemble that of granite-porphyries. This microscopically coarse-grained aggregation consists of roundish, water-clear grains of quartz, more numerous, roughly quadrangular sections of feldspar, which are somewhat dull, and often somewhat fibrous, rare plates of brown biotite, and grains of ferrite. This decidedly Tertiary rock contains, moreover, some pale-reddish grains of perfectly isotrope garnet, measuring up to 0.2^{mm} in diameter. This, by the way, is not the first time garnets have been observed in rhyolites. Macroscopical individuals of garnet were found by v. Richthofen in the rhyolite from Mount Hradek, Hungary, and others were discovered by v. Hochstetter in the felsitic rhyolite from Mount Misery, Malvern Hills, South Island of New Zealand.[1]

In Clover Cañon, East Humboldt Range, a dark glassy rhyolite, having a resinous lustre, occurs [471]. It is remarkable for containing a large number of quartz-grains, which are traversed by a multitude of cracks, the cracks being filled with dark yellow ochre. The sanidin and plagioclase contain an enormous quantity of half-glassy inclusions, which are so thick as to form a sort of net-work. The quartzes of this rock, contrastingly, do not have any inclusions at all. Fresh crystals, which are quite undichroitic and of a grass-green color, (doubtless augite), and thick magnetites, are also present; but biotite and hornblende are wanting. The groundmass consists

---

[1] v. Hochstetter, Geologie von Neuseeland, 1864, 203.

of a brownish glass, densely crowded with colorless feldspar-microlites and pale-green microlites, which are in all probability augite rather than hornblende. Here and there in the mass, however, may be seen larger microscopical spots of pure glass-base.

A rhyolite from the Antelope Hills, south of Leech Spring, Nevada, presents macroscopically faint, undulating stripes or waving fluidal phenomena, which the microscope discovers to be an alternation of fine, sphærolitic fibrous strings, with strings of an imperfectly granular nature, without any tendency to fibration. The rock contains the mos⁺ characteristic concretions of tridymite, a few quartzes, some biotite, apatite, and highly altered hornblende.

The specimen from the Antelope Hills, southeast of Leech Spring [472], does not contain tridymite. The sanidins bear extremely large glass-inclusions with indented, pronged outlines. This peculiarity of the periphery is quite common to the glass-inclusions of sanidins; but it never happens in quartzes, the glassy particles of which always have a linear border.

Rhyolites of the Wachoe Mountains embrace many varieties. One, a very compact rock resembles hornstone, is pretty rich in quartz and feldspar, both with beautiful glass-inclusions [473]. Under the microscope, the groundmass is made up of a combination of axial and central fibrations, the former varying from yellowish-gray to greenish-gray. There is no biotite.

Another rock from the Wachoe Mountains [474] contains, in a dirty, rhyolitic groundmass rather rich in crystals, black, seemingly half-glassy stripes, possessing a greasy lustre. These stripes consist of colorless or brownish glass, in which an enormous number of extremely fine black grains are aggregated. They run parallel to one another; but are very much distorted and curved. The limits between these stripes and the rhyolitic groundmass are very sharp; there being no sign of passage from one to the other, so that the stripes seem very much like included fragments. Quartzes of the rock contain the most beautiful inclusions of pale-brownish glass, often with several bubbles.

At the north end of the Wachoe Mountains, a pale-reddish rhyolite occurs [475], in which a number of dark red, jasper-like stripes and spots are visible to the naked eye. Many quartzes and sanidins are also present. The dark-red parts of the mass are found, by the use of the microscope, to consist of a small quantity of a homogeneous, yellowish-red, glassy substance. They are, for the most part, excellently sphærolitic, being made up of bristling globes densely heaped together. The centres of these balls are a more intense red; the looser ends of the bristling fibres being more yellow. At their outer extremities, all of these globes and half-globes have their limits towards the lighter portions of the groundmass, and their bristling points project into it. This effect is particularly pretty where one globe intrudes into a quartz, and its tender, yellow fibres pierce the water-clear mass. The prevailing light groundmass has for a base a genuine pale-yellowish-gray microfelsite, in which, beside small, colorless, polarizing particles, are dispersed the most perfect, small, isolated, fibrous globules; intimate aggregations of these forming the dark red stripes mentioned above. A lighter color is here merely the result of the presence of a smaller quantity of sphærolites; so it is evident that the red portions are only massive concretions of a primary rock-element, not strange fragments. Larger quartzes and feldspars are very poor in microscopical inclusions, with the exception of a few glassy and half-glassy grains in the quartzes. A remarkable phenomenon discovered in this genuine rhyolitic rock, was a quartz which contained the most characteristic fluid-inclusions, with moving bubbles, in as great profusion as they are found in the quartz of granites and gneisses. This rhyolitic quartz individual is the only one of the thousands and thousands that have been examined with the microscope which has been found to bear fluid-inclusions. In this connection, the fact is significant that to this curious quartz was joined a quite dull and entirely decomposed feldspar, like those in granites; all the rest of the observed feldspars in these rhyolites being extremely fresh and perfectly pellucid. Since so many of these rhyolites contain sharply angular, microscopical fragments of other rhyolitic varieties, the observer is permitted to conclude that this singular quartz and the adjoining altered feldspar are also foreign inclusions.

The seemingly half-glassy rhyolite [476] from Spring Cañon, Wachoe Mountains, is rich in crystals containing sanidin, a comparatively large amount of plagioclase, beautiful dark-brown hornblende, less pale-yellowish augite (with penetrating apatite prisms), but no quartz, therein approaching trachyte. Hornblende sometimes has a black border of more or less intensity; and some black, impellucid, granular, tail-formed bodies, which are present, appear to be altered hornblende, although they lack the slightest trace of the original brown color. The groundmass is a dense aggregation of almost colorless microlites intimately imbued with glass. Along traversing cracks, the groundmass has become quite dull and almost impellucid. The glass-inclusions of all the crystalline ingredients except hornblende are enormously large: in the hornblende, they are small and rare.

Desert Buttes, Utah, furnishes a normal rhyolite [477] of quite a light-grayish color, bearing quartz, which is rich in glass-inclusions and feldspars. The groundmass is imperfectly granular, showing, at intervals, a tendency to form rough sphærolites. Biotite and hornblende are wanting, but the tridymite, occasionally found in hollows, seems to be of a secondary nature; for it is often found overlying iron-ochre or earthy ferrite.

The interesting rhyolite from Passage Creek, Desert Gap, Nevada [478], has macroscopical stripes 2^{mm} broad, much curved and undulated, which wind around and among the sanidins and quartzes and also encircle some cavities with lithophyses, which are present. Under the microscope, these stripes are found to be individually composed of three different zones: a, grayish-yellow middle zone, quite sphærolitic, with small fibres, and rich in ferrite needles, which give the zone a somewhat darker color, and are sometimes grouped radially in the sphærolites; b, bordering this, on both sides, dull-gray zones, not fibrous, and seemingly rather homogeneous, which have fewer ferrite needles but a considerable quantity of ferrite grains; c, boundary zones, extending along the two sides, of almost crystalline aggregations of colorless grains, destitute of ferrite, developing out of zone b : the third zone, peculiarly, surrounds the cavities.

The rhyolite from Forellen Butte, Nevada [479], seems to be a brecciated variety, composed of, a, broken crystals of sanidin and quartz, the latter shivered into a great multitude of pieces, one individual sometimes being separated into fifty parts, all lying close together; b, pieces of dark-gray rhyolite, resembling hornstone, rich in glass; c, stripes and bands of a dull whitish rhyolite, including an enormous number of sharply angular quartz-splinters, and winding like a stream among the other ingredients. This is surely not a clastic rock deposited in water, but an eruptive breccia.

Upon the northeast slopes of the River Range, a light-gray rhyolite is found [480], which has excellent axially fibrous strings, splitting two or three times into diverging ramifications, and very much curved. The rock is extremely poor in opacite and ferrite. There are very fine microscopical crystals; some feldspar and quartz being occasionally detected. Under the microscope, nearly all the feldspars are sanidins. Finely lamellated biotite is present.

On the east slope of the Cortez Range, north of Palisade Station, a yellowish-gray rhyolite, very similar to that last described, occurs [481]. It contains some plagioclase but no quartz, with sanidin as the only micro-scopical constituent. The groundmass is a finely sphærolitic body, with very thin and delicate black hairs grouped between the radial fibres. There are numerous cavities which are covered with a verrucose or papillary, light-gray crust, consisting of a number of fine layers, which are often of different colors. This substance, which is not fibrous and is not affected by polarized light, seems to be a hyalitic opal-matter.

The rhyolites next to be described are from the Mallard Hills, Nevada. In strong contrast with the last-described rocks, these varieties are all characterized by large quartzes, often exceeding the size of a pea. In the rock from North Point, Mallard Hills [482, 483], the light-brownish groundmass looks somewhat trachytic, macroscopically; but, under the microscope, it is very beautifully sphærolitic. The large, fibrous sphærolites consist of loosely grouped, single bunches, the ends of which diverge, like the straws of a broom, from a usually darker centre.

Light-colored rhyolite from Deer Cañon, Mallard Hills [484], shows macroscopically feldspars and larger quartzes. The groundmass is chiefly a distinct aggregation of colorless ledges and grains, and black grains. Larger crystals are surrounded by a narrow ring or zone, visible even to the naked eye in the thin sections, which is an extremely fine, granular modifi-cation of the groundmass. Occasionally, this predominating aggregation

200 MICROSCOPICAL PETROGRAPHY.

gradually passes into dull, distinctly fibrous spots, whose outlines have become indistinct.

In the Goose Creek Hills, a rhyolite is found [485] which looks very much like porcelain. The small macroscopical secretions of quartz and feldspar are distinct only in the thin sections. The groundmass is a mixture of colorless, polarizing particles and somewhat duller, pale, yellowish-gray bodies, which are either radially fibrous, or, as in the rhyolite of Trinity Mountains, back of Montezuma (see page 178), consist of confusedly-grouped bunches and systems of parallel fibres, showing hardly any action in polarized light.

East of Goose Creek Hills, there occurs a rhyolite having something of a violet color [486]. It is rich in crystals, which are unusually free from interpositions. The groundmass contains beautifully fibrous globes; in some cases the spheres being perfect, and in others only single segments of diverging bunches appearing. Fully developed sphærolites reach a diameter of 0.5^{mm}, and are often found to have for a centre or kernel a small feldspar-individual. Ferrite needles are found scattered without order or grouped radially. This rock, too, bears tridymite.

A very peculiar rhyolite is seen at White Rock, Cedar Mountains, Utah [487]. Its gray groundmass does not appear as compact as is usual in most rhyolites, but is very rough and trachytic, containing, macro-scopically, many riven sanidins closely resembling those of trachytes, numerous brown biotite plates, and large quartzes. Beautiful augites, which cannot be seen with the naked eye, are discovered by using the microscope. The groundmass is an almost wholly crystalline aggregation of comparatively large grains and individuals of feldspar, quartz, and augite. There are no microscopical biotite plates. The quartzes, and more especially the smaller ones, are remarkable for containing an unusually large quantity of little glass-inclusions, each with a dark bubble. In sections of quartz crystals which measured only 0.075^{mm} in diameter, as many as fifty glass-inclusions were observed in one plane; the most extraordinary surcharging of them ever seen in this mineral. And, in very curious contrast with this, the sanidin associated with the quartz is almost free from glassy interpositions. The biotite is noticeable for containing a great quantity of black grains and brownish, acicular needles of the same material; the latter being isolated or grouped into thin bunches precisely as in the biotites of granites, gneisses, and mica-slates. It is impossible to distinguish this rhyolitic mica from that of the old crystalline slates; for each in turn repeats the characteristic phenomena of the other. Since augite is so abundant in this highly quartziferous rock, it is remarkable that hornblende is wanting. The crystalline groundmass contains locally some roundish, microfelsitic spots of a dull gray color, which cannot be resolved into individual crystals.

Another very interesting rock is found on the summit of Hantz Peak, Elkhead Mountains [488]. It is a grayish-white mass, and, as the thin sections show better than the hand-specimens, rich in quartz and sanidins. No plagioclase was observed. Some of the quartzes have the most perfect dihexahedral glass-inclusions, with dark bubbles; others, undoubtedly fluid-inclusions, grouped into heaps and strung out into lines, having rapidly moving bubbles: these two types of inclusion do not, how-however, occur in one quartz. Polarized light discovers that all the quartzes, but more especially those having fluid-inclusions, are broken into fragments. A greater quantity of fluid-inclusions than the quartzes contain is enveloped in the feldspar. They are generally irregularly shaped, and are far more distinct than is usually the case in this mineral. No inclusions were seen which could be taken for glass. The somewhat porous groundmass contains many minute polarizing grains, among which there seems to be some microfelsite that occasionally passes into indistinct fibrations. The rock is destitute of hornblende and biotite A little ferrite and opacite is present. Particular attention should be called to the fact that this rock, the only one of this division whose doubtless primary quartz bears fluid-inclusions, can be pronounced a rhyolite by its other petro-graphical characteristics. It properly belongs to the trachytes, and there-fore dates further back than any other of the described rhyolites.

In Good Pass, North Park, another rhyolite is found which contains single, large quartzes.

The foregoing descriptions show in what abundance those fibrous bodies in which the fibres are not grouped radially around a centre, as in sphærolites, but arranged axially along a longitudinal line, are disseminated through these rhyolites. The presence in these rocks of such fibrations was formerly unknown, notwithstanding they are also common in the often-examined Hungarian and Euganean rhyolites. These axiolites usually consist of distinct, uniformly thin fibres, or of wedge-like particles.

Another phenomenon to which attention was never before directed is that found in some of these Fortieth Parallel rhyolites, where fibres of the same kind as above decribed are arranged in parallel form, producing bunches. So we see in the arrangement of the fibres in these rhyolites four different types: a, centrally radial; b, longitudinally axial; c, parallel; d, confused and orderless. The development of fibres is, indeed, a phenomenon very characteristic of rhyolites : though the tendency to fibration may in many cases be feeble and imperfect, it is seldom entirely wanting. Trachytes, on the other hand, are remarkable for lacking all signs of fibres.

The rhyolites of the Fortieth Parallel are generally poor in tridymite; occurrences of the mineral being comparatively rare. This may in some way be consequent upon the great quantity of quartz present in most of these varieties; for it has been stated, as a result of observations of European rocks, that an abundant secretion of quartz is unfavorable to the formation of tridymite in the same rock.[1]

Augite is more frequent in these rhyolites than was formerly supposed, being associated with hornblende. There are even occurrences where hornblende is wanting, and augite is associated with quartz and sanidin. In earlier times, as is well known, it was a petrographical law based upon macroscopical observations, that quartz-bearing rocks never contained augite as an ingredient.

Neither macroscopical nor microscopical white potash-mica (muscovite) could be detected in any of the examined rhyolites of the Fortieth Parallel. The only mica found was a dark magnesian biotite. The muscovite seems to have died out and totally disappeared since the beginning of the Tertiary formation.

In some rhyolites here, the feldspar contains fluid-inclusions, each with a moving bubble, in unexpected profusion; being often as rich in them as the feldspars of old granites.

---

[1] F. Z., Poggendorff's Annalen, CXL, 492.

But out of the many thousands of quartzes which have been carefully examined, only two were discovered with liquid-inclusions. (All the others were, characteristically, filled with the most perfect glass-inclusions.) And of these two quartzes bearing liquid, one occurred under such circumstances as to make it appear highly probable that it was nothing else than a foreign fragment in the including rock; while that bearing the other quartz was only a rhyolite petrographically, belonging geologically to the older trachytes.

Our study of the rhyolites of the Fortieth Parallel, therefore, corroborates the result obtained by the examination of similar European rocks, that the quartzes in genuine members of this group have no inclusions except of glass.

One of the convictions which this section most strongly enforces is, that the microscopical structure of rhyolite develops in a far greater variability and variety of types than that of any other rock.

In conclusion, we shall try briefly to sum up the most characteristic of the many types of structure in which the rhyolitic groundmass appears in these extremely complex rocks:

a. Crystalline throughout, entirely composed of individualized, polarizing grains, and generally rich in large secreted crystals; the groundmass sometimes possessing an unquestionably microgranitic structure, being made up of easily determinable grains of quartz and feldspar: this is a rare type.

b. Microfelsitic, becoming in spots and passing by the different steps of transition into an imperfectly granular structure, often containing more or less perfectly developed sphærolites, and generally bearing ferrite and opacite: a frequent type.

c. Aggregation of colorless, polarizing particles and colorless glass: very rare.

d. Alternating bands of light-colored genuine glass and microfelsite: rare.

e. Predominating microfelsite, showing some polarizing particles, and bearing single, dark, tail-formed axiolites, or short, longitudinal, axially-fibrous bodies.

f. Microfelsite, which is traversed by a net-work of axially fibrous or cuneate strings, having a distinct middle suture.

g. Net-work of axially fibrous or cuneate strings, with concentric, radially-fibrous sphærolites in the meshes

h. Net-work of axially fibrous or cuneate strings, with more or less distinct crystalline-granular aggregations in the meshes: rare.

i. Plain aggregation of sphærolites.

j. Confused aggregation of bunch-formed systems of accurately parallel fibres.

k. Confused, felt-like aggregation of short fibres.

l. Aggregation of cumulites, occasionally mingled with sphærolites.

m. Half-glassy mass, made up of an aggregation of thin, little microlites, fully imbued with glass, passing into obsidian; rocks, generally rich in larger crystals of quartz, sanidin, and biotite.

n. Fluidal bands of dark-brown grains, undulating and contorted, which include homogenous glass.

o. Bands identical with those last described, which include fibrous sphærolitic or axiolitic bodies, instead of homogeneous glass.

p. Light-colored homogeneous glass, traversed by pearlitic cracks, which are associated on both sides with narrow zones of microfelsite.

It is doubtful if these sixteen different types represent all the varieties of the rhyolitic groundmass; but that they comprehend the most characteristic and common ones is proved by the fact that the comparative study of more than one hundred and fifty thin sections of rhyolites from Hungary, Transylvania, Rhenish Prussia, the Euganean Hills, Iceland, and New Zealand, did not discover a single variety which is not represented and described among those of the Fortieth Parallel.

Our examinations prove that the waving fluidal phenomena of rhyolites are produced:

a. By the different amount of coloring particles (needles and grains of ferrite and opacite), alternating in layers, while the nature and structure of the main mass remains the same throughout the rock.

b. By the band-like alternation of different varieties of structure (generally with a gradual passage between one another); for instance, by the *c.* Alternation of more or less distinct crystalline-granular layers with sphærolitic ones;

d. Of microfelsitic and more or less perfectly crystalline layers;

e. Of imperfectly and distinctly granular layers;

f. Lastly, of layers of colorless and fine brownish-yellow globulitic glass, of which the former have, very characteristically, either an indistinctly crystalline or a fibrous structure, and usually contain dark, hair-like microlites, which generally have their root in the darker glassy bands.

SECTION III

GLASSY AND HALF-GLASSY (HYALINE) RHYOLITES.

The rocks described under this head are distinguished by consisting, entirely or in very large part, of glass. Obsidians, pitchstone-like rocks, pumicestones, and pearlites belong geologically to the rhyolites, of which they are only a petrographical modification.

On the left river-bank at Truckee Ferry, in Truckee Cañon, such rocks outcrop through and over trachytes. There is one curious occurrence [489], which shows in the hand-specimens a brown, obsidian-like glass, that has a vivid orange color in the thin sections. It is remarkable that this pure glass has no microlitic secretions whatever, except occasional rudiments of microscopical feldspars.

Another beautiful variety of obsidian from the same locality (Plate VIII, fig. 4) has a greasy lustre, and consists of laminæ and layers of two kinds of glass, twisted and entangled together in the most confused manner. One is a quite colorless, pellucid glass, the other a somewhat pale-brownish glass, with extremely fine, brownish grains, measuring only 0.0005^{mm}, imbedded in it. Indeed, the intermingling is as if the thin layers of these two kinds of glass were kneaded together artificially; and their entanglement or confusion, the sections appearing as narrower or thicker waving fluidal lines, is often comparable to a gnarled and knotty tree-trunk. Some of the layers are twisted into the shape of the blades of a screw-propeller.

The largely semi-hyaline rock from the Rhyolite Peak north of Desert Station, Truckee Range [490], is a dark-gray glass-mass, containing many feldspars and biotite plates, with some hornblende. It is destitute of quartz. The thin, sharp, oil-green laminæ of mica in the glass, often measuring only 0.01^{mm} in diameter, are very pretty. This rock is very instructive as to the character of aggregations of small globulites in glass (Plate IX, fig. 1). The simple elements are very pale-greenish, rounded or angular, isotrope grains, from 0.002 to 0.003^{mm} in size. Sometimes these grains are isolated; at others, two or three, or more, are conjoined into a little lump or star; and, at others, they are strung out in lines, like pearly strings, an interval between the grains being usually distinctly visible, but in rare cases they touch one another. Towards one end, the globulites gradually grow smaller, so that the needles seem to be pointed. Two of these strings are often seen diverging from a thicker globulite, or from a heap of them, like the arms of a pair of compasses. This is occasionally repeated three or four times, producing manifoldly knee-formed objects. In other cases, the aggregation of globulites takes the form of the most perfect, curved and twining tendrils. Sometimes a number of these radiate from a centre, suggesting a spider with many legs. The curvature is in some cases very great, and the torsion occurs in widely different planes, as in a cork-screw. In short, all the interesting phenomena are repeated here in natural glass, which Vogelsang has described in the artificial slags from the Friedrich-Wilhelmshütte near Siegburg.[1]

South of Warm Spring, near old Fort Churchill, Nevada, there occurs a light pumicestone, or (as proved by the microscope) more properly a pumicestone-breccia [491], the rock being made up of angular pieces welded together. This is made evident by the variety and independence of direction of the glass-lines in the single fragments. They consist of densely-woven, parallel strings, ropes, and lines of colorless glass, occasionally with long, cylindrical hollows between them. The few feldspars of the rock, which are mostly striated, are remarkable for the wide difference in size of the bubbles in their glass-inclusions: large lumps of glass are seen which have the most minute bubbles; and thick, dark bubbles are found, surrounded with but a thin zone of glass.

A dirty, yellowish-gray pumicestone occurs at Mullen's Gap, west side of Pyramid Lake [492], in conjunction with rhyolites and breccias. It is a more homogeneous rock than that last described, and bears feldspars with glass-inclusions, which are made remarkable by the number of their bubbles. Some of these glass-grains contain five or six small bubbles, and some are quite finely porous. The pumicestone-glass contains brown biotite plates, and, as foreign fragments, rounded, bluish-gray particles, 1^{mm} thick, of a felsitic rhyolite.

---

[1] Die Krystalliten, 1875, page 25, Plate II.

A splendidly devitrified pumicestone comes from the same locality. It contains, in its light-colored glass (rich in large and small cavities), a great number of small, almost colorless, belonites, averaging 0.02^{mm} in length, and 0.0015^{mm} in thickness, which are arranged parallel, and form excellent bands of waving lines that wind around the oval cavities; also sharply hexagonal and triangular plates of specular iron, of which the thinner ones are orange-colored and pellucid, and the thicker brown-black and impellucid; and, lastly, some brownish-yellow microlites and quadrangular magnetites. The rock contains, porphyritically, large feldspars, measuring 3^{mm}.

But the two best regions for glassy rocks are the Pah-tson Mountains and Montezuma Range, where they occur in connection with rhyolites. The beautiful pearlites found here, which contain grains and balls of obsidian, that are often as thick as a hazel-nut or walnut, merit particular attention. A bluish-gray pearlite from Basalt Ridge, Pah-tson Mountains [493], is shown by the microscope to be a nearly colorless glass-mass, with concentrically curved cracks, not unlike the layers of an onion. They are never complete rings, but only segments of circles. This mass is devitrified by very small and rare, colorless, or feebly-greenish microlites; by larger dark-green prisms, very much crippled and indistinctly crystallized, which, though undichroitic, cannot be pronounced augite, because neither the cleavage nor the prismatic angle is to be observed; by larger feldspars (of which a part are triclinic); and, lastly, by a considerable number of biotite plates, varying from light brown to black-brown in color, which are sometimes only rudimentary and sometime sharply outlined hexagons.

A rather dull-looking, yellowish, or bluish-gray pearlite from Aloha Peak, Pah-tson Mountains [494], owes its appearance to an abundance of microscopical products of devitrification, which here also are rounded globulites, isolated and in peculiar aggregations (Plate IX, fig. 2). The small grains are arranged in long needles, not unlike crystals and tendril-like forms; the latter often so much curved and twisted as to resemble knots. These twisted tendrils usually have undulated borders, produced by the lateral disappearance of the lineally arranged globulites. It would seem that these distorted and twisted, line-like cilia are characteristic of pearlites; for they have also been observed everywhere in the classic pearlites from

Hungary (for instance, in that from Glashütte near Schemnitz, Telki-bánya, Bereghszász), Cattajo, Euganean Mountains, Italy, and Mount Sommers in the southern island of New Zealand; a development, on the other hand, strikingly rare in obsidians, pumicestones, and pitchstones, otherwise so closely related to them. All these crystallites are not straight, linear bodies, but present distinct, waving fluidal phenomena, being grouped together in undulating bands. The rock contains splendid brown hornblende sections, measuring 0.8^{mm} along the orthodiagonal. Some of these crystals are excellent twins (parallel to $\infty P \infty$); the field on one side of the orthodiagonal axis in the horizontal sections becoming, in one position of the nicols, entirely black, and at the same time on the other side dark yellowish-brown. Some individuals of feldspar are present.

At Grass Cañon, Pah-tson Mountains, a pearlite occurs [495] which has the most excellent onion-like or layer structure. The glass-bulbs vary from the size of a pea to that of hazel-nuts. Products of devitrification in the nearly colorless glass (Plate IX, fig. 3) are chiefly cylindrical, needle-formed microlites, not exceeding 0.01^{mm} in length, and either of a pale-greenish hue or almost colorless; shorter, prickly bodies, of the same kind, grouped into very minute, bristly lumps or loose stars; black, opaque grains; straight and undulating, short, black, line-shaped microlites (trichites). Small, pellucid grains often cleave to the surface of the black microlites, giving them the appearance of being covered in part with powder or a granular dust. In consequence of fluctuations, all these microlites are arranged in parallel bands; a phenomenon well known from examinations of pearlites of other regions.[1] The grouping is without any reference to the concentric structure of the pearlitic glass globes; the bands traversing independently the shells of the glass-grains, and passing directly through many of them. This evidently proves that the microscopic devitrification and the concentric layers of the pearlitic shells are entirely independent of each other. The latter seems to be merely a phenomenon of contraction. Considering this intimate analogy, it is very remarkable that, in these typical American pearlites, sphærolitic formations, which are so well and widely developed in the Hungarian varieties, are rarely found.

[1] F. Z., Zeitschrift d. d. geolog. Gesellschaft, XIX, 1867, 768.

The obsidian which is found in the form of kernels and balls in the pearlite of Grass Cañon [496], as in the Siberian marekanite from Ochotsk, is of an intensely dark, blackish color. It gives, under the microscope, curiously, a light-gray section, which is hardly at all devitrified. This is one of the purest obsidians known, being only surpassed by the green bouteillenstein, or pseudochrysolite, from Moldauthein, Bohemia, and it contains only extremely rare and thin black microlitic lines, which are often knotted (trichites). Its compactness and freedom from gas-cavities is remarkable, because the other very pure obsidians, for instance, the marekanite, the pseudochrysolite, and the famous obsidian from the Hrafntinnuhryggr in Iceland, are extremely rich in microscopical pores.

Some pearlite lumps which occur in the pumicestone-tufas of Grass Cañon [497] are also hardly at all devitrified, with the exception of a sparse sprinkling of delicate, water-clear microlites; but they contain a great number of long and narrow, pointed-oval pores that are often twisted like a paragraph-mark.

In the Montezuma Range, west of Parker's Station, a pearlitic rock occurs, bearing black, dull, conchoidal glass which has a resinous lustre, and rounded clods of obsidian [498]. The latter (Plate IX, fig. 4) is prettily devitrified by subtle black trichites, which are usually sharply twisted, and often entwined in indistinct little flocks. The surface of the straighter and stronger ones is often powdered with extremely minute, pale, pellucid grains and prickles. Here also the microlites show, by waving fluidal lines, a distinct parallel arrangement, presenting excellent phenomena of distortion. In a single thin section, the lines of trichites here project into the plane of the section, and there form an angle with it. In the latter case, the ends of the black microlites appear like mere dark points or small grains.

The intensely devitrified pearlite from above White Plains, Montezuma Range [499], is imperfectly conchoidal, and contains large foldspars, 1.2^{mm} in size, which are mostly triclinic, together with thin, brown biotite plates, which, if cut transversely, form nothing more than short, black lines.

A rock of a gray color, and possessing a dull lustre, which is found forming fine columns in the Montezuma Range, back of Lovelock's Knob [500], is an intermediate member between pearlite and rhyolite. It is rich

in glass, has an imperfect globular structure, shows the interesting phenomenon of globulites aggregated into needles and tendrils, and includes, in
its almost colorless glass, beautiful quartz crystals, with glass-inclusions,
some biotite plates, dark-brown hornblende in sharply developed crystals,
possessing a splendid cleavage, and some lighter sections of undichroitic
augite, characterized moreover by normal contours and the nearly rectangular cleavage. This latter ingredient, which some time ago was not
supposed to exist in such highly silicated rocks, will also be found mentioned in some of the half-glassy masses hereafter to be described, where it
is present in such quantity that it sometimes predominates over the hornblende. It is very likely that augite will also be discovered in analogous
European occurrences, most of which were studied microscopically before the
distinctions between augite and hornblende were definitely known. Many
of the dark-green crystals occurring in obsidians, pitchstones, etc., which
have been described as hornblendes, may, upon more careful examination,
prove to be augites.

Yet there occur, in Montezuma Range, typical, concentrically globular
pearlites [501], which bear, beside the other elements producing devitrification that are mentioned in the rocks heretofore described, those colorless
crystals or crystallites which probably belong to feldspar. Their ends
either terminate in two acicular points of varying length, are regularly
serrated like stairs, or are irregularly lobate and deeply riven, so that they
look like the shattered ruins of crystals (Plate I, fig. 20). Nevertheless,
they are not broken at the ends, but are simply in a rudimentary state,
imperfectly developed. Such a pearlite is rich in biotite plates, partly
in the form of sharply outlined crystals, and partly as irregular, ragged
patches.

Some singular rocks were found on the foot-hills of the Montezuma
Range, near White Plains [502, 503, 504]. They exhibit at once a structure
very much like that of pearlite, and a linear lamellation produced by the
varying composition of their zones. The microscope discovers a great
quantity of products of devitrification, nearly all the bodies found in the
above-described pearlites being present: pellucid globulites, dark grains,
globulitic needles, spikes, tendrils, and cilia; the screw-like and spider-like

formations, and black trichites. The crystallites terminate in pinnacles. Feldspar crystals, some quartzes, rare apatite prisms, rather many biotite plates, and extremely beautiful brown hornblende, of which the transverse sections measure as high as 0.15^{mm} in length, are also met. The linear lamellation, forming in the sections dull, delicate, and often rather fine, undulated lines, is partly the result of the exceedingly dense aggregation into bands of some quite small, pellucid, round grains, through which the glass is hardly visible, partly of the zonal grouping of small, yellowish-gray, sphærolitic globules composed of exceedingly fine fibres. The sphærolitic stripes are generally somewhat broader than the granular ones. That the sphærolites do not occur elsewhere in the glass, being limited to these zones, is a point worth mentioning.

A member intermediate between pearlite and rhyolite occurs at the Shoshone Mesa [505]. An arrested tendency to form pearlitic globules is seen in the gray, half-glassy mass, which also contains sphærolites nearly as thick as a walnut, that develop, by decomposition, the concentric layer-structure. Some of the single shells or layers are less easily decomposed than others, and those which are least affected become isolated; so that the altered sphærolites seem to consist of single, partly loose, convex layers, like the crystal of a watch. There occur all the stages of transition between sphærolites in the natural state and cavities in which there are five or six shells with their isolated borders. Such occurrences in Hungarian rhyolites have been named lithophyses by v. Richthofen,[1] who described them as bladder-like, vesicular swellings of the molten material. J. Roth has expressed the well-founded opinion, however, that these lithophyses are nothing but mechanically and chemically altered larger sphærolites;[2] a view which has also been put forward by Szabó with respect to those from Tokaj, and which is doubtless confirmed by the American occurrences. In microscopical structure, the rock resembles the pearlites from Grass Cañon, although the mass of the predominating small, pellucid microlites has a very pale, but distinct, greenish color. The rock also contains larger quartzes, with fine glass-inclusions, feldspars measuring 4^{mm} in length, brown horn-

[1] Studien aus den ungarisch-siebenbürgischen Trachytgebirgen, 1861, 180.
[2] Beiträge zur Petrographie der plutonischen Gesteine, 1873, 168.

blendes, and some dark-green, undichroitic, larger grains and prisms doubtless belonging to augite, notwithstanding their form and cleavage are not
easily discernible. If the question were asked, whether the small colored
microlites which are not feldspars belong to hornblende or to augite, it could
only be said that they seem most like the latter.

In the western foot-hills of the Owyhee Bluffs, a black rock, appearing to
be very glassy, is found [506]. Under the microscope, it is seen to consist of
colorless and brown stripes of glass, which are very much bent and of varying
thickness. The colorless ones contain a great many straight and twisted
pellucid microlites, while the brown are much poorer in them. There are
not many larger crystalline secretions, but among those present are distinct
green augites and sanidins with irregular, ragged inclusions of the brown
glass variety.

The summit of Mount Nova, Cortez Range, is formed of a rock rich in
both crystals and glass [507] The base is a gray glass containing numerous
microlitic prickles, needles, stars, loops, and tendrils, with quartz, sanidin,
plagioclase, and an unusual amount of beautiful biotite in larger crystals.
Neither hornblende nor augite is visible.

Some very interesting obsidians occur at the Ombe Bluffs, Utah, just
south of the Union Pacific Railway. One of them [508] is a red-brown
glass rock, with imbedded feldspars and quartzes measuring 8ᵐᵐ (Plate
X, fig. 1). The quartzes bear, in unsurpassed perfection, macroscopical
inclusions of the glass, retaining the natural color, and almost as thick as a
pepper-corn. Such splendid macroscopical inclusions as these are very rare,
though minute microscopical ones are not infrequent. There is only one
other occurrence of the kind known. This is in the famous pitchstone from
the island of Arran, Scotland, the feldspars of which include thick grains of
the prevailing deep-green glass easily visible to the unaided eye. The microscope discovers that the chief mass of the rock is made up of two differently
colored kinds of glass. The sections consist of prevailing yellowish-red and
nearly colorless glass, the dividing lines between which are sharply drawn.
They are in the form of much contorted, alternating bands and stripes. The
thin sections look as if thin layers of red and colorless glass had been artificially laid upon one another, thoroughly kneaded together, and then drawn

out longitudinally. The red glass contains a great number of long and quite narrow cavities arranged parallel to the direction of the stripes, but is almost destitute of products of devitrification. The colorless glass is more compact, and bears quite an abundance of black grains and irregular trichites. Orange-colored, microscopical glass-grains with large bubbles are imbedded. in great quantities in the quartzes. If the section passed through a bubble, the latter of course only appears as a delicate, rounded ring, being incapable of producing the optical effect of a cavity.

In the same locality, a rock occurs [509] which is composed macroscopically of black, red, and yellow bands, streaks, and dashes of glass, intricately woven together. The microscope reveals the proper ground-substance to be a water-clear glass, colored macroscopically, as above described, by a variety of mechanically included bodies. The black stripes are made up of little angular and rounded, opaque, black grains and thin, short trichites. The colorless glass also bears narrow, linear fathoms and broader, curved microscopical dashes of a reddish-yellow color, which are generally somewhat darker along the borders than in the middle. Where these streaks are abundant, the glass has a red color; where they are less frequent, it is yellow. Microscopical stripes and bands of the same nature are much contorted, and sometimes form fantastical undulations. Quartz and sanidin are the crystalline secretions.

On the east slope of the Goose Creek Hills, a largely half-glassy rock is found [510], which shows a distinct tendency to form pearlitic globes, and contains quartzes nearly as thick as a pea. The microscopical crystalline ingredients (Plate X, fig. 2) are, a, quartz in imperfectly formed dihexahedrons; b, sanidin; c, plagioclase; d, highly lamellated brown biotite; e, very beautiful, feebly yellowish-green augite (sometimes crystallized in form ∞P. $\infty P \infty . \infty R \infty . - P$); f, quite rare, dark-brown hornblende; and, g, magnetite. The quartz, sanidin, and plagioclase contain excellent inclusions of colorless glass. The mass between these ingredients is a throng of microlites, with an abundance of glass, and it presents the most perfect, waving, damming and encircling fluidal phenomena. The microlites are naturally a very pale green, and, judging by the secreted crystals, there can be little doubt that they belong to augite; more especially since the pronounced transition between augite crystals and thinner, lighter, and more irregularly shaped (augite) prisms can be easily traced.

In the same locality, on the east slope of the Goose Creek Hills, there is another rather curious rock [511]. Macroscopically, it is composed of a pale grayish glass, in which many rounded and angular bodies, of a deep isabel-colored substance, having a dull or waxy lustre, are dispersed. These bodies reach the size of a pea, and are encircled by a somewhat darker, dirty, yellowish-gray border. In the sections, the central mass and its border strongly contrast; the dull portions being but slightly transparent. The glass which forms the main mass bears quartzes (including glass-inclusions with delicate, green crystals) and feldspars, together with the same microlitic products of devitrification found in the other hyaline rocks. The microlites conspicuously exhibit the phenomena of fluctuation, and they are disseminated so loosely that the pure, compact glass appears distinctly among them. It is surprising to see that these microlitic lines traverse the dull yellowish-gray portions without altering their direction at the entrance or exit, so that the spots present, with respect to the nature, quantity, and arrangement of microlites, precisely the same behavior as the prevailing glass-mass. And it is also very remarkable that in the isabel-colored portions no pure, homogeneous glass lies between the microlites, its place being taken by a fine fibrous glass or sphærolitic substance (if the expression is allowable), the direction of the extremely delicate fibres being, upon the boundary, usually rectangular, even in the irregularly shaped spots. The fibrous substance produces the dullness and feeble pellucidity above mentioned, and between crossed nicols it in some places sends out an indistinct play of light. A development of sphærolitic fibres has therefore happened locally in this rock. It did not, however, advance so far as the production of real sphærolites, and did not occur until after the microlites were all solidified and dispersed through the rock by fluidal waving, so that it did not at all alter their nature or direction. Moreover, these portions appear to be somewhat richer in iron than the main glassy mass of the rock.

CHAPTER VIII.

BASALTS.

SECTION I.

GENERAL REMARKS.

Of the younger Tertiary eruptive masses, the basaltic, in a general sense, are the opposites of the trachytic rocks, namely, rhyolite, trachyte, phonolite, and hornblende-andesite. They are characterized by the presence of augite, the total absence, or very small amount, of quartz and sanidin, the frequent occurrence of olivine, an abundance of magnetite, a more basic constitution, a higher specific gravity, and a darker color. It is only in comparatively rare cases that they present their mineralogical constituents in forms visible to the unaided eye.

A great multitude of dark, heavy, basic rocks have been collected for basalts. Their chief mass seemed macroscopically to be homogeneous, and their mineralogical composition gave rise to conjectures and interpretations as untrustworthy as they were numerous, until microscopical study achieved a solution of this much-vexed question.[1] The examinations show

---

[1] F. Z., Untersuchungen über die mikroskopische Structur und Zusammensetzung der Basaltgesteine, Bonn, 1869.

that these rocks, very similar in their exterior behavior and in their chemical constitution, are not, as was accordingly inferred, made up of the same principal mineral ingredients; but they are clearly divisible into three large groups, possessing different mineral combinations. The microscopical association of ingredients discovered here are not, as such, however, at all new or strange, but are merely a phanerocrystalline repetition of types which have long been known. As stated above, the basalts may be arranged into three divisions, the behavior of each being quite different from that of the rest; and, according to the principles valid in macroscopical petrography, they are three separate and well-characterized types of rock. With respect to the chief silicate, which is free from iron and rich in alumina, that always accompanies the never-wanting augite, which is rich in iron and poor in alumina, there exist the following: *a*, feldspar-basalts, characterized by the presence of plagioclase, usually wanting in leucite, occasionally with some nepheline, which correspond to the more distinctly grained dolerites and anamesites; *b*, nepheline-basalts, occasionally containing some leucite, and, when rich in nepheline, usually free from feldspar, corresponding to the nephelinite, for instance, from the Löbauer Mount, Saxony; *c*, leucite-basalts, which are almost always free from feldspar, but generally contain nepheline in comparative abundance, although less than the leucite. Contrary to the previously entertained opinion, therefore, feldspar is not a principal ingredient of all so called basalts. The members of all the three groups always bear magnetite, almost always olivine, and sometimes titanic iron. Mellilite and haüyne only occur separately, and are limited to the nepheline and leucite-basalts.

The microscope also proves that the separation into three groups not only refers to the massive, proper basalts, but to all the basaltic lavas. These latter are divided into:

Feldspar-basalt-lavas.
Nepheline-basalt-lavas.
Leucite-basalt-lavas.

And not only all the varieties of constituent combinations which are met in the proper basalts, but all the most special relations presented in their microscopical structure, are exactly repeated in the basaltic lavas.

Whether a basalt is a feldspar, a nepheline, or a leucite rock must always be decided in each case with the microscope; for the simple black *ensemble*, common to them all, completely hides the difference of their interior mineralogical composition, and even the most careful chemical analyses do not afford material for a rigid determination.

Yet it becomes evident, by a comparative review of the examinations thus far made, that, taken in general, the basaltic occurrences assembled together in one region differ but little in their composition The stronger contrasts are obtained when rocks from different regions are compared. For example, the German basalts of the Siebengebirge, and the enormous basaltic and anamesitic depositions of Scotland, the Western Islands, the Faeröer, and Iceland, are all feldspar-basalts, and not a particle of leucite has yet been discovered in them. The proper basalts of the Erzgebirge, between Saxony and Bohemia, on the other hand, bear only leucite and nepheline, and are free from feldspars. No lava from the environs of the lake of Laach, Rhenish Prussia, has been examined in which there was not to be observed an abundance of leucite. For aught that is now known to the contrary, leucite is totally wanting in the numerous basalts and lavas of Central France (Auvergne, Velais, Vivarais, Cantal), which bear feldspars, and are free from, or poor in, nepheline.

The nepheline-basalts sometimes contain leucite, and the leucite-basalts usually bear nepheline; so that these two groups appear to be much closer connected with each other than either of them with the feldspar-basalts. Moreover, the nepheline and leucite groups often occur together in one region; for instance, at Erzgebirge, Rhön, in Germany, and Northern Bohemia. And where feldspar-basalts are abundantly developed, there is little probability of finding with them members which are rich in leucite and nepheline, the latter almost always occurring separately.

These rules, deduced from a comparative study of European basaltic regions, are found to hold good of the occurrences along the Fortieth Parallel in Western America. Notwithstanding the enormous number and extent of development of the basaltic eruptions here, the rocks are, with very few exceptions, and those confined to the eastern limit of the examined territory, feldspar-basalts; which, in general, are no doubt the most frequent type in all parts of the globe. If on this account the petrographer finds himself confined to the monotony of one general type of composition, and searches in vain for those interesting mineral combinations exhibited by the leucite and nepheline-basalts, he is amply compensated by the great number of remarkable and characteristic varieties of microscopical structure offered by the numerous feldspar-basalts.

Beside the proper and genuine feldspar (i. e., plagioclase) basalts, which always contain olivine, often in abundance, there are some closely allied rocks which show sufficient persistent differences to make it proper to arrange them into a subdivision. They are distinguishable from the proper feldspar-basalts, although the two are almost identical macroscopically, in these respects: a, besides the plagioclases, there are always distinct sanidins, which are often in Carlsbad twins, but never predominant over the plagioclases; b, olivine is generally wanting, which characteristic feature happens where the sanidins are present in considerable quantity; c, the behavior of the microscopical structure is quite unusual in genuine feldspar-basalts, the chief mass of the rocks being a felty accumulation of small microlites evenly impregnated with glass, and accordingly the larger feldspars are much more highly charged with glass-inclusions than are those of the proper basalts, beside which the glass gives the rocks a rather distinct resinous lustre; d, they sometimes contain hornblende as an accessory ingredient, which is generally unknown to the true basalts; e, the chemical analyses show that they all have a higher amount of silica than the proper basalts, rich in olivine, free from sanidin, and poor in glass; f, lastly, it may be mentioned that the apatites of these rocks are generally dusty, which is more common in andesites and trachytes than in basalts. The points, therefore, in which the rocks in question differ from the genuine basalts are evidently of only secondary importance, the chief constituents of both being augite and plagioclase; and they will always, upon merely a macroscopical examination, be classed as basalts, and geologically the two are closely connected; possessing the same forms of occurrence and being likewise of younger eruption than even the rhyolites. They differ from the common trachytes in the predominance of plagioclase and the abundant presence of augite, although they are pretty closely related to that rare variety, the augite-trachytes, which contain, beside invariably though often but slightly predominating sanidin, a good deal of plagioclase, augite instead of hornblende, and are likewise free from olivine; but geologically and geographically they are distinct from the trachytes. These basaltic rocks, of course, differ from the hornblende-andesites by the amount of augite they contain. If a name is to be conferred upon them, that of augite-andesite seems the most suitable. When the special chemical composition of the plagioclases was a leading feature by which rocks were determined, and when oligoclase and labradorite were considered as fixed species, this name was applied by J. Roth to the Tertiary combination of oligoclase and augite. But now, when only a contrast of the triclinic nature of the feldspar-constituent with that of the orthoclase or sanidin is valuable in petrographical nomenclature, such an application of this name becomes superfluous; for the so-called rocks come within the general class of plagioclase-augite mixtures, becoming members of the basalts, the more as it has appeared highly probable of most of the latter that their plagioclase is richer in silica than the so-called labradorite. It therefore seems that the name augite-andesite may unhesitatingly be transferred, without causing any confusion or changing its original meaning, to those feldspar-basaltic rocks in which (beside the predominating plagioclase) sanidin has a certain part, and which are either free from or extremely poor in olivine, whose presence is more characteristic of the wider-spread genuine basalts. At any rate, these rocks are the augite-bearing equivalent of the hornblende-andesites, but on that account are also petrographically more nearly related to the basalts. In a certain sense, however, they occupy an intermediate position, presenting a kind of passage between the two; and, therefore, the description of the basaltic rocks may properly be begun with them.

SECTION II.

AUGITE-ANDESITES.

To this sub-division of basaltic rocks belong those from Java, Gambirán, Rogodjampi, Grad Takan, Widodarin, Sungi Pait, which Rosenbusch has examined microscopically.[1] These occurrences, which have also been named by him augite-andesites, would seem, according to his description, to agree perfectly with the similar American rocks which have been analyzed. The rocks from Tunguragua, Cotopaxi, and Antisana, in the Andes, which were called quartz-augite-andesites, on account of the large amount of silica they contain (63. to 67. per cent.), have been proved to be totally wanting in quartz, but rich in brown glass.[2] But if these rocks agree petrographically with the other augite-andesites, the large quantity of silica they contain removes them from the basalts. The lavas of Santorin, poured forth in 1865, are also rightly classed among the augite-andesites by such writers as Roth, Stache, Leonhard, and Urba. The black rock with a resinous lustre, from Bagonya, Hungary, which was formerly taken for a trachyte, also belongs under this head. An excellent augite-andesite from the Palau Islands, Australia, was quite recently described by Wichmann.[3] Dr. Ulrich sent from Melbourne to the Mineralogical Museum of Leipsic some rock-specimens from Kyneton, Victoria, Australia, which represent the most typical augite-andesites. It is very astonishing that these rocks, from such remote parts of the earth, should offer in the sections so detailed a resemblance to one another that it is impossible to distinguish them except by reference to the labels.

Among the augite-andesites of the Fortieth Parallel, one of the most typical varieties is that first found in passing from west to east on the knoll west of Basalt Creek, Washoe [512]. It is a brownish-black mass, with a somewhat resinous lustre, containing white, ledge-formed feldspar crystals. which are seldom tabular; and it is both macroscopically and microscopi-

---

[1] Über einige vulkanische Gesteine von Java, Ber. d. naturf. Gesellsch. zu Freiburg, i. Br., 1872.

[2] F. Z., Die mikroskopische Beschaffenheit u. s. w., 418.

[3] Journal des Museum Godeffroy, 1875, Heft VIII.

cally very similar to the well-known Hungarian rock from Bagonya, which is found in most mineral collections, by reason of bearing excellent hyalite in its hollows and fissures. Under the microscope, the Washoe rock consists of a brownish-yellow glass-ground; larger spots and insular bodies of it appearing quite pure and unaltered in many places. An enormous quantity of yellowish-green augite, colorless feldspar-microlites, and black magnetite grains, together with larger crystals of feldspar and augite, are imbedded in the rock. The feldspars are largely sanidins in simple individuals and Carlsbad twins; but plagioclase, with its rich striæ, evidently predominates. Both feldspars contain the most beautiful and numerous inclusions of pale-yellowish, glass-bearing bubbles. Of these inclusions, nearly all, even the smallest ones, are rectangular in shape, and they are often arranged in lines which run surprisingly near to a parallel with the outlines of the crystal section. There are also larger inclusions of glass of a darker color; their shape being irregular and disfigured. The thicker augites are sharply outlined, having the usual eight-sided section-forms ($\infty P . \infty \!\!+\!\! P \infty . \infty \!\!\mathcal{P}\!\! \infty$), are traversed by nearly rectangular cracks, show only the slightest trace of dichroism, are entirely fresh and filled with oval, glassy inclusions. There is no vestige of hornblende in this rock, nor yet of olivine. Some dusty apatite prisms are present. The quantitative determination of silica gave 58.015 per cent., an amount which entirely agrees with that found in other characteristic augite-andesites. For example:

Top of Pico Teyde, Teneriffe	59.68	(Bolton.)
Widodarin, Java	58.35	(Rosenbusch.)
Chimborazo (17,916 feet elevation)	59.12	(Rammelsberg.)
Masaja Nindiri, Nicaragua	56.58	(Marx.)
Klausenthal, Hungary	57.79	(Doelter.)
Tuhrina, Hungary	58.76	(Doelter.)
Palau Islands, Australia	57.54	(Wichmann.)

No genuine basalts possess so large an amount of silica as these typical augite-andesites contain. The newly discharged lavas from Santorin, which also belong to this group, are even still more acid.

Another excellent augite-andesite occurs on the hill west of Steamboat

Valley, Nevada [513]. It is very similar to the last described rock, except that the glass-base impregnating the felt-like aggregation of microlites in the groundmass, is not brownish, but light-gray. Many larger, colorless feldspars measuring up to 1.5^{mm}, among which are some sanidins, are present. Most of them are no doubt triclinic, and all are evidently built up by surrounding zones, and surcharged with glass-inclusions. Augites in sharply-defined crystals are present, and magnetite and apatite are found. Hornblende and olivine are wanting.

There are some rocks which are connected with the genuine basalts of the Truckee River, a part of which only seem to belong while another part without any doubt do belong to the proper augite-andesites. The occurrence in the ravine north of the Truckee Road, a few miles west of Clark's Station [514], macroscopically very much resembles the foregoing, and is likewise rich in brown glass, which is here, however, of a somewhat darker color. The feldspars are mostly sanidin. There is at least as much orthoclastic as plagioclastic feldspar present; and one might therefore be inclined to petrographically classify this rock, which also contains exceedingly well-crystallized, green augites and is devoid of hornblende, as an augite-trachyte, if it did not bear fresh, and, characteristically, half-decomposed olivine, which establishes its relation to the basaltic family. The association of an abundance of sanidin and of olivine in a single rock is, however, extremely rare. So that the characteristics of both augite-andesites and genuine basalts are here united. This olivine, curiously, is immediately surrounded by a circle of tangentially placed, little, yellowish-green augite prisms.

In the near vicinity, there occurs another augite-andesite [515], which also bears olivine. But the glass in this variety is a little lighter brown than that of the other, and is filled with small, glassy granules of a darker color. The globulitic development of glass-mass is much more distinct and beautiful here than even in the so-called melaphyre-pitchstone from the Weisselberg, near St. Wendel, Rhenish Prussia, which is famous on that account. The inclusions of the feldspars also consist of this hyaline modification. These rocks from the ravine north of the Truckee Road, are, indeed, identical in composition, both as regards the nature and the quantitative proportion of their crystalline constituents; but they are different in structure.

Nevertheless, there occur in this region, near the Truckee River, south of Wadsworth, in the foot-hills, on the southern side, very well characterized augite-andesites [516, 517]. Among the larger feldspars, there are. as many sanidins as plagioclases; but the smaller individuals seem chiefly to be triclinic. In the aggregation of very small feldspar and augite-microlites, and magnetite, which forms the groundmass, glass seldom appears, except indistinctly as a cement. Occasionally, however, it may be seen in pure, homogeneous, little, brown spots. The feldspars are highly charged with foreign substances; the longer sections showing even macroscopical kernels of groundmass set in narrow frames of colorless feldspar substance. These rocks contain some hornblende beside the prevailing augite, and are instructive as to the difference between the two minerals, presenting the peculiarities of each in striking contrast: the augite sections are always very sharply outlined in the usual form, have nearly rectangular cracks, are of rather a pale-yellowish color, and are almost undichroitic: the hornblende is of a light-brown color, surrounded with a narrow, black border (never found in the augite), having obtuse angles of cleavage, very high dichroism, and changing under the polarizer from a light brown to a deep, dark brown, with a very strong absorption. The hornblende never assumes its regular shape, but always appears in larger, broken crystals and fragments: all the smaller individuals and microlites belong, without exception, to augite. In short, here, as in so many other basaltic rocks, the hornblende has the appearance of an erratic, secondary ingredient, originally foreign to the rock. Olivine is here wanting; a fact, as has been seen, characteristic of augite-andesites

Rocks of this class next appear in Antimony Cañon, Augusta Mountains [518]. The specimens from this locality can hardly be distinguished, either macroscopically or microscopically, from those heretofore described. The base is a brownish glass without any globulitic secretions, penetrating everywhere. It cements microlites of plagioclase and augite and grains of magnetite, and in some places it forms more noticeable spots. The larger feldspars (a few of which are sanidins) and the yellowish-green, sharply

outlined augites imbedded in this groundmass, are filled with an enormous
quantity of egg-like and irregular bodies, and often large stripes of the brown
glass. Olivine is wanting.

The rock from the north slopes of Jacob's Promontory, Reese River
Valley, Nevada, is also quite similar [519]. It contains very little sanidin;
most of the feldspars being larger plagioclases, bearing a great quantity
of excellent inclusions of brown glass with thick bubbles, accurately rectangular in shape. The glassy grains in the augites are so large that they
sometimes include augite-microlites. No olivine can be detected, nor any
hornblende. As usual, it is superfluous to mention the groundmass, which
is the common glass-cemented aggregation of feldspar and augite-microlites
and magnetite grains.

At Susan Creek Cañon, Nevada, a real augite-andesite occurs, which
looks half-glassy, and has a somewhat resinous lustre [520.] The larger,
zonally built feldspars (some of which are orthoclastic) bear the most beautiful
inclusions of the yellowish-brown glass which constitutes the cement of the
rock, together with microlites and eggs of glass, containing one or more
dark bubbles, being often finely porous, sometimes possessing a crenate
border. Some feldspars have an insular position in almost entirely pure
glass; the light-brownish inclusions being woven together on the sides so
that the feldspar scarcely appears between them; but the bubbles of the
single particles are easily seen (Plate XI, fig. 2). A still greater quantity of
glass-inclusions are found in the yellowish-green augite; one crystal section,
0.3^{mm} long and 0.12^{mm} broad, having in one plane not less that 95 oval
particles, each with a bubble. In this ratio, there would be 2,650 glass-
grains on the surface of one square millimetre of augite; and assuming
that these inclusions are evenly disseminated through the entire crystal,
a cubic millimetre of augite would have more than seven millions (7,022,500)
of glass-inclusions. Microlites are often set tangentially around the thick
magnetite grains, encompassing them on all sides and presenting distinct
traces of former fluidal phenomena. Here also olivine is absent.

In the foot-hills of the Cortez Range, Independence Valley, Nevada,
an augite-andesite occurs, which closely agrees with that from the hill west
of Steamboat Valley [521.] Plagioclases up to the thickness of a hazel-nut

15 M P

predominate, exhibiting macroscopically rag-like, grayish-yellow particles of glass measuring 0.1^{mm}, whose edges curiously ramify like digits, as if they had been squeezed flat by the crystallization of the feldspar. At the periphery of the largest feldspars, which appear quite impellucid in the sections, the minute glass-grains decidedly predominate over the crystal sub-. stance. There are many microlites in the sharply crystallized augites, imbedded parallel to the zonal structure. Olivine is wanting. The glass base cementing the microlites of the groundmass is of a gray color.

A blackish augite-andesite, having a resinous lustre, occurs in Wagon Cañon, Cortez Mountains [522]. Beautifully zonal feldspars are visible macroscopically (all of which are plagioclases), and so also are some dark yellowish-brown crystals of augite, both being rich in glass-inclusions. There is no olivine. Glass cementing the microlitic aggregation constituting the groundmass is not brownish, but of a light-gray color. It is evident that all these rocks which possess a grayish glass-base, are much richer in larger and microlitic augites than those with brownish glass; and it therefore seems highly probable that the iron of the original magma in the first case mostly entered into the augites, and in the second has remained in the glass. Considering this, it is interesting to remark that the feldspars of the rocks with a gray glass-base often contain inclusions of brown glass, showing that at the time they were taken up, the differentiation of the magma and the secretion of augite had not happened. Occasionally, the glass-base appears in somewhat purer little spots, which are sometimes darkened by straight and curved black trichites interspersed with small, light-colored grains, similar to the products of devitrification in obsidians.

One specimen of augite-andesite from the same locality contained some hornblende in dark-bordered and apparently erratic fragments [523].

At South Point, Wachoe Mountains, is an augite-andesite [524] so similar in the most subtle details to that from the North Pass, Cortez Range, that the sections cannot be told apart without reference to the labels. It bears augite crystals 3^{mm} long.

The rock from the foot-hills of Spring Cañon, Wachoe Mountains [525], contains considerable sanidin; but plagioclase decidedly predominates. Olivine is wanting. There are also rather dark-yellowish, well-crystallized, fissile, and faintly dichroitic augite-sections, and some very strongly dichroitic, yellowish-brown hornblende-fragments, with dark borders and the characteristic cleavage. There is no olivine. The glassy base is of a light-gray color.

An augite-andesite which seems to be half-glassy occurs at the west of White Rock, Cedar Mountains [526]. Almost all the larger feldspars are plagioclases. The augites are built up zonally. There are very few dark hornblende sections here. Some brown, sharply and straightly lamellated biotite is present this is a rare ingredient in these rocks, and, in connection with the hornblende, produces a resemblance to hornblende-andesites. The groundmass contains a very light glass-base, and exhibits good fluidal phenomena. There is no olivine.

It is perhaps worth mentioning that the augite-andesites possessing a pale-gray glass-base, herein examined, are largely limited to the eastern, and those with a brownish glass-base to the western, regions of the examined territory.

The foregoing descriptions suffice to show the extraordinary similarity between the augite-andesites, both macroscopically and microscopically, notwithstanding the individual occurrences are widely separated.

A remarkable rock from the north bank of Palisade Cañon, Cortez Range [527], which occupies a quite isolated position petrographically, should be mentioned before closing this section. Upon examination with the unaided eye, it would appear to be a hornblende-andesite; but the real composition of the rock cannot be discovered macroscopically, for it is very cryptomerous. Under the microscope, it is found to consist of predominating plagioclase, which looks something like that in the German basalts, a little sanidin, not very abundant brownish-yellow augite, a considerable brown biotite, and some curiously angular quartz grains, with very minute glass-inclusions. Hornblende and olivine are absent. The presence of the quartzes is surprising; but they are easily identified by their compact substance and their very vivid chromatic polarization. It is remarkable that in the larger individuals, but more especially in the feldspars, numerous extremely fine crystals, scarcely larger than 0.003^{mm}, are imbedded, which exhibit the hexagonal pyramid very accurately formed, and for the most part belong to quartz, though in some measure to apatite. The rock has a wholly granular-crystalline structure, and it shows no vestige of a glass-base or other amorphous substance. This occurrence seems best to merit the name of quartziferous augite-andesite. In a certain sense, it is the dacite of augite-andesite, but with a different structure. The common augite-andesites are in every case entirely free from quartz, being always essentially half-glassy rocks; and the amount of biotite present gives the rock a certain resemblance to the hornblende-andesites rather than to dacites. The quantitative analysis of this rock made by Mr. Reinhard, at Leipsic, resulted as follows :

Silica	62. 71
Alumina	12. 10
Sesquioxyd of iron	14. 79
Lime	8. 34
Magnesia	1. 31
Potassa	1. 15
Soda	0. 73
	101. 13

SECTION III.

TRUE BASALTS.

The proper basalts are, as is well known, subdivided into feldspar-basalts, anamesites, and dolerites. These three varieties differ only in point of structure: the same principal constituents are common to all. Dolerite comprises the middle and coarse-grained members. The granular structure of anamesite is visible macroscopically, but the individual elements cannot be detected with the naked eye. The basalts include those widely spread rocks whose mass would appear homogeneous but for the macro-porphyritical crystals that occasionally occur in it.

Beginning at the west, the first basalt found has a very characteristic type of microscopical structure. It occurs north of American Flat Creek, Washoe [528]. In every point, it bears the closest resemblance to the rocks from the Kieshübel near Dilln, and not far from Schemnitz, Hungary, from the Tungfernberg in the Seven Mountains, Rhenish Prussia, from Tunchal and the Puico Rivo, Madeira, and also to those from many other localities. The most important characteristics of this interesting structure-type (Plate X, fig. 3), which so often reappears along the Fortieth Parallel, are the absence of any amorphous, glassy or half-glassy base, and the way in which its macroscopical and larger microscopical porphyritical crystals of feldspar (which are often accompanied by similar olivines) contrast with its very fine-grained mixture of rounded, drop-like, or crippled augite grains of a pale color, and sharp, black grains of magnetite. The aggregation here described, whose individuals are seldom larger than 0.01^{mm}, take the part of ground-mass. Feldspar crystals, some of which are sanidins, are imbedded in it; and sometimes colorless particles are visible which would at first be considered as colorless glass, but which prove in polarized light to be feldspar. Olivine never occurs in this ground-mixture, but only in larger porphyritical crystals, which are generally well-developed, like the feldspars. The augite of the rock, however, is confined to the groundmass. Other characteristic points are, that the two long, parallel borders of the ledge-formed feldspar sections are not usually drawn very sharply; that extremely minute augite grains are often interposed in the large feldspars, being arranged in lines which correspond with the triclinic striation; and that two feldspar individuals lying close together have a line of augite grains running between them.

The basalts from the second ridge of American Flat Cañon, Washoe, are rather peculiar [529]. They are not characteristic types, but present exceptions to the general behavior consisting of white plagioclase and a blackish-green constituent, which would seem, by its outlines, to be augite, but it possesses a singular fibration, which at first suggests uralite, the well-known pseudomorph of hornblende after augite. The thin sections prove, however, that the mineral (which is here dark green) is not at all dichroitic, and therefore cannot belong to hornblende; so that the only alternative is to consider it some other fibrous product of augitic alteration. The plagioclases are beautifully lamellated, and are, besides, extremely well built up in single wrappings: crystal sections, 0.5^{mm} in length, consist of more than a dozen striæ of involution. There is neither olivine nor apatite nor any amorphous substance; but there are some magnetites. The rocks are in one place coarser-grained, or doleritic, in another fine-grained, or anamesitic.

The next excellent basalt occurs in the Virginia Range, east of Spanish Spring Station [530]. The plagioclase is well striated, and is often built up zonally. With it is greenish augite, and olivine also occurs, its larger crystals altered along the borders and cracks and its smaller filled with a brownish-red, somewhat fibrous substance, which is, without doubt, of a serpentineous character. It may here be mentioned, in advance, that this phenomenon of decomposition is evident in all the olivines of our American basalts, in which respect they correspond with those from other parts of the globe which have been examined (see Plate X, figs. 3 and 4, showing the half-metamorphosed crystal of olivine belonging to another rock). Olivine is the substance in all rocks first falling a victim to alteration, which process begins on the exterior of the grains and crystals and pushes inward along the microscopical fissures which traverse the individuals in all directions; and since the walls of these irregularly ramifying cracks are first altered, the larger crystals in one stage of metamorphism appear to be checkered with veins of a strange material, which divide the original substance into little insular spots or grains, which remain quite fresh.

The product of this alteration (as appears in the wet way) is in most cases serpentine, possessing in one place a darker or lighter and in another a reddish-brown, brownish-red, or even a yellowish-red color, and a delicate, fibrous structure. There is scarcely any olivine to be found which does not show at least a tendency to decomposition. A quite common phenomenon is to find smaller olivines which have been totally metamorphosed by the action that is manifest in the larger ones only along the cracks and borders. The gradual transformation of these insular spots and grains of the normal olivine substance marked out in the larger individuals by the serpentineous lines of alteration, which represent the middle stage of change, can be easily traced, even in different parts of a single thin section. In this rock, olivine sections measuring 1^{mm}, and encircled by a red border, the interior being somewhat yellowish, may be seen macroscopically in both the thin sections and the hand-specimens, the latter of which are sometimes a little porous. Magnetite is the fourth constituent. Apatite and sanidin are wanting. The rock is not altogether crystalline; for there exists between the individualized elements a small quantity of an extremely fine, brown, globulitic, amorphous mass, which is sometimes pierced by delicate, colorless rays. This is better observed between the diverging sections of feldspars than between the augites. It forms quite thin, interposed layers, and can be examined to the best advantage when cut obliquely. Irregular bodies and stripes of this mass are inclosed in the larger feldspar crystals parallel with their twin-striation.

Between Peavine Mountain and Virginia Range, a somewhat decomposed and bleached basalt occurs [531], which bears macroscopical olivines.

The hill behind Steamboat Spring, at the foot of Geiger Grade, is composed of basalt [532].

Truckee Cañon is rich in basaltic varieties. The augite-andesites of this cañon have been already mentioned (page 124). Common feldspar-basalts occur here [533], which are rather coarse-grained microscopically, yet contain very little brown, globulitic, half-glassy substance between the crystalline elements. It is exceptional to come upon so small an amount of this base; for, where it occurs at all, it is generally much more abundant. There are macroscopical feldspars in the sections, but the augites and olivines are confined to microscopical individuals. A great many very small, always brownish, metamorphosed olivine grains are disseminated through the rock.

A basalt from the south flank of the entrance to Truckee Cañon [534] is similar to that last described; but it is still more coarse-grained. Indeed, it is nearly anamesitic, resembling the famous typical anamesite from Stein- heim near Hanau, Germany, with which it in other points corresponds; namely, by being almost or wholly destitute of olivine, and by possessing an abundance of a brownish-gray, partly globulitic and partly fibrous, amorphous mass, which is flattened out between the crystals, and is altering into a dirty-green, fibrous substance, precisely as described and represented in the anamesite from Steinheim.[1] There is a very gradual and distinct passage between the original substance and the alteration-product. There is some apatite, also, as in the Steinheim rock.

Another variety of the Truckee Cañon basalts, occurring in the Truckee Valley, ten or twelve miles below Wadsworth [535], is a very porous and even somewhat vesicular rock. It is rich in comparatively large feldspars, whose prevalence can be detected with the unaided eye in the thin sections. A small part of these feldspars are sanidins. The remainder of the rock-mass is, as it were, only crowded in between the long and broad ledge-formed feldspar sections. The beautiful plagioclases include very neat, roundly crystallized, but somewhat altered, olivines, measuring up to 0.012^{mm} in length. This phenomenon was never before observed. The rock is poor in augite, rich in small olivines and aggregations of magnetite grains, and contains considerable amorphous matter. The latter is a pale-yellow-ish glass-mass, bearing the usual small, brown, roundish globulites, and pierced by numerous long, colorless, acicular rays. These prisms or rays probably belong to some undeterminable product of devitrification, for they cannot be identified with any of the rock-constituents; and they stand parallel with one another, like the teeth of a comb, or are grouped in the shape of fascicles and bundles. Their surfaces, strangely, are often thickly covered with very minute, black, opaque grains, which are probably mag-netite.

---

[1] F. Z., Basaltgesteine, 98.

On the left bank of the river, at Truckee Ferry, Truckee Cañon, a black, vesicular basalt [536] makes its appearance. It is distinguished from the others by containing many sanidins among the larger feldspars, most of which, however, are triclinic. Its dark groundmass consists of feldspar crystals and a smaller number of greenish-yellow augites distributed in a globulitic, glassy mass, exactly as in the basalts below Wadsworth. Olivine is entirely wanting here, so that the rock in one point resembles the augite-andesites of the region.

Some basalts occur in Berkshire Cañon, Virginia Range, which are not well characterized, and are so highly altered that their composition is sometimes undeterminable [537, 538, 539].

One of the most representative basalt regions is found on both sides of the Truckee Valley, in the foot-hills of the Virginia and Truckee Ranges, in the vicinity of Wadsworth, and the surrounding hills, where a rich variety of the most splendid and highly characteristic types are found overflowing older diabase rocks. The predominating black variety appears, for the most part, to be rather homogeneous, is seldom distinctly grained, and has a somewhat resinous lustre, which indicates the presence of a half-glassy substance. Little hollows of the rock are covered with a thin, milky-blue, cacholong-like deposit of silica. These rocks resemble, in the most minute details, the nature and the relative proportion of the constituents, and the microscopical structure of that peculiar basaltic type which has been described in specimens from Strathblane, near Dunglass, Scotland; from Mount Smolnik, near Kremnitz, Hungary; from Soleyjarhofdi, Iceland; from Beaulieu, Auvergne; and from Mount Hecla [540]. And it is worth the while to pause here and remark that in these widely remote quarters of the globe, the product of the solidification of a molten mass, although exposed to many casualties, has, nevertheless, maintained a surprisingly close identity of microscopical composition. These basalts (see Plate X, fig. 4) are made up of crystalline elements in an unindividualized, amorphous base, which is sometimes present in considerable quantity. This latter is generally a nearly colorless or very pale yellowish-gray glass substance; some little globules, a product of devitrification, being imbedded in it. These globules have been mentioned in the foregoing pages as occurring in some of the rocks, but they have not been found characteristically developed until now. They measure on an average 0.0015^{mm} in diameter, have a dark brown color, and show with a high magnifying power a lighter central spot. They do not polarize, and are no doubt of a glassy nature, corresponding to the globulites in artificial slags. The glass often contains, beside these globules, long, narrow, acicular needles and rays, which are sometimes dichotome, and either lie parallel, or cross each other confusedly, like the fibres of a felt. The longer and stronger needles not infrequently pierce the adjoining feldspar crystals. These globulites are always much better characterized than the undeterminable microlitic secretions in the glass. The base is crowded in between the diverging crystalline elements of the rock, forming wedge-shaped bodies, whose microscopical structure is best studied where they are cut obliquely, and in an extremely thin layer overlap the border of a colorless feldspar crystal. In thicker layers, this glass-base, rich in dark globulites, appears grayish or brownish-black, and is almost perfectly impellucid. Cases are rare where it does not occur in narrow, cuneiform or arrow-head-shaped masses, but in larger, rounded, insular spots. It sometimes shows a tendency to molecular alteration. The peculiar wedge-shaped places between the feldspar crystals, which it usually occupies, are instead occasionally filled with amygdaloidal formations, consisting in the sections of undulated and curled concentric rings, having an alternately lighter and darker grayish, or brownish-yellow color (see Plate XI, fig. 1), where it is easy to see how the glassy mass is gradually altering, the process beginning on the surface and working toward the middle. While the centre is still fresh, a gradual passage between it and the surrounding rings of alteration is plainly visible. In some cases, even in the same rock, this globulitic base is replaced by a pure glass-mass destitute of grains; and it is interesting to observe that this mass has a dark brown color, showing that the equivalent of the iron which formed the globules in the pale glass-mass is here evenly distributed, and produces the uniform color. A considerable proportion of the feldspars of this characteristic basalt variety are monoclinic; but plagioclases, which are often Carlsbad twins, largely predominate. These plagioclases are sometimes built up zonally, in one case more than one hundred zones being found in the thickness of 0.3^{mm}; and they generally contain inclusions of the globulitic glass in the form of long, irregular bodies, parallel with the twin-striation, a phenomenon which is common to all like rocks throughout the globe. Here again, curiously, the plagioclases include minute crystals of olivine and drop-formed, greenish grains of augite. Larger crystals of augite are comparatively very rare; the mineral here generally forming only small irregular and crippled individuals, destitute of that morphological beauty which is a feature of those seen in the augite-andesites. Moreover, some occurrences are rather poor in augite; and it is interesting to observe that the rocks which are rich in the brown amor-phous base, are the same that prove to be comparatively poor in augite, and *vice versa;* so that it seems highly probable that one is the equivalent of the other. Olivine is hardly ever lacking, being usually present in numerous individuals that sometimes attain macroscopical size. The olivines exhibit the well-known phenomenon of successive alteration into a serpentineous mass, which is mostly of a reddish-brown color. They are often well crystallized, and contain very distinct but minute, sharply octahedral crystals having a greenish-brown color, translucent on the edges, which belong to picotite, a variety of chromiferous spinel, a mineral found occurring in precisely the same manner in innumerable basaltic olivines of Germany, Bohemia, Hungary, Italy, and Scotland. They resist alteration, and are consequently found entirely fresh when the whole surrounding crystal mass has become decomposed into serpentine. They never occur as independent constituents of the rock, but are confined to the interior of olivines. Here more than in any other known basalt variety the magnetite is strongly inclined to form skeleton-like or cross-formed groups of crystals, which are very pretty; three longer or shorter lines of grains standing perpendicularly one above the other, according to the axes of the regular system (Plate 1, fig. 12). Apatite is occasionally present in small quantities, and is sometimes altogether wanting: in general, it is proportionally rare. Hornblende and nepheline never occur here. Experiments have proved that the globulitic glass base is not at all affected by hydrochloric acid. A powder of these basalts boiled five hours, and treated four days with this acid, showed under the microscope that the small fragments of the base were still fresh and unaltered. The glass, therefore, cannot be of a tachylytic nature, but must possess a more acid character. The feldspars also remained unattacked after the long treatment with acid. Olivine and magnetite alone disappeared under the test; and so it is comprehensible why these rocks gelatinize so little with hydrochloric acid. The quantity of silica in the whole rock (i. e., in one of the most typical specimens of this division) was determined by Mr. Councler, of Leipsic, to be 56.53 per cent. This is considerably more than the average amount in basalts. In the quantity of silica it contains, and in the frequent presence of sanidin, this variety resembles the augite-andesites; but its abundance of olivine precludes the observer from classifying it with these rocks.

Nearly all of the basalts of this region are constituted as above described, but with them are some exceptional rocks [541, 542, 543] which are entirely crystalline, the amorphous glass base being wholly wanting. Nevertheless, these varieties are also rich in olivine and comparatively poor in augite, or at least in well-developed individuals of this mineral. There are larger feldspars 3^{mm} long, and large metamorphosed reddish olivines; and between these porphyritical crystals is a kind of groundmass which is a wholly crystalline, small-grained aggregation of feldspar prisms and microlites, exhibiting a good fluidal structure, and of little, crippled, greenish-yellow augites and magnetite.

The low hills in the region of Diabase Hills, Truckee Range, present a brownish, somewhat porous basalt rock [544], although its structure is the same as that of the predominating variety. But its feldspars are smaller and narrower, its augites and olivines extremely minute, and the globulitic grains in the glass-base are not blackish-brown but brownish-red, producing the peculiar color of the rock-mass.

The above-mentioned type of basalts, which is porphyritically crystalline throughout, is also found scattered here and there in the remoter neighborhood of Wadsworth. The hill three miles north of Diabase Hills has some excellent specimens of this variety [545.]

At the same place (Diabase Hills), a basalt was discovered [546] representing, in striking contrast with the rest, the other variety which abounds in a globulitic glass-base.

This interesting occurrence of the union of the two types of structure at one point is repeated on the road from Clark's Station to the entrance of the Truckee Cañon, where a crystalline, micro-porphyritical basalt [547] is accompanied by a globulitic half-glassy one [548]. In some parts of that first named, fine, predominating magnetite grains have been grouped with augite grains into dark roundish heaps, whose outlines gradually pass into the general groundmass. A curious and rare phenomenon is that where a countless number of the most minute, brown or black grains are irregularly scattered through the mass of the somewhat larger augites, giving it the dusty appearance so common to apatites and noseans.

In one case, the micro-porphyritical type, which is elsewhere entirely crystalline, was observed bearing also an amorphous base. A basalt discovered near King's Station [549] contains in the groundmass, in which the larger feldspars are imbedded, an excellent light-brown glass, occurring in comparatively large insular spots and patches. This glass is either quite pure or is penetrated by delicate, prickly microlites, and its color is the same as that in the lavas of Vesuvius. All the other peculiarities of the genuine micro-porphyritical type are faithfully detailed here: feldspars with indistinct outlines; the minuteness and paleness of the crippled, grain-like augites; augitic interpositions in the feldspars; the crystals of black magnetite unusually sharp; a few small olivines altered into a dirty-green serpentineous substance.

The basalts from the high peak in the Truckee Range, northeast of Wadsworth, are in part very similar to those from the region of the Diabase Hills. There is one [550] in which the globulites of the interwedged, half-glassy base have a light yellowish-brown color and are comparatively large. The larger feldspars contain kernels composed of loosely aggregated, irregular bodies of this mass, through which the feldspar substance can hardly be seen.

Other varieties [for instance, 551] represent the evenly granular type; a regular mixture of crystalline constituents, without any tendency to micro-porphyritical or macro-porphyritical structure, and destitute of any conspicuous amorphous substance. Apatite is more often found in these basalts than in any other modification; but this mineral seems to be rarer in the American basalts than in the corresponding German rocks. They abound in larger or smaller olivines, whose altered brownish mass sometimes imparts to the rock a dark yellowish-brown color [550.] One specimen [552] contains a great quantity of quite small reddish-yellow and yellowish-red spangles, laminæ, and lobes of specular iron disseminated throughout the rock, and sometimes pierced with numerous holes. It seems to be of secondary origin, which is connected with the fact that there is not much fresh and unaltered augite in the rock.

Basalt from the low hill west of Carson River [553] contains cuneiform masses of globulitic base, and has the structure and composition of the prevailing type of the Truckee Valley.

The basalts from the Kawsoh Mountains and their environs are often somewhat porous; thin, pearl-gray deposits covering the small hollows. That from the east end of these mountains [554] is rich in a globulitic, half-glassy mass, which, although it has the behavior so often described, does not occur in interwedged cuneiform bodies, but penetrates the rock like a ground-paste. This amorphous mass, together with its included brown globules, and the delicate, colorless prickles, which also occur here, is plainly seen decomposing into a seemingly quite homogeneous, yellowish-brown substance, which in polarized light is resolved into a number of parts like mosaic, each showing a chromatically different or an aggregate polarization. Considerable sanidin accompanies the prevailing plagioclase.

The principal rock from the central peak of the Kawsoh Mountains [555] is a basalt. It contains a globulitic base; beautiful, zonally built feldspars; larger, red-spotted olivines; quite small augites, and a thick grain of magnetite inclosing a particle of olivine, a new phenomenon. The feldspars appear in the slides in colorless sections 2.5^{mm} long.

At West Spur, Kawsoh Mountains, an almost crystalline, even-grained basalt occurs [556], in which, nevertheless, there is a small quantity of a thickly globulitic, amorphous base. Many laminæ and serrated dendritic lobes of specular iron unite with altered, smaller and larger, brownish-red olivines, to give the rock a dirty-brown color. Even in this variety, augites are not very frequent, and are poorly shaped. The feldspars have many gas-cavities. Numerous colorless microlites, which are often dichotomous, are scattered through the rock, and they would appear to belong to those so often found secreted in the globulitic base, but surely not to apatite.

In the south end of the Kawsoh Mountains, there is a basalt [557] whose structure is intermediate between the micro-porphyritical and the even-grained. Curiously enough, it contains microscopical aggregations of tridymite in the form of subtile, often regular hexagonal laminæ, which partly cover one another like tiles and are grouped into rounded heaps, exactly as in the rhyolites and trachytes; but they do not look as if they were produced by a secondary infiltration of silica. This is the first time tridymite has ever been observed in basaltic rocks. Since this basalt comes to the surface either through or near strata of infusorial silica, it is not impossible, as Mr. Clarence King has suggested, that an included fragment of silica is the true origin of the tridymite, in which case it would of course be a substance originally foreign to basalt.

There also occur in the same locality [558], in the southern end of the range, nearly due west from Wadsworth, and at Fossil Hill, at the extreme northern end of the Kawsoh Mountains [559], some excellent basalts, having the cuneiform masses of amorphous base, which is here a beautiful brownish glass with only a few pale, globulitic secretions. Some of the feldspars are colored a quite dirty yellow by hydrous oxyd of iron, which is deposited in innumerable confused cracks.

All other basalts from the environs of the Kawsoh Mountains which were examined, exhibited a globulitic base. That from the central peak [560] is a dark reddish-brown rock, containing feldspars 3^{mm} long, the capillary fissures of which are filled with numerous lobes of oxyd of iron, evidently secondary. The abundant olivine present is altered into a reddish-brown substance, and the interwedged base has here and there received the color of iron-rust, and its structure is gradually becoming obliterated.

The amorphous mass in the rather porous rocks from the Basalt Hills, at the south end of the Kawsoh Mountains [561, 562, 563, 564, 565], has some peculiarities. This light-brown, glassy substance sometimes contains, beside the globulites, short, black, impellucid, little needles, which appear to be embryo trichites. Augites of these specimens are remarkably pale. In other rocks, the globulitic mass only forms extremely thin septa between the polysynthetic individuals of plagioclase. If the section is oblique, this almost immeasurably narrow wall strongly contrasts with the colorless mass bounding it on each side, and its structure can easily be studied. The mass consists of colorless glass, with a multitude of very dark globulites, so that there is little of the colorless substance to be seen, and the thicker layers are impellucid. And as the thin sections show narrow feldspar ledges in this dark mass, it looks hachured. Here and there the amorphous base has begun to alter into a dirty-green substance, with which, however, there was only previously joined a feeble and indistinct fibrous formation. All these rocks are rather poor in olivines.

The basalt from the western foot-hills of the Truckee Range, four miles northeast of Wadsworth [566], is totally different, being an entirely crystal-line, even-grained rock, composed of plagioclases; comparatively thick, roundish augite grains; olivine and magnetite. Its macroscopical olivines are very accurately formed and bear excellent glass-inclusions, with bubbles.

In the Lake Range, on the east shore of Pyramid Lake, are some basalts with large pores, which are wholly crystalline, and destitute of amorphous base [567, 568, 569]. Plagioclases 4^{mm} long and 1.5^{mm} broad are sometimes far more highly charged with devitrified half-glassy inclusions and grains of augite and magnetite than is common in basalts; and in this they are like the plagioclases of andesites and trachytes. There are many crippled individuals of augite and olivine. Much lamellar oxyd of iron has settled on the rock, and the surfaces of the augites seem browned. One specimen from this locality is remarkable for the unusual length of its augitic microlites and its poorness in olivine.

The basalts with a somewhat resinous lustre, from the Lake Range on the northwest shore of Winnemucca Lake, have, on the contrary, an abun-dance of a quite pure or feebly globulitic glass-base [570, 571]. The augites are pale and stunted, and they very rarely show crystal faces. The olivines are rare but comparatively large and fresh. In one specimen from this locality, feldspar crystals occur which measure three-quarters of an inch in length, and appear very impure even in the hand-specimens. The strange particles imbedded in them are nearly as thick as a poppy-seed, and are simply fragments of the basalt-mass with the structure and elements complete. There are also innumerable, smaller, irregular particles of brownish, globulitic glass, nearly colorless, flat glass-inclusions, with bubbles which are only a few thousandths of a millimetre large, together with many gas-cavities, imbedded in the feldspars. And yet, curiously, these enormous feldspar crystals do not show any striation, and prove in polarized light to contain smaller individuals of sanidin, which are oriented in a different position. All the smaller feldspars are doubtless triclinic.

Basalts from the Lake Range, at the east shore of Pyramid Lake, are not very different [572]. The glass-base contains very thick and dark globulites; the augites are better crystallized, some being well formed; the feldspars, again measuring up to 4^{mm} in length, are very rich in glassy fragments, but all are true plagioclases, of which the fine striation is not at all disturbed by innumerable foreign inclusions: the glassy lobes often form a kind of net.

The most characteristic dolerites occur at Black Rock Mountains, Nevada, and in their immediate neighborhood, among them being a variety new to the herein-examined regions. That from Black Rock Hill, at the southernmost point of the group, consists of plagioclase, intensely colored augite, olivine, magnetite, and apatite. It shows, both in hand-specimen and thin section, a mass that appears macroscopically to be rather coarsely-crystalline throughout; but the microscope discovers that a little amorphous mass is present. The plagioclases are beautifully clear and fresh, and are splendidly lineated. There is no sign of sanidin. The augite is very fresh, of a light brownish-yellow color, and perfectly pure, with the exception of some glass-inclusions. Feldspar is better crystallized than augite, masses of which devoid of individual forms fill spaces between the plagioclases. Olivine is slightly altered. Magnetite is in fresh, thick grains. There is no titanic iron. Quartz is wanting here; indeed, it seldom occurs in the Tertiary dolerites, although it is very often present in the otherwise similar ante-Tertiary diabases. The augite differs from that in the freshest older diabases in that it shows no trace of chloritic alteration. The globulitic amorphous base, seen in thin section to be interwedged between the crystalline constituents in cuneiform masses, is traversed by colorless and very pale, yellowish rays, which sometimes protrude from it and pierce the

16 M P

feldspars, and by short, black microlites. Its mass is here and there slightly browned.

The dolerite from the south end of the Black Rock Mountains [573] agrees in every point with that just described.

A remarkably beautiful amorphous mass is found in a quite similar coarse dolerite which forms a butte in Black Rock Desert [574]. It is dotted with fine, black globulites and broad, acicular rays, composed of small, black grains arranged like beads on a string. The olivine is altered into a brownish substance.

To this same class of rocks also belongs the dolerite from Round Hill, Black Rock Mountains [575].

These dolerites, which are rich in olivines and darker augites, are a very characteristic type, which does not seem to be at all represented in other basaltic regions ; for instance, they are not found among the rocks of the Lower Truckee Valley.

Neighboring basalts from Snowstorm Ledge and Cañon, Black Rock Mountains, are entirely different from those of this locality thus far described [576, 577, 578]   They are homogeneous, destitute of macroscopical constituents, and the presence of much glassy mass is proved by their resinous lustre.   In some varieties, the globulitic base occurs in extremely minute particles, and the crystalline elements are also strikingly small.   In all the rocks of these localities, the infrequent augite is very pale, and it is often found in small, thin prisms or thicker microlites, on both sides of which subtile prickles of augite have fastened, pointing at different angles like the needles of a fir-tree, and some of them are covered with real bristly cilia (Plate I, fig. 19).   A striking contrast between these rocks is produced by the fact that they do not all contain distinct olivine.   In some of them, the magnetite is altered into brownish-yellow, hydrous oxyd of iron, which is somewhat translucent at the edges.   This decomposition is a rare phenomenon, even in the oldest diabases and diorites.   The passage from the original substance to the product of alteration can be nicely observed where one of those crossed or dendritic aggregations so common in this globulitic variety has suffered metamorphism in all its particles.   A most frequently observed phase of transition consists of a black, opaque kernel with light-brown border; usually, however, only a feeble obliteration of the outlines happens, the quadratic form being generally well preserved. One specimen, which appears somewhat altered and bears green-earth in small pores, contains titanic iron. In its fresh state, it can hardly be distinguished from magnetite; but it is sufficiently characterized when covered with the dull, porcelain-like crust of alteration, which makes it very conspicuous in reflected light.

A low hill west of the Kamma Mountains [579] yields a good dolerite, resembling those from the Black Rock Range, except by being less coarse-grained. It is more beautiful than the others, however, on account of the distinctness of the cuneiform bodies of dark, globulitic base between the feldspars and augites. This base is easily studied by reason of its distinctness. Thicker, almost black, globulites are rather rare, and lie isolated in the colorless or pale-grayish glass-mass, which also bears the acicular rays so often mentioned. When the contrast between these rays and the light glass is observed, it is discovered that they are not also colorless, but possess a pale yellowish-green tint. It is, therefore, probable that they are augitic microlites. They are often grouped in the form of stars, and arranged parallel, like the teeth of a comb. In some spots, this intermediate mass has begun to alter, and the black grains disappear, producing a seemingly homogeneous, and often rather intensely yellow material, in which the long, difficultly altered microlitic needles lie unchanged. The last stage of change is to really amygdaloidal products, built up of differently colored, concentric layers. The yellow substance polarizes indistinctly, yet evidently reacting under polarized light, the fresh glassy base being, of course, quite isotrope. Beside the fine magnetite grains, the rock bears rather many sharply hexagonal laminæ of specular iron, measuring 0.02^{mm} in diameter. These laminæ are violet-brown when very thin, and dark-brown when thicker. There are large augites and a very little olivine.

The dolerite from the desert between the Kamma and Pah-supp Mountains [580] is in every respect similar to the above.

Basalts from the Pah-tson Mountains closely resemble those from the Lower Truckee Valley, but they are richer than the former in microscopical olivines. The rocks from the west ridge of Blue Peak [581], Basalt

Peak [582], the northwest ridge of Black Peak [583], and the Grass Cañon Camp [584, 585], possess larger or smaller cuneiform bodies of amorphous globulitic base, which is more or less translucent, and often appears with a low magnifying power in the thin sections as a black, opaque mass, with light, short, linear incisions produced by the imbedded feldspars. The microscope also discovers that the feldspars contain numerous, long, brown glass-inclusions. There is more olivine (also with glassy grains) found here than the other basalts of the same type generally contain.

A rock capping the north peak of the Pah-tson Mountains [586] is somewhat different. In places, it is almost wholly crystalline, and it is composed of plagioclase, greenish augite, much olivine, and magnetite, exhibiting in parts of a single thin section light-brown and in other parts deep, dark-brown insular spots of homogeneous or slightly globulitic glass.

The same type, characterized by a globulitic base, occurs still further on, and is found in the basalts from Montezuma Range, their external aspects agreeing with those from the Truckee Valley.

In the basalts back of Oreana, Montezuma Range [587], the glassy mass is less frequently found in interposed cuneiform bodies, but serves more as a microscopical groundmass. As usual, the augite seldom occurs in the exactly formed, thick, dark crystals common to the more crystalline varieties, but in pale, crippled, and distorted, long prisms. The olivines are, without doubt, much better crystallized than the augites.

The glass-base of a rock from Basalt Hill, near White Plains, Montezuma Range, has an interesting structure [588]. It is a dark, grayish, globulitic glass, and contains, beside the globulites, opaque, quadrangular individuals of magnetite, whose well-known forms are powdered with grains, small augite crystals, and prisms of apatite, the sections of which often shine like little six-sided holes in the thicker, dark parts of the base. The apatites are very thin and delicate, and occasionally have a black, longitudinal centre or axis running from end to end. Sometimes extremely thin, line-like prisms are affixed to the six vertical edges of a larger individual (Plate I, fig. 10). It will, therefore, be seen that the base is unusually differentiated. There are very fresh, large olivines, with many included crystals of picotite. As a proper constituent, equivalent to plagioclase and olivine, augite is almost wanting; being confined to the extremely small grains and crystals in the glassy base. There are splendidly built crosses of magnetite grains. The globulites of the base are often not isolated, but are sometimes joined and form half-circles and horseshoe-shapes.

Another specimen from the same locality [589] contained only globulites in its base, being even destitute of the acicular rays; so the rock is, of course, much richer in independent individuals. Pale augites, of course, occur.

As a contrast to these, the basalts of the West Humboldt Mountains generally have an almost entirely crystalline structure. That near Buffalo Cañon [590] shows only a feeble trace of a globulitic, amorphous base, the presence of which would hardly be recognized if the observer had not become familiar with its behavior by recent previous examinations. The larger feldspars are highly charged with half-glassy inclusions. Here also the augites are much crippled. There are larger olivines, which are sometimes very nicely crystallized. It is here easily observable how the brownish-yellow product of alteration of the olivines works in long, delicate fibres from the fissures toward the interior, through the still fresh mass.

Better crystallized augites occur in the almost wholly crystalline basalt east of Oreana, in the West Humboldt Range [591, 592]. Under the microscope, this rock very closely resembles the German basalts from the Seven Mountains; but macroscopically it appears somewhat altered, and has developed calcite in its mass.

A rather rare composition is that of the basalt from Eldorado Cañon, West Humboldt Mountains [593]. It is an entirely crystalline rock, and its only macroscopically visible constituent is olivine, which occurs in the thin sections in numerous almost colorless grains. There are no larger feldspars, but only microscopical ones, and these are generally in the undeveloped state of microlites. Augites are very abundant, without doubt predominating over the feldspars. The augites are not especially large, but most of them are well crystallized, the sections in the different directions presenting very sharp and straight linear outlines; the horizontal sections, shaped by (∞P, $\infty \mathcal{P} \infty$, $\infty \mathcal{P} \infty$), showing the most beautiful and faultless zonal structure. They are accompanied by many rounded or irregular, brownish-yellow augite grains; and these grains and small prisms are often included in the larger, sharply outlined augite crystals. The olivines contain finished crystals of picotite, which are often gathered into heaps or groups, and are metamorphosed along the borders and cracks. There is a faint trace of colorless glass between the crystalline constituents.

The porous basalts from the hills north of Sou's Springs, Pah-Ute Range, resemble those from Buffalo Cañon [594, 595].

Specimens of all these rocks in which there is no glassy base, or only minute bodies of it, are quite dull and destitute of the resinous lustre. The striation of the feldspars is uncommonly rich, and the larger ones contain many inclusions. All the feldspars are plagioclases. An abundance of sanidin, in basalts, in fact seems to depend upon the presence of a globulitic glass-mass. There are olivines measuring 2^{mm}, which have been metamorphosed into a vivid red substance. The augites are poorly crystallized.

A basalt from Mountain Wells Station, south end of the Pah-Ute Range [596], and another from the divide at the head of Clan Alpine Cañon, Augusta Mountains [597], belong to the type which has a globulitic glass-base. That first named bears feldspars measuring up to 3^{mm}, which one can discern with the naked eye to be sanidin. All the lesser feldspars belong to the largely predominating plagioclase. The glass-base has the usual form, interwedged between crystals; and it is thoroughly altered into amygdaloidal nests (Plate XI, fig. 1). That the feldspars of the latter locality are built up of numerous schists, although very highly charged with foreign, half-glassy particles, can be seen in unusual distinctness. There are some olivines which bear glass-inclusions that are pressed flat and stretch out many dendritical arms, carrying near the end a small, dark bubble (Plate I, fig. 13). It may perhaps be remembered that a typical augite-andesite occurs in Antimony Cañon, Augusta Mountains.

Along the western foot-hills of the Fish Creek Mountains is a fine and large stream of porous basalt [598], containing feldspar crystals an inch long, part of which do not show any striation in the hand-specimens or any lineature in polarized light; they, therefore, belong to sanidin. But the microscope proves that all the smaller feldspars are plagioclases. The chief mass of the rock is in a very micromerous condition. There are no larger augites, and smaller individuals of this substance are not abundant. The rock is destitute of olivines. Its prevailing dark mass, which contains only macroscopical and microscopical feldspars, is very feebly transparent, and generally appears to be in the globulitic, half-glassy state; which condition agrees with the fact that delicate, irregular bodies of a globulitic base lie in the pellucid mass of the larger feldspars. Leucite and nephelino are surely not contained in this basaltic lava. Incrusting all the protuberances of the interior of the pores is an isabel-colored material, which is evidently a product of alteration; but its nature cannot be ascertained either macroscopically or microscopically.

A reddish-brown rock, from east of Winnemucca, near the mouth of Little Humboldt River [599], is seen, both macroscopically and microscopically, in the thin section, to be an excellent, genuine dolerite, bearing plagioclase, augite, many small olivines, and magnetite. The rock would appear at first sight to be entirely crystalline, but a closer examination proves that there are a very few globulitic, amorphous particles present. It is an interesting fact that these bodies, notwithstanding their rareness and smallness, have the common modification of solidification.

The low hills northeast of the Havallah Range are composed of a true, medium-grained basalt [600]. It would be exactly like the most common German variety, if it were not for the occasional finding of a very thin wall of globulitic glass-base between two plagioclases lying close together. The glass-mass is as rare in the German, Bohemian, and Scotch feldspar-basalts, as it is almost universal in those of the Fortieth Parallel.

At the top of the plateau at Stony Point, Shoshone Mesa, is a very small-grained basalt [601], which is rather poor in augite. Included between the constituents, more frequently, however, between the plagioclases, is an amorphous mass of the usual structure. But the glass is a light-grayish yellow, and the globulites are, therefore, comparatively pale. The constituents of the rock appear somewhat blended and confused on account of their minuteness. The small, reddish-brown, somewhat transparent grains scattered through the rock are olivines. Close observation is necessary to distinguish them from the magnetite grains, which here often possess an ochreous, peripheric zone, the centre or kernel being opaque.

The cliffs of the Shoshone Mesa exhibit a thoroughly characterized dolerite [602], similar in composition to those from Black Rock and the Kamma Mountains. Its well-formed plagioclases include rounded, greenish-yellow, drop-like augite-grains and little olivines, which are often crystallized, and even here are partly altered into a brownish substance. The rock also contains well-individualized augites, rather much olivine, magnetite, some apatite, and a little amorphous mass which bears more rays than globulites. There is no titanic iron. The rock is porous, the pores being sometimes as large as peas: this is not common in coarser-grained dolerites.

A similar dolerite occurs on the summit of the Shoshone Mesa, in company with the above-mentioned basalt [603].

The basaltic rocks of Egyptian Cañon, Mallard Hills, Nevada, afford a great variety of rare types. One of the less curious occurrences [604] has for its chief mass an extremely fine mixture of almost indistinguishable microlites and grains of plagioclase and augite, the largest elements being scarcely longer than 0.003^{mm}. This groundmass contains, without gradations of dimension from the smaller members up, macroscopical porphyritical, colorless feldspars, which are largely sanidin, and yellowish-brown augites. There are no olivines.

A very strange blackish-gray homogeneous rock [605] occurs in this cañon, bearing constituents which are in a certain sense porphyritical, although not exactly macroscopical, namely, impure sanidins and predominating plagioclases and augites. Olivines are wanting. These elements are imbedded in a groundmass which a high magnifying power proves to be in the globulitic, half-glassy state, relieved here and there with a secondary brown color. In this rather opaque groundmass, very peculiar products appear (Plate XI, fig. 4). They are colorless, line-like bodies looking like incisions or notches in the mass, most probably a feldspathic crystalline product of devitrification which are usually only 0.005^{mm} wide, and are straight, crooked, or curved into two-thirds of a circle. These parts of circles are sometimes arranged concentrically, sometimes with a tail like a paragraph-sign. The bent ones are sometimes placed radially, and sometimes they represent little trees, irregular branches projecting from a stronger stem. Often thinner, curved bodies are joined to a larger, like ribs to a spine, and again thinner, straight individuals are arranged like the teeth of a rake, not being on either side very sharply separated from the globulitic glass-mass. These curiously shaped and arranged lines pass into better-individualized bodies, which are recognized as identical with some that often occur in obsidians, pitch-stones, and artificial slags.[1] They have rectangular crystalline forms, the four corners tapering out into long teeth or prongs (see Plate I, fig. 20). The structure developed by these crystalline products of secretion is elsewhere entirely unknown to basalts; and when a thin section is considered only superficially, it might easily be supposed to belong to the rhyolites; but a globulitic base never occurs in the latter, and besides, the combination of plagioclase and augite is sufficient to prove the rock a member of the basalt family, amongst which it constitutes an exception: apatite, for instance, is far more plentiful than in other basalts.

At Whirlwind Peak, Shoshone Range, is a usual type of fine doleritic basalt [606]. It contains plagioclase, augite, olivine, magnetite which is rather coarse-grained under the microscope; and between these are small bodies of blackish-gray, globulitic base, its rays being powdered with minute grains.

In Agate Pass, Cortez Range, the same type reappears: it is finer-grained, however, and contains more base, paler augite, very little olivine, and unusually thick grains of magnetite. Fine specimens of chalcedony are found in this basalt; large stalactitic pieces, which in the interior often pass into a dull, milky, cacholong-like substance.

A common type of somewhat lustrous, porous basalt appears at Shepherd's Ranch, on the south fork of the Humboldt River [607]. The grayish-black globulitic base, however, serves more as a pervading ground-mass than merely as an interwedged body. In some places, the base is altered into the familiar isabel-colored fibres; and it now becomes evident that the interposed rays, which are powdered with minute grains, belong to augite, for the thicker and stronger ones are decidedly green. The rock is extremely poor in olivine.

---

[1] Vogelsang, Die Krystalliten, Plate VII, figs. 10, 11, 12.

In the Ruby Valley Range, the basalts bear a curious, finely porous, blackish-brown mass, which has a pitch-like lustre, and appears largely glassy [608]. It is destitute of macroscopical secretions. Under the microscope, it proves to be a brown glass free from any trace of a devitrification-product excepting some feeble traces of fine grains. Along some irregularly running, narrow lines, the glass has become pale and quite colorless; but these places do not show any polarizing action, the whole thin section appearing entirely dark at every point between crossed nicols. This basaltic glass-mass would be mistaken at first sight for a very pure tachylyte; but it is easily ascertained that it will not gelatinize, even when treated with boiling hydrochloric acid, the only effect of which is to give it a slight yellowish tinge. It is therefore only a tachylytic-looking substance; for it is destitute of the most characteristic feature of real tachylyte, namely, a readiness to form a thick gelatine of silica. It belongs rather to that division of basaltic glasses (the obsidians of basalt) which has been named hyalomelane (pseudotachylytes), since the rock is unaffected by acids. In Germany, these basaltic glasses, which were referred to the tachylytes on account of their external appearance, but have since been proved not to gelatinize, occur at Ostheim, in the Wetterau, and at the Sababurg, in the Reinhardswald.[1]

At the northern end of the Ombo Mountains is a common middle-grained basalt [609], containing but a very little amorphous, globulitic base. It is richer in augite than most of the other basalts, but, curiously, there is no olivine to be seen.

At Watch Hill, Elkhead Mountains, a rather coarse-grained typical dolerite occurs [610]. It bears large feldspars, augite, olivine, and magnetite. Much dark globulitic substance is interwedged between the crystals.

The top of Anita Peak, Elkhead Mountains, is composed of an excellent basalt [611] representing that well-characterized variety in which the amorphous base is free from globulites, being a pure glass of a chocolate or coffee-brown color, with occasional acicular microlites. Olivine alone appears macroscopically in the rock and in the thin sections as rather large grains, containing sharply outlined crystals of picotite and glass-inclusions.

---

[1] Rosenbusch, Mikroskopische Physiographie, 134.

The augites are of a darker-brown color, and are generally very well crystallized. All the feldspars are beautifully striated. Its augites include many quadrangular magnetite grains. An abundant brown glass-base is not interwedged in cuneiform shapes between the crystals, but serves as a pervading groundmass. In short, the rock combines all the peculiarities of the analogous German rocks from the Stillberg, in the Habichtswald, from Elfershausen, and from Weissholz, near Lütgeneder.

A rather remarkable rock is found in that from the Benches of the Upper Little Snake River [612]. It is a grayish-black mass containing small, greenish-black grains and large grains of quartz. Narrow, ledge-formed, microscopical plagioclases exhibiting a distinct fluidal texture, little crystals, and grains of pale greenish-yellow augite and black magnetite grains unite to form a mixture which appears macroscopically in the thin sections as a dark-grayish groundmass. Very dark grains, measuring 1^{mm}, may be seen macroscopically in this mass. These are the greenish-black grains of the hand-specimens, and a high magnifying power discovers that they are either a very intimate aggregation of opaque, black grains of magnetite, with augite grains, which sometimes possess crystal outlines, or a micaceous mineral larded with black grains. There is no olivine present. The quartzes, which appear in a certain sense as a foreign substance, are each surrounded by a narrow, coroniform zone of small augite grains. Possibly this rock is in some way connected with the curious quartziferous trachytes of the neighboring Elk Mountain.

Near the fork of the Yampah River is a common, medium-grained basalt, which has only faint signs of a globulitic base [613]. The plagioclases are fresh and richly linear; the augites pale green and poorly shaped; the olivines altered into an intensely brownish-red substance; and the colorless feldspars include a great quantity of angular, Prussian-blue grains, which are somewhat transparent, hardly 0.003^{mm} long, and of an unknown nature (possibly haüyne).

A very good basalt is found in the dikes west of Buffalo Peak in the ridge between North and Middle Parks, Colorado [614]. It is a plagioclase rock, rich in augite, bearing olivine, generally of a crystalline structure. The augites are mostly noteworthy for the excellence of their crystallization, the well-defined green kernels in their prevailing brownish-yellow mass, and the completeness of their zonal structure. One horizontal augite section 0.06^{mm} square was composed of no less than 42 layers. The olivines (Plate XI, fig. 3) are also very evenly shaped, the smaller ones being entirely metamorphosed into a brownish-yellow substance, which at first sight would not be easy to distinguish from that of augite. In the larger individuals, alteration has not proceeded beyond the borders and the walls of cracks, so that serpentineous veins wind in all directions through their sections. Each of these alteration-bands is made up of several layers of varying colors, slightly undulated ; some of them showing brown, yellowish, and green tinges, and the effect is very pretty where these variegated veins traverse the otherwise fresh and almost colorless olivine-substance. In many places between the crystalline elements of the rock are the most perfect bunches of trichites, aggregations of straight and curved, black, opaque, hair-like microlites of varying thickness, and with exactly the same behavior as they exhibit when scattered through obsidians. Basalts bearing groups of such trichites are not rare among the German occurrences, which are in general similar to this. Rectangular, dendritic, or skeleton-formed groups have not been observed here. The long microlites surely do not belong to magnetite, for there is no sign of passage between them and the common angular magnetite grains. It is probable that they are not proper ingredients of the rock, but are rather confined to small patches of colorless glass, which are not distinct. The rock contains a few quite small laminæ, of strongly dichroitic and absorbing brown biotite. And it has one strange phenomenon : some augite crystals standing close together form a compact group measuring about 3^{mm} in diameter. These crystals have sharp outlines, are traversed by the characteristic fissures of a yellowish-brown color common to the rest, and their substance here is perfectly pure. Inside they are much paler, becoming quite light aquamarine and pale greenish-blue, and a large quantity of foreign bodies is here interposed; rounded, opaque, black grains ; straight and black, longer or shorter needles of varying thickness arranged parallel into two systems pointing different ways, so that they cross each other obliquely in a similar manner to those which have been observed in diallages and hornblendes ; and small brown biotite plates, especially in those augites which contain the black grains, for those which bear the needles are generally destitute of other interpositions. Inclusions of biotite plates have never before been observed in basaltic augites, and are even wanting in the smaller and more isolated augite individuals in the same rock. Between the augites of this group are large sections of apatite, a mineral which does not appear elsewhere in the rock. Perhaps the black needles (0.02^{mm} long and generally 0.003^{mm} thick) are in some way connected with the above-mentioned trichites.

Buffalo Peak, North Park, presents a light basalt [615] which is entirely crystalline, rich in plagioclase and well-shaped light olivines, and rather poor in augite, mostly in the form of pale microlites Many sharp, six or three-sided, thin, brownish-violet plates of specular iron are scattered singly and in little groups through the rock. There is no brown mica. The glass-inclusions abounding in the olivines often contain, beside the bubble, many short, black microlites, which project from near the border toward the interior (Plate I, fig. 18).

Upon trying to separate into groups the different varieties of microscopical structure in these feldspar-bearing basaltic rocks of the Fortieth Parallel, we find the following distinctive groups :

a. Rocks of an evenly granular-crystalline composition, without any disposition to porphyritical microstructure, and poor in amorphous, glassy or half-glassy base. But a very slight trace of globulitic glass is often interwedged between the crystalline ingredients. This type of structure is presented by the true coarse or medium-grained dolerites, and by some of the seemingly homogeneous, genuine basalts. Nevertheless, the rocks possessing it are rather rare along the Fortieth Parallel, as compared with Germany or Northwestern Europe (Ireland, Scotland, Faeröer, Iceland), where this type is the most common one.

b. Rocks possessing a microscopically very fine-grained, totally crystalline aggregation of crippled microlites, largely feldspar and augite, which serves as a groundmass in which micro-porphyritical and macro-porphyritical, larger crystals of feldspar and olivine, with occasional augites, are distinctly and sharply imbedded. This type is rather restricted.

c. Rocks in which a homogeneous, pure glass-base, usually of a yellowish-brown color, is largely developed, but hardly in such abundance as to exceed the crystalline ingredients. This type is very rare.

d. Rocks composed of larger and smaller crystals, with a globulitic glassy base interwedged in cuneiform bodies between them. Without doubt, this variety has the closest affinities to augite-andesite. This well-characterized type, which occurs in other basaltic regions only as a well-known exception, is the most common one along the Fortieth Parallel; a fact that tends to sustain a previously mentioned result, namely, that the mode of structure which most frequently occurs in the European basaltic regions, is rare in the herein-examined territory of North America.

SECTION IV.

APPENDIX TO TRUE BASALTS.

There are two rocks which differ somewhat in mineralogical composition from the true feldspar-basalts described in the preceding pages, and yet are most intimately connected with them geologically. These basaltic occurrences are the subject of the following notes.

The principal rock of the hills between Haws's and Reed's Stations, near the Carson River, south end of Kawsoh Mountains [616], is of a blackish-gray, but not so dark or dull as most of the basalts, possessing a peculiar shimmering lustre. It looks something like a phonolite, and is fissile in rather thin and flat plates. Macroscopically, it is perfectly homogeneous, without any distinct porphyritical secretion. Under the microscope, a confused mass of badly formed crystals and needles appear, their substance ranging in color from a pale brownish-yellow to totally colorless. By comparison with other occurrences, these crystals and needles prove to belong to augite. Between the thin, delicate prisms, which are arranged without order, and are seldom longer than 0.045^{mm} or thicker than 0.015^{mm}, lie colorless sections of feldspar, mostly quadrangular in shape, and for the greater part polarizing monochromatically. But this is not proof that they are all sanidins, for the sections might belong to plagioclases cut parallel to $\infty \breve{P} \infty$. Distinctive striated plagioclase is, however, quite rare. There is no hornblende or biotite, leucite or noscan, and, curiously, no olivine, in this rock. Another irregularly shaped and even externally unindividualized, colorless, polarizing ingredient is found between the augite prisms. Judging from its behavior, this substance can only be considered as nepheline; for it occurs here in the manner so often found in the genuine nepheline-basalts. A great many small magnetite grains are disseminated through the mass. Upon being treated with hydrochloric acid, the rock immediately produces a gelatine, which is not very abundant or very stiff. This gelatine is occasioned by the presence of nepheline; for olivine is entirely wanting, and no other ingredient of the rock is thus decomposed by the acid.

Some conical hills at the north end of Kawsoh Mountains produce a variety similar to this in both macroscopical and microscopical respects [617, 618.] Larger fresh augite crystals, possessing the characteristic shape and cleavage, occur here, and they throw light upon the numerous, acicular, light brownish-yellow prisms belonging to the same mineral. There are also larger feldspars, which form small, white, macroscopical spots in the light-gray rock-mass; but here the larger and microscopical feldspars are, for the most part, plagioclases, accompanied by some sanidin. These specimens are also destitute of olivine. Apatite is present in many dusty, brown prisms, occurring precisely as so often found in phonolites, trachytes, and andesites, but rarely in genuine feldspar-basalts. Sometimes one apatite prism is partly imbedded in a larger feldspar and partly in the groundmass, another proof of the early solidification of this mineral. There is also considerable magnetite and some of the colorless, unindividualized nepheline-substance.

A comparatively very light rock from the eastern point of the Kawsoh Mountains is precisely the same as the above-described. The small prisms and ledges of feldspar show a distinct fluidal structure.

At the north end of the Kawsoh Mountains, the same variety is found in an altered state [619.] In the thin sections, numerous, little, pale, macroscopical veins can be seen traversing the dark-gray mass in reticular forms. These veins indicate avenues of alteration along which the rock is decomposed into a dirty, greenish-gray substance, whose nature cannot be determined. It is remarkable that the parallel layers of which this product of alteration consists, in many places contain, as the innermost portions of these veins of decomposition, small, rounded aggregations of tridymite laminæ, which, more than probably, are secondary depositions, although they have all the peculiarities of the mineral where it is supposed to be a primary, original constituent; such as the scaly accumulation, the tenderness, the regular, but more often irregular, six-sided shape, as in those within the pores of andesites, trachytes, and rhyolites.

The rock from Fortification Peak, Colorado [620], is a microscopically rather coarse-grained basalt rich in well-shaped, zonally built augites. At first sight, the rock appears closely to resemble the famous dolerite from the Löwenburg, in the Seven Mountains, on the Rhine. There are larger crystals of olivine. The colorless ingredient between the augites, olivines, and magnetites, however, in part only belongs to triclinic feldspar; other parts, polarizing monochromatically in colors of low orders, are unindividualized nepheline. Neither rectangular nor sexangular forms of this mineral could with certainty be detected. The sharply pointed ends of the augite crystals pierce this colorless nepheline mass in the usual manner, and it is also streaked with long, thin augite microlites. This ingredient is sometimes slightly altered into a less pellucid, dull substance, exactly like the first product of the decomposition of nepheline in the typical nepheline-basalts from the environs of Urach, in Würtemberg, from the Wartenburg, near Donaueschingen, Germany, and from the Fiji Islands, near Australia. Sharp, six-sided laminæ of brown biotite are not rare here, being more abundant than in any true and pure feldspar-basalt. There is much magnetite. Olivines are rich in beautiful crystals of picotite and in glass-inclusions. The augites also have glass particles imbedded in them, which are remarkable for their thickness and the included bubbles. This rock, like those next to be described, much more strongly gelatinizes when treated with hydrochloric acid than could olivine alone; and the presence of nepheline is thus chemically substantiated.

The rock from the summit of Navesink Peak, Elkhead Mountains, is exactly the same [621], except that the nepheline, and with it the biotite, are a little less abundant. Glass-inclusions of the olivines measure as high as 0.008^{mm} in length.

A dike on the Yampah River, south of Fortification Peak, also presents precisely the same composition. The less abundant augites are well crystallized, which is especially observable where they project into the colorless nepheline.

The mixed, coarsely and finely porous rock from the summit of Bastion Mountain, Elkhead Mountains, would appear, also, to belong to this variety [622]. Nevertheless, it is rich in narrow plagioclases, which in some places possess an excellent fluidal structure. Some colorless spots are probably nepheline. There occur, beside the dark augites, some unknown needles, which are apparently flat and of a citron-yellow color when very thin, and varying from an orange to brownish-red when thicker. They are totally undichroitic, with rudimentary and crippled ends. In some places, these prisms are very numerous, and measure 0.06^{mm}. They are neither hornblende, augite, olivine, nor biotite; but perhaps they belong to göthite; yet the rock contains but little less magnetite than the others. A very little globulitic glass-base is occasionally seen.

The rock from the ridge running east from Hantz Peak, Elkhead Mountains [623], surely belongs to this series. It bears plagioclase, unindividualized nepheline, augite, olivine, some biotite and apatite.

A very curious rock was found at Fortification Rampart, Elkhead Mountains [624]. It belongs geologically to the basalts, although it differs from them at first sight by the lighter-gray color of its specimens and by the presence of a not inconsiderable quantity of macroscopical brownish-black biotite plates, which appear as foreign elements even macroscopically. The thin sections do not show in polarized light a single triclinic feldspar. A great quantity of freely cleavable and partly well-crystallized yellowish-green augites, finely lamellated biotite, laminæ measuring 1^{mm}, with sharp borders and a darker or lighter brown color to their sections, according to their thickness, and a colorless ingredient, which is equal in amount to both the others, and polarizes monochromatically without any striation, are present. Notwithstanding there is no olivine, the rock gelatinizes, which, by all analogy, proves nepheline. But only a part of the colorless spots above mentioned can belong to nepheline; for after the powdered rock had suffered a long treatment with boiling hydrochloric acid, a large quantity of the colorless grains and fragments remained unaltered. It is unquestionable that these latter belong to sanidin. Sometimes the colorless bodies are bordered on each side by parallel lines, perpendicularly upon which the substance has become somewhat fibrous, as so often happens when alteration has just begun in nepheline. Apatite is more abundant than in any genuine plagioclase-basalt. Hornblende is wanting.

CHAPTER IX.

LEUCITE ROCKS.

More than twenty years ago, Alexander von Humboldt published his conclusion that leucite was a mineral only found in Europe; and it is rather curious that this casual remark has not been disproved until very recently. This mineral, up to the year 1868, was only known as a constituent of several lavas of Italy, of the Laacher See, and of the Kaiserstuhl, in Baden. Since that year, it has been discovered to be a microscopical ingredient of many basalts of Saxony, Bohemia, the Thüringer Wald, and the Rhön Mountains, occurring in unexpected frequency[1] But all these localities were European; so the remark still held good; and the other extra-European basic rocks, examined in large quantity, were never found to contain leucite.

In 1874, Vogelsang discovered an Asiatic leucite. It occurred in a basaltic rock from the Gunung Bantal Soesoem, upon the small island of Bawean, north of Java.[2]

And now the microscopical study of the rocks of the Fortieth Parallel establishes the existence in America of the most classic leucite rocks. Moreover, these rocks are richer in the mineral than any occurrence in the Old World, besides which their general composition is very peculiar. Leucite was always considered, as is well known, one of the most perfect members of the regular system, until, in 1872, G. von Rath stated[3] that it belonged to the tetragonal or quadratic system, the apparent icositetrahedron

[1] F. Z., Die mikroskop. Structur u. Zusammensetzung der Basaltgesteine.
[2] F. Z., Neues Jahrb. f. Mineralogie, 1875, 175: which was a communication after the lamented death of Vogelsang.
[3] Monatsber. d. k. Aknd. d. Wissensch. zu Berlin, 1. Aug. 1872.

259

being a combination of (P . 4 P 2). The colorless crystals, which generally show in the section a more or less regular or rounded octagon, have the peculiarity of containing a great quantity of strange, little crystals and grains grouped into a small, central heap or (which is more often the case) concentric zones, of which the sections are also octagonal or roundish. These corpuscula, which are supposed to be intruded into the leucite, are, instead, situated on the surface of the leucite forms or globular figures.

The first occurrence of these American leucite rocks was found in the Leucite Hills, northwest of Point of Rocks, Wyoming Territory [625, 626]. They have a light yellowish-gray, felsitic-looking, and very finely porous mass, in which the only macroscopical inclusion is some brownish-yellow and reddish-brown mica. This mica is not in six-sided or rounded plates, but in the form of remarkably long stripes and dashes, such as have seldom been observed. No other ingredients are visible to the naked eye, and the specimens do not disclose their rich secretions of leucite. At the first glimpse of the rock under the microscope (Plate V, fig. 4), the leucite appears, with its innumerable, very sharply outlined, colorless, octagonal sections 0.035^{mm} in diameter. None of the known European rocks are as rich in leucite as these, and there is scarcely one in which the forms of the sections are so regular and so similar. As is the rule with all such small bodies, the sections are entirely dark between crossed nicols, and do not show the curious systems of alternating dark and polarizing lines caused by polysynthetic twin-formation. The most minute leucites, measuring but 0.003^{mm}, with their fine, clear octagons, seem to have perfected their crystalline form. All of these leucite sections (Plate I, figs. 21, 22, 23) include quite pale-green augite-grains, which themselves bear very minute glass-grains, with included bubbles, arranged into pretty wreaths or rings, being, in fact, the American counterpart of the leucites in the famous lava stream flowing from the Alban Mountains to the Tomb of Cæcilia Metella, near the Capo di Bove, near Rome. From five to eight rounded grains are grouped in these rings. A very nice phenomenon is that where light-green augite-microlites, radially arranged and very evenly distributed, occasionally protrude from the surrounding rock-mass into the larger leucites. In rare cases, leucites are found which entirely include club-formed augite-needles. These needles are not arranged zonally or tangentially, but radially; the long axis of each pointing to a common centre, precisely as the phenomenon has been observed in some leucites of Vesuvian lava streams.[1] There are mixed with the leucites in this rock, as independent ingredients, pale-green prisms, acicular needles, and microlites, which surely belong to augite; although their shape is indistinct, and larger, better-crystallized individuals do not occur. In this fine aggregation and intermixture of leucite and augite, the large biotite stripes are imbedded, and none of them of microscopical size was observed. This curiously colored mica, which resembles ormolu, and whose long, thin streaks appear in surprising distinctness in the light rock-mass, is remarkable for its comparatively very feeble absorption. When examined with one nicol, its transverse sections never appear deep-brown or black, but only reddish-brown. Sometimes several delicate zones, each of a different color, compose the mica plates. These plates seem for the most part to be scattered through the rock with some measure of parallelism; and hence the sections prepared parallel to the rock-cleavage show no transverse sections of mica, but only basal ones. There is no trace of monoclinic or striated feldspar, and hornblende, olivine, mellilite, haüyne, and noscan are wanting. A small quantity of magnetite is present, and also a considerable number of comparatively thick apatites, possessing a basal cleavage, and often a longitudinal dust-line in the interior. Occasionally, indistinct, colorless, rectangular or oblong bodies appear, which possibly belong to nepheline. No corresponding hexagons are visible; but, in any case, this mineral must be relatively very rare. Some brownish-black, opaque microlites occur at intervals, and a few of them are included in the mica.

The external aspect and the mineralogical composition of these rocks differ not a little from the other leucite-bearing masses. Their unusual light-gray color is produced by the extraordinary abundance of leucite, and their comparative poorness in augite. Moreover, the augite occurs only microscopically. The European leucite rocks commonly bear thicker individuals of augite, and much more of it, and also more magnetite, so that their color is a great deal darker. The entire absence of feldspar is as remarkable as the abundance of large macroscopical biotites.

---

[1] F. Z., Neues Jahrbuch f. Mineralogie, 1870, 810.

CHAPTER X.
CLASTIC ROCKS.

SECTION I.

OLDER CLASTIC ROCKS.

Only a small number of occurrences belonging to this group has been examined, for the series does not possess great petrographical interest. The following rocks, however, seem to deserve mention.

An old Carboniferous conglomerate from Penn Cañon in the River Range, Nevada [627], is mostly made up of angular grains of black and brown lydite, quartz, and hornstone. The quartz-grains bear a great multitude of fluid-inclusions and frequently also delicate lamellæ of mica; both of which inclusions prove that the grains are derived from shattered and disintegrated old granites or crystalline slates. .

Another old Carboniferous rock from Penn Cañon [628], which occupies a middle place between sandstone and graywacke, consists of rounded grains of quartz and decomposed feldspar and lydite. Here, also, the quartz grains include very neat, sharp, six-sided mica lamellæ, measuring only 0.003^{mm}.

A reddish conglomerate occurs in the same locality, which bears grains of quartz and kaolinized feldspar in a cement that is sprinkled with unknown black grains and is itself entirely indifferent to polarized light. This cement is therefore an opal-like substance or an amorphous silicate.

262

In another old clastic rock found in the Fountain Head Hills, Nevada [629], which is a rather coarse-grained graywacke similar to arkose, the microscope discovers a phenomenon that was previously known only macroscopically, namely, the impressions made by egg-shaped fragments of neighboring rocks, as they occur, for instance, in the pebbles of the nagelflues in Switzerland. Here rounded, oval, worn grains of quartz have caused very distinct and often rather deep impressions in the surface of other clastic constituents with which they come in contact, especially in the pebble-like pieces of decomposed feldspars of a mass similar to felsite, and also in lydite.

SECTION II.

YOUNGER CLASTIC ROCKS—BRECCIAS, CONGLOMERATES AND TUFAS OF TERTIARY AGE.

The character of a clastic rock is easily recognized under the microscope if the thin section is made up of several fragments and not of a single one. Rhyolitic and trachytic rocks of this series are still rather fresh, while the basaltic and andesitic ones are much altered or decomposed, which renders them very difficult to study. If little bits of rock form the clastic material, the characteristic structure of certain mineral constituents can be seen very distinctly; for instance, the quartzes in the rhyolitic fragmentary rocks are seldom free from glass-inclusions, and the olivines in the basaltic group show the traversing veins of serpentineous matter.

It should be remembered that these clastic rocks are to be divided into two genetically different classes; on the one hand those in which the cement binding the larger and smaller fragments, is only a very finely ground detritus of the same petrographical material, and on the other hand an eruptive crystalline rock-mass, which, for the most part, presents a variety of cemented fragments. In the latter case, the imbedded clastic pieces generally have a remarkably sharp-edged form. The Tertiary clastic rocks to be examined in the following pages may be separated into two divisions: one made up of rhyolitic or acid, and the other of basaltic or basic material. Trachytic and andesitic clastic rocks are very rare about the Fortieth Parallel.

RHYOLITIC CLASTIC ROCKS.—The rhyolites of Western Nevada are often accompanied by numerous tufas and breccias. They are abundant, for instance, on the ridge at the head of Winnemucca Valley and about the Warm Springs and the Hot Springs.

West of the Warm Springs, near old Fort Churchill, Nevada, a tufa [630] forms a lake deposit, consisting of predominating, light-colored and brown rhyolitic detritus.

In the neighborhood of the Hot Springs, west base of Kawsoh Mountains, a rhyolitic breccia is spread out [631]. It is very finely clastic and highly porous. The microscope discovers the walls of the pores to be incrusted to the depth of 0.2^{mm} with a homogeneous substance of a pale-yellowish color, entirely isotrope in polarized light, and without doubt opal as a product of decomposition.

The Tertiary hills between the Kawsoh Mountains and Montezuma Range are rhyolitic tufa deposits [632, 633], in former fresh-water lakes, made up of nearly colorless, predominating, little, microscopical splinters, chips, and shards of very porous glass, accompanied by some fragments of diatomes (*Melosira, Navicula*).

One of the most remarkable clastic rocks of those herein described is an obscure rhyolitic breccia from Mullens' Gap, west side of Pyramid Lake [634]. It is composed of sharp-edged fragments of a light-gray and a dark-gray rhyolitic rock, as large as hazel-nuts, imbedded in a predominating dirty-gray material. The structure of the clastic particles of the light-gray and dirty-gray rhyolitic substance are not especially noteworthy; but the fragments of the dark-gray rhyolite, which have a somewhat pitch-like lustre, merit particular attention. Under the microscope, they are found to consist (Plate XII, fig. 1), in the main, of a pellucid glass, which has a very strange tone of color, best described as a pale-brownish-violet. Some feld-spar crystals, which are mostly sanidins, a considerable quantity of little feldspar microlites, and some black-edged grains, probably belonging to magnetite, are scattered through this glass-mass. Distinct and beautiful, waving, fluidal phenomena are caused by the direction of those secreted bodies which have a longitudinal axis. The glass also bears dark-bordered gas-cavities, roundish in form, egg-shaped, or drawn out parallel to the direction of the fluidal lines. But the most remarkable feature of all is, that the glass contains the most perfect fluid-inclusions, with a movable bubble in each. For a moment the bubble will roll slowly around in the liquid, presently it shows a trembling motion, and again rests immovable; but it can easily be set in motion by a slight elevation of temperature, for instance, by the heat of a lighted cigar held under the thin section. These liquid-inclusions attain the comparatively large size of 0.012^{mm}, being seen at the first glance, and there is a great quantity of them, for the most part of an oval form, but many are stretched out parallel to the lines of fluctuation. Since heating the thin section to a high temperature will not cause the bubble to be absorbed, the liquid cannot be pure carbonic acid. It is probably water holding in solution a slight amount of the acid.   The presence of fluid-inclusions in a real glass-mass is indeed striking.   To be sure, such inclusions were known in the con-stituents of rocks that had doubtless been solidified from a molten material, as in the leucites and olivines of basaltic lavas.   But these latter masses have, by cooling, become a wholly, or almost wholly, crystalline aggregation which does not contain any, or hardly any, glassy base as a solidified residuum of the molten magma.   On the other hand, fluid-inclusions in the larger crys-tals of glassy and half-glassy rocks were, as far as is known, totally wanting. In the feldspars, quartzes, hornblendes, etc., of the pitchstones, pearlites, and obsidians, and of the trachytes and rhyolites, rich in glass, all included amor-phous particles are, conformably, of a hyaline nature.   But in the rhyolitic fragments of this American rock, a part of a liquid, or of a gas condensed to a liquid, has been arrested by the molten mass and preserved in the glass produced therefrom by cooling.   The conclusions which are to be drawn from these observations as to the physical state of the former molten matter, are so near at hand that they should be explained in this connection.   The presence of liquids does not necessarily exclude the idea of a former molten state, and *vice versa.*   The fact that fluid-inclusions occur, for instance, in the quartzes of granites cannot, by any means, be used as an argument against the igneous origin of this rock.   This interesting breccia presents yet another rare phenomenon.   A colorless crystal, 0.14^{mm} long and 0.024^{mm} thick, one end terminating in a point, lies in the violet glass.   On account of its daz-zling clearness, the roughness of its surface, its transverse basal cracks, and its association with hexagonal sections of the same substance, it would appear most probable that it belongs to the almost omnipresent apatite.   This crystal contains an inclusion of light brownish glass, 0.02^{mm} long and 0.009^{mm} thick, imbedded parallel to the chief axis of the crystal, as is usual in apatites; and there is a moving bubble within this fluid-inclusion.   This isolated hyaline particle, entirely separated from the crystal mass, therefore possesses precisely the same peculiarity as the chief glassy mass of the rock.   This phenomenon invests with new importance an older and perhaps half-forgotten observation made in 1868, where the leucites of the lava from Capo di Bove, near Rome, of that from the Solfatara, near Naples, and from the Burgberg, near Rieden, Lake of Laach, were found to contain analogous glass-inclusions,[1] which bore, instead of the usual interior empty cavity, a liquid in which rolled a moving bubble. Beside these combined interpositions, there occur in the same leucites, single glass and fluid inclusions. Since then no such curious associations have been seen. They merit attention now, because here, in *one* microscopical object, proofs of the presence of both factors in the rock-formation of molten material and liquid (or gas) are evidently united.

At Cold Spring, Forman Mountains, Nevada, a characteristic rhyolitic breccia occurs [635]. It is a predominating brownish-red rhyolite, in which there are so many small splinters and chip-like, sharp-edged fragments imbedded, that in a thin section the size of one's finger-nail more than thirty can be seen with the naked eye. It seems to be a real friction-breccia, not a product of aqueous accumulation, nor yet a solidified, ejected tufa; for under the microscope the brown-red rhyolite mass is seen to fill up the very smallest spaces between the strange fragments. There is great similarity between it and the massive quartziferous rhyolite found in the Forman Mountains [362]. The gray fragments of this mass very closely resemble the material of which a rhyolitic breccia of Snow Storm Cañon, east slope of the Black Rock Mountains, is mostly composed [636], and which again appears in the desert near Utah Hills, Black Rock Mountains [637]. It may be remembered in this connection that among the described massive rhyolites there are many that contain a few very small fragments of strange varieties without exhibiting either to the unaided eye or under the microscope the true characteristics of a breccia.

In Snow Storm Cañon, Black Rock Mountains, there is a pumice-breccia [638] which the microscope discovers to be composed of numerous fragments welded or cemented closely together. The single fragments are mostly skeins of a gray glass, with a few crystals and ledges of feldspar. Individual glass-lines follow different directions in the adjoining pumice fragments. Under the microscope, the character of the mass as a breccia is very distinct. Broken pieces of a brown rhyolite mass are also interposed between the pumice particles.

Another series of rhyolitic tufas and breccias develop in the Kamma and Pah-tson Mountains. Three varieties were examined from the Kamma

---

[1] F. Z., Zeitschrift d. d. geolog. Gesellsch., XX, 1868, 117, 132.

Mountains [639, 640, 641], one from the ridge north of the Kamma Mountains [642], and four from the vicinity of Grass Cañon, in the Pah-tson [643, 644, 645, 646]. The rocks from these places are made up of very small fragments of rhyolite heaped together, sometimes in actual contact with each other, and sometimes included in a cement, which is not of a clastic nature, and often itself predominates. The most diverse varieties are represented here; strongly half-glassy ones, little sphærolitic rhyolites, including glass, and possessing microscopically an excellent fluidal structure; some whose texture is entirely orderless, and brownish-gray ones with a reddish tinge. They chiefly belong, however, to varieties which are very poor in larger crystals or entirely free from them. One of the nicest rocks of this neighborhood is a pumice-like breccia from Ball Rocks, Grass Cañon, Pah-tson Mountains [644]. It is for the most part composed of pieces of variously colored glass, which are very rich in pores. There are no crystalline secretions, but the single glass-fragments contain shards and bits of differently colored glass.

Tufas and breccias are also associated with rhyolites at Lovelock's Knob, foot-hills of the Montezuma Range. It is difficult to determine whether the principal part of a dirty-gray product from this place [647] is a solid, massive rock, or a very intimate accumulation of fine, clastic fragments. To be sure upon this point would be rather interesting, for the cavities of the rock contain an enormous quantity of the most beautiful and characteristic aggregations of comparatively large tridymite crystals. This occurrence of tridymite, supposing the rock to be composed of fine clastic fragments, can only be explained as a secondary formation, which would be very remarkable genetically; there being no unquestionable proof of the epigenetic nature of this mineral.

Another specimen from Lovelock's Knob is an accumulation of entirely isotrope shards and splinters of glass, varying in color from yellowish-gray to almost colorless, and very rich in pores. On account of its porosity, the rock shows no polarizing ingredient, and for the same reason it passes into the pumice-like variety.

In the Mopung Hills, West Humboldt Mountains, a compact crystalline quartz and some which is distinctly fibrous, forming the nicest sphærolites, with an admirable aggregate polarization, serve as the cementing material of the rhyolitic fragments [648].

The rhyolites of the Mopung Hills are associated with fine breccias, in which massive, not clastic, rhyolite material is the chief binding mass of the small fragments [649, 650]. Very coarse, light-colored bits of a sphærolitic rhyolite, in a quite dark, brownish-red cement, appear in the breccias of the Sou's Springs, Pah-Ute Range [651], bearing in its hollows small, botryoidal and well-stratified deposits of siliceous matter. The sphærolites are rather poorly developed, consisting merely of the first rudiments or of segments of a circle: the formation of a somewhat regularly outlined, globular secretion has nowhere taken place.

Grayish-green rhyolite-breccias are found in the Desatoya Mountains [652, 653]. They are chiefly made up of a pale-greenish, twisted, conchoidal glass, which is traversed by curious stripes of colorless glass, sometimes straight and sometimes curved like a sabre, a linear aggregation of the most fine, green, microlitic prickles running like a longitudinal axis from end to end of each. This aggregation is bounded on both sides by the colorless glass. The latter bears quartzes which include apatites containing glassy particles and monoclinic and triclinic feldspars. In the prevailing glassy rock-mass, there is a great number of sharp-edged little fragments of glass of the most diverse texture, but usually possessing a very distinct fluidal structure, the direction of which, of course, varies a great deal in the single shards. So many kinds of glass are here fused together that with a magnifying power of 300, as many as six glass splinters of a different texture may often be seen at once included in the chief mass.

Real pumice-tufa occurs in the Fish Creek Mountains. It is, for the most part, an accumulation of very porous and undulated streaks of yellowish-gray glass.

A breccia from Mount Airy, southern end of Shoshone Range [654], consists of sharp, angular fragments of dirty-grayish and greenish rhyolitic varieties, isolated crystals of quartz, which are often broken, with perfect glass-inclusions, feldspar, and biotite. The pores of the rock are covered over with curious microscopical crystals, the nature of which is unknown. These crystals measure 0.1^{mm} in length, are entirely colorless, sharply crystallized, and belong either to the tetragonal or the rhombic system, having a rectangular, and often apparently quadratic, prism, with two horizontal terminating faces. The prismatic faces bear a vertical striation. It is difficult to think of a mineral known macroscopically which could be supposed to occur in this manner, and capable of connection with these secondary crystals. May it not be the zeolite, comptonite, or thomsonite, the prismatic angle of which is 90° 40′, and whose prismatic faces are vertically striated?

Penn Cañon, River Range, contains very fine clastic rhyolitic tufas [655, 656, 657], which contrast with many of the above-mentioned rocks, that contain strange fragments in a predominating crystalline mass. Here are striped and striated, gray, brownish, and yellowish varieties which are perfect likenesses of the felsitic tufas or claystones of the Lower Permian (Dyas, Rothliegendes) in Germany, originating in the old felsite-porphyries; in every respect, the true precursors of the Tertiary rhyolites.

Dirty-gray rhyolitic tufa from Carico Cañon, Shoshone Range, whose individual particles on an average measure only 0.05^{mm} in diameter, is similar to the last described [658].

A coarser tufa from the slope toward Indian Creek [659] has, upon the surface of its rounded, clastic particles, crystals like those in the rock from Mount Airy, here also protruding into the chasms.

The same locality has another variety which looks like a light, coarse-grained graywacke. Under the microscope, there are to be observed: a, several kinds of rhyolitic-felsitic groundmasses; b, fragments of feldspars that are partly striated; c, rounded quartzes, in some of which glass-inclusions appear; d, broken pieces of biotite; e, brown hornblende. All these ingredients are closely massed together without any visible cement, but there are minute spaces between them.

Rhyolitic tufas of Sacred Pass, Humboldt Mountains, are very finely clastic [660, 661, 662]. One of them was made up in pretty equal parts of fragments of rhyolitic rubbish, and bits of crystals measuring 0.1^{mm}.

A clastic rock from Citadel Cliff, Holmes' Creek Valley, is a very interesting one. It is a nearly compact brown mass, which the loupe shows to be made up of little splinters of glass. The composition of the rock is a fine volcanic ash, consisting of very thin splinters of obsidian fused together into a cohering mass. Under the microscope, the thin sections have a very beautiful appearance. The thin bits of glass, destitute of secretions, are of a lighter or darker brownish-yellow color. They are orderless, pointing in different directions, and can often be seen to be welded together on the border crosswise. Between them, as independent clastic ingredients, are fragments of feldspar and quartz, the latter bearing comparatively large glass-inclusions.

Before closing this section, some occurrences which are genetically or geologically connected with the rhyolitic, clastic rocks, should be mentioned.

The tufas from Boone Creek, Shoshone Range, include opal, the colorless mass of which shows, in the thin sections, white, milky stripes, less pellucid than the surrounding substance [663, 664]. They are an intimate aggregation of little siliceous sphærolitic globules (Vogelsang's cumulites[1]), sharply separated at the borders from the predominating colorless material. The latter appears perfectly homogeneous in ordinary light, and it is astonishing to observe between crossed nicols that they form an aggregation of single-edged polarizing grains which are set together like mosaic. Where this aggregation is coarser, but particularly where it is finer, there appears in polarized light a very pretty speckled, spotted, and stippled surface, such as could not possibly be reproduced by artificial coloring. In some places, the larger grains have very fine, radiating fibres. Independent of the fact of the presence of water in the mass, it is not very probable that the grains belong to crystalline quartz. It seems more likely that they are particles of opal, which have been endowed with double refraction by mutual pressure. The polarizing qualities of the noble opal were detected by Reusch in 1865, who has been corroborated by Behrens.[2]

A chalcedony from Grass Cañon, Pah-tson Mountains, possesses an exquisite structure [665]. It does not originate from the tufas, however, but from the massive rhyolites. Under the microscope, the section shows little globules and botryoidal concretions in a seemingly homogeneous, colorless

---

[1] Die Krystalliten, Bonn, 1875, 134.

[2] In his capital examinations of the microstructure of opals—Sitzungsber. d. Wiener Akad., LXIV, 1871, Dec. Heft.

substance. The globules are very nicely concentric, and become entirely
dark between crossed nicols. Viewed through the nicols, the colorless
substance proves to be an aggregation of siliceous sphærolites, which
richly polarize (Plate XII, fig. 2). They are fibrous, the fibres radiating,
although the outlines are not rounded, but have become polygonal by
reciprocal compression.

A whitish, sinter-like, siliceous deposit resembling chalcedony, from
the hills between Kawsoh Mountain and Montezuma Range [666], gives a
thin section, in which small pellucid spots alternate with less pellucid ones.
The microscope discovers that the whole mass is crystalline, and it presents
a variegated, glittering picture. It is a pure, proper hornstone, made up of
an aggregation of the finest quartz particles, closely resembling the hornstone from the metalliferous veins of Schneeberg, Saxony, which is, however, somewhat coarser crystalline. The dull spots are caused by an
enormous quantity of angular and rounded, dark-bordered cavities, averaging 0.01^{mm} in diameter, which lie associated in this hornstone. They
are always empty, never showing a bubble, the sign of a surrounding
liquid. Otherwise this siliceous deposit is wholly free from anything like an
inclusion, and no particle which could possibly belong to an opal substance
can be detected in it. It is remarkable, and, as far as is known, hitherto
unobserved, for a sinter produced by siliciferous springs to take the form
and condition of cryptocrystalline quartz instead of that of amorphous,
simply reflecting opal, called a siliceous sinter.

BASALTIC CLASTIC ROCKS.—The massive basalts do not seem to be as
often accompanied by corresponding fragmentary rocks as the rhyolites.
Only those which are in some respects especially interesting will be mentioned in these closing pages.

At the Black Rock (which will be mentioned hereafter as the location
of a palagonite tufa), a blackish-gray rock [667, 668] is found which appears
rather homogeneous and looks like a basalt; but under the microscope it
proves to be a basaltic tufa. Angular, dark splinters and little bits of
basalt are first distinguished, together with colorless ledges of plagioclase.
They seem to belong to a very dark, globulitically devitrified variety of
basalt, and are often browned. Other basalts are represented, but they are

much decomposed, and cannot well be made out. There are also rounded spots, mostly of a green color, sometimes composed of undulated stripes and sprinkled with black grains. These are probably products of the alteration of olivine and augite. The cement is mostly of a calcareous nature. Even larger and purer portions of calcite bearing the characteristic twin-striation appear in some places.

A remarkable basaltic tufa comes from Basalt Ridge, east of Grass Cañon, Pah-tson Mountains [669]. It is principally composed of many-cornered splinters, of a brown, somewhat porous, and entirely isotrope glass, in which only the traces of crystalline secretions can be detected. There are also some polarizing fragments of dark-brown augite and color-less feldspar crystals. These clastic constituents are joined without cement, so that the rock is very loose and easily triturable. The brown glass will not gelatinize, even after a long boiling with hydrochloric acid : it therefore does not belong to tachylyte, but to hyalomelane (page 250). Indeed, it is allowable to call this rock a hyalomelane tufa. It was probably once in the state of volcanic sand ; and it may be remarked in this connection that, among the clastic, dust-like particles of ejected volcanic material, glass-masses far more largely predominate than in the massive lavas which have flowed out of the same crater.[1] Petrographically, if we disregard their insolubility in acids, such materials are not very different from palagonitic tufas.

At Bastion Mountain, Elkhead Mountains, a curious basaltic tufa occurs [670] which the microscope shows is composed of, a, fragments of a basaltic, light greenish-yellow glass, as thick as peas, with augite crystals, color-less feldspar-microlites, arranged like stars, black magnetite grains, and numerous small, oval cavities ; b, rounded quartzes, traversed by many band-like lines of fluid-inclusions, and the long, often curved, very thin, blackish needles that are so often observed in the quartzes of granites or crystalline schists ; c, fragments of a decomposed, dull, untransparent min-eral, which appears to be altered orthoclase ; and, d, a cement of calcite. It is probable that predominating basaltic detritus has united with metamor-phosed granites to form this rock-mass.

PALAGONITE TUFA.—The mineral known as palagonite, which was first

_____
[1] Neues Jahrb. f. Mineralogie, u. s. w., 1872, 16.

detected by Sartorius von Waltershausen in the basaltic tufas from Militello, Sicily, and from several places (but especially Seljadalr) in Iceland, has since been found in many other localities as a constituent (sometimes predominating) of basic fragmentary rocks; for instance, at the Beselicher Kopf, near Limburg, and at the Lahn, Nassau; in the Eifel, at the Kaulesborg, in the Westerwald, Germany; at Le Puy en Velay, France; near Montferrier, north of Montpellier; at the Szigliget Mountain, and at Leányvár, near Battina, Hungary; at James Island, Galapagos; in the district of Dyampang-Kulon, Java; in the Canary Islands; at the foot of Mount Somers, New Zealand. This list may be lengthened with some excellent occurrences of palagonite in Nevada. They have been hitherto unknown in the United States. Localities where these occurrences are found are in the Tertiary strata at the south end of the Kawsoh Mountains, near the Overland Road; west of the Kawsoh Mountains, near Hot Spring; and at Black Rock, Nevada. They are tufas, composed for the most part of grains and little fragments of a lighter or darker, yellowish-brown, amorphous mass, totally indifferent to polarized light. This substance indeed looks glassy, and is enormously rich in very dark-bordered, larger and smaller, microscopical gas-cavities, usually of a rather regular, oval form. There is no trace of augite, olivine, magnetite, or nepheline. Colorless ledges of striated plagioclase are the only secretions. Here and there sharply outlined bodies of a glass-mass are seen to be imbedded, differing from the surrounding mass by a different tone of color; so that this is most probably a hyaline breccia (Plate XII, fig. 3). In some places, the inner walls of the larger empty hollows have been remarkably altered, particularly in a stratum which outcrops southeast of Haws' Station. The alteration progresses in zones from the walls of the cavities inward through the surrounding mass, changing this originally homogeneous substance into a fibrous aggregation of short needles, the color only being retained. A section running through such a cavity shows plainly the structure of the walls, although it is not easy at first sight to distinguish the radiating external circle, or altered outer wall, from the fibrous mass which forms the inner parts, and the bottom of the hemispherical cavity laid open by cutting through the hollow. Between the nicols, these objects aggregately polarize; and even a colored cross, changing its color and position by turning the thin section or the analyzer, may be distinctly seen running over them (Plate XII, fig. 4). The rocks from near White Plains and from Black Rock are finer-grained tufas. That from Fossil Hill, Kawsoh Mountains, is more of a breccia. In it the black palagonite grains are often distinctly arranged in the form of schists. According to Sartorius von Waltershausen,[1] whose opinion formerly received general approbation, the palagonitic substance is to be compared with a hydraulic mortar, being the secondary product of a submarine alteration of basaltic tufa rocks. It would therefore be a hydrous, iron-bearing silicate which belonged to the class *porodine*, amorphous bodies produced like opal by the solidifying of a mass resembling gelatine.

As the result of his recent microscopical study of several palagonites, Rosenbusch has expressed the view[2] that these tufas are chiefly accumulations of ejected hyaline volcanic sands and ashes, consisting of basic glass. But he is inclined to think that the amount of water in the palagonites is not primary, but is derived from a molecular alteration of this glass, which is poor in silica. The substance which has been analyzed and named palagonite is indeed a mechanically inseparable mixture of the primitive anhydrous glassy palagonite (the sideromelane of Sartorius von Waltershausen, with only 0.349 per cent. of water), and the products of its easy decomposition. Rosenbusch's conclusions would appear to be accurate, for the microscopical study of this new Nevada palagonite does not at all contradict him. But the differently colored, red, yellow, and brown, band-like zones which appear in the amorphous substance of, for instance, the Icelandic palagonites, as well as others, and which probably represent separate stages in the progress of alteration, do not occur here. The only proof of decomposition in the Nevada occurrences is the fibrous walls of the cavities. This American palagonite being, therefore, a comparatively rather fresh one, approaching sidromelane, it may be allowable to conclude that a chemical analysis will demonstrate it to be poorer in water and richer in silica than are most of the more highly metamorphosed types.

[1] Die vulkan. Gesteine v. Sicilien u. Island u. deren submarine Umbildung.

[2] Neues Jahrb. f. Mineralogie, 1872, 152; Mikrosk. Physiographie d. petrogr. wichtigst. Mineral., 141.

GENERAL INDEX.

292

GENERAL INDEX.

www.ingramcontent.com/pod-product-compliance
Lightning Source LLC
Chambersburg PA
CBHW031358270326
41929CB00010BA/1229